HOLYFIELD
THE HUMBLE WARRIOR

Evander Holyfield and
Bernard Holyfield

A
JANET
THOMA
BOOK

THOMAS NELSON PUBLISHERS
Nashville • Atlanta • London • Vancouver

Published in Nashville, Tennessee, by Thomas Nelson, Inc., Publishers, and distributed in Canada by Word Communications, Ltd., Richmond, British Columbia.

The Bible version used in this publication is THE NEW KING JAMES VERSION. Copyright © 1979, 1980, 1982, 1990 Thomas Nelson, Inc., Publishers.

Library of Congress Cataloging-in-Publication Data

Holyfield, Evander.
    Holyfield : the humble warrior / Evander and Bernard Holyfield.
      p.   cm.
    "A Janet Thoma book."
    ISBN 0-7852-7693-9
    1. Holyfield, Evander.   2. Boxers (Sports)—United States—
Biography.   I. Holyfield, Bernard.   II. Title.
    GV1132.H69A3   1996
    796.8′3′092—dc20
    [B]   96–32674
                                                                          CIP

Printed in the United States of America.

2 3 4 5 6 — 01 00 99 98 97 96

DEDICATION

This book is dedicated to the loving memories of our Humble Warriors: our grandmother, Mrs. Pearlie B. Hatton, our mother, Mrs. Annie L. Holyfield, our brother, Willie B. Holyfield, and Evander's first coach, Mr. Carter Morgan.

ACKNOWLEDGMENTS

I would like to thank almighty God for sharing His blessings on my life in the sport of boxing and for giving me a mother who loved, encouraged, and guided me throughout her life. Also, I would like to pay special honor to Mr. Carter Morgan, my former coach, who was my mentor and motivator at an early age. He taught me the true meaning of being all that you can be, and the importance of setting goals. May the Lord shine His light on all their loved ones.

—Evander Holyfield

Loving thanks to my wife, Renee Holyfield, for her patience and encouragement; our children, Norris, Jasmine, and Joi Holyfield, for their love and inspiration; my sisters, Joe Ann McCoy, Eloise McCoy, Priscilla Wimby, and Annette Holyfield; my nephews, Mike Weaver, Anthony and Jesse McCoy, for standing in the gap; my niece, Angela Woodard, for always looking out for me; and to my entire family for their love and support.

A special thanks goes out to my pastor and his wife, Rev. Dewitt and Helen Sherrer at Unity Missionary Baptist Church, for their prayers, support, and encouragement.

Special literary thanks goes to Barton Green and Gary L. Thomas for editing, attorney Lisa Roberts for transcribing interviews from tape to paper, and Dr. and Mrs. William Sheffield, Pastor Bonnie and Hattie M. Gaston for their patience during long interviews. A heartfelt thanks goes out to the following ministers for their prayers and encouragment throughout my brother's boxing career: Rev. Gerard Ancrum, Rev. James Henderson, Rev. Cornelius Henderson, Rev. Parker Scott, Rev. Jasper Williams, Rev. Eddie Long, Rev. Cameron Alexander, Rev. Frank Sherrer, Rev. Randy Jordan, Rev. Creflo

Acknowledgments

Dollar, Rev. Kirby J. Caldwell, Rev. W. J. Buchanan, Rev. A. L. Tyson, Dr. Robert Schuller, Rev. Billy Graham, Rev. Pat Robertson, and Rev. Binny Hinn.

TEAM HOLYFIELD: Lou Duva, Dino Duva, Kathy Duva, Tim Hallmark, Ed Solomon, Mike Boorman, Don Turner, Sharon Magnuson, Tommy Brooks, Anne Merrem, Maria Kennett, Lee Haney, Ronnie Shields, Dr. Christopher Vaughn, Levert Robinson, Michael Weaver, Eloise McCoy, Tammy McGowan, Tammy Stewart, Jennifer Bryant, Delinia Jackson, Charles and Jennifer Watson, Earl Peak, "The Great" Eddie Gilbert, Mike Tyson, Marvin Rucker, Tyrone Eggleston, Willie Crowder, Ray McCoy, and everyone who takes care of the estate.

WARREN MEMORIAL BOY'S CLUB: Herman B. Guinn, Ron Osborne, Jack L. Roebuck, Ricky Roebuck, Guinn Roebuck, Bobby Smith, Jeannette Hornsby, Inez Hawkins, Jimmy Hawkins, Charles Pender, Carl Hines, James Hines, Carter Morgan, Ted Morgan, Ed Morgan, Bob Jones, John Swain, Buddy and Bo Davis (GABF), Lawrence Baker (ABF), Dr. Ron Stephens, Mary Flournoy, Charlie Mae Harris, Angela Nelson, Billy Nelson, Alex Stone, Janice Scott, Gwen Simms, Jerry Tipton, John Mack, Charles Reeves, Alicia Morgan, Gail Johnson, Patricia Jackson, Eric Osborne, and Albert Lindsey.

THE THOMAS NELSON TEAM: Janet Thoma, Rolf Zettersten, Ron Land, Esther Fitzpatrick, Lillian Roadman, Belinda Bass, Todd Ross, Sharon Gilbert, Phyllis Williams, Jonathan Merkh, and Jennifer Willingham.

LIBERTY ENTERTAINMENT GROUP: Attorney Jay Acton, Inge Hanson, Lennison Alexander, Dave Fagenson, Derrick Miles, Newton Hinds, Tom Brionos, Brock Stanton, Terry Kane, Maurice Madden, Steve Lash, Parrish Preston, Ronald W. McKinney, Gregory and Yolanda Collins, Ira and Celeste Collins, Luther and Marjorie Harris, Wayne and Felicia Becca, Rosemary and Clyde Meeks, Barbara Stewart, Al Franklin, Carol II. Dawson, Winston Green, Robert Head, Andrea L. Mills, Bobby L. Olive, Ukeme Usange, Les "Big Daddy" Bradford, Francine Dangerfield, Ricky Seals, Tony Barrs, Claude Perry, Alfonso Wesson, Butch Lewis, Donna Boortz, Alton "T C" Woodruff, Alfonso Thrash, Bobby "The Reverend" Smith, and attorney Lagrant Anthony.

—Bernard Holyfield

CONTENTS

CHAPTER 1

RINGSIDE SEAT

The postor taped to the wall read:

NOVEMBER 6, 1993
HOLYFIELD VS. BOWE II, THE REMATCH

The closer the time came for the round one bell, the more the dressing room seemed to shrink. The small cinder-block chamber was like a miniature Grand Central Station, bustling with the sounds of clanking ice buckets, ripping masking tape, and the loud voices of trainers, reporters, and well-wishers—all offering their predictions for the night's big fight.

Oblivious to it all, the robed boxer sat motionless, quiet, solitary. Ignoring the TV lights and cigar smoke, he stretched out his muscular legs, bowed his head, and closed his eyes. It was as if he were somewhere other than on a bench in that loud, crowded room. A look of calm concentration was on his face—a familiar expression, one that often appeared when he slipped off to that inner place our grandmother used to call "the prayer closet." In that self-created solitude Evander Holyfield shut out the chatter of a world that had made him the talk of the town, and he concentrated on the true source of his strength.

From across the room I recognized the moment. Its appearance made me smile. Over the years that calm, confident air had become a familiar feature of my brother's face. The expression and its calming affects were contagious. Even in that shrinking, cinder-block room, as thick with anxiety as it was with people, I found myself virtually unconcerned about the outcome of the night's contest. I simply knew that when the bell finally rang for round one, there would be a struggle, and that Evander could—and would—go the distance.

This was not a notion based on hopeful speculation. It was a fact founded on three decades of intimate, firsthand knowledge. Being Evander's older brother (by one year) I've had a ringside seat to every fight he's faced, on both sides of the rope. From diapers to boxing briefs, we've shared a kind of "tag-team" relationship. We've always been there for each other. Therefore, seeing what I've seen, and knowing what I know, I can be confident about what I put down here in black and white.

Blow for blow I've watched his struggles and witnessed his training. I've seen him learn the subtleties of not only how to fight but when to fight. And on every occasion I've observed, he's walked away from the battle stronger and wiser than before it began. Evander "Real Deal" Holyfield has discovered the secret of becoming a warrior of the highest order. And having been a party to this adventure, I too have learned the lessons of strength, confidence, and calm.

Realizing all of this, standing across that loud, cluttered room, I couldn't help but smile. The boxer's calm, familiar countenance put me at ease. He was ready to face the fight, and I knew it. Whatever the outcome, I was confident that the kid I still call "Chubby" would emerge from the struggle a champ.

The lessons of struggle and opposition were among the first we learned as children. Being the two youngest of eight siblings, "Chubby" and "Lightning" (my childhood tag) had to catch on fast to the strategies of survival. We discovered early that conflict was not something we could avoid. It was a part of life, a training exercise that must be experienced, endured, and mastered.

Our first training camp was the southern Alabama town of Atmore, where we were both born during the Kennedy administration. Although our birthplace was just down the road from Mobile and Montgomery, our village was far removed from the riots and marches of the stormy sixties. If anything, Atmore was a pleasant, industrious little mill town, full of scampering squirrels and high-gliding bluejays.

Like most of the black families in that small hamlet, ours was an energetic, enterprising, hardworking bunch. Mama, Grandma, and our older brothers and sisters put their backs into whatever work Atmore offered. From picking cotton and harvesting pecans to restaurant cooking and waitressing, they did what was necessary to attain that "something better." They worked sunup to sundown, each one maintaining the constant hope that some day, as a family, we too could finally have our chance at more.

Yet no aspiration is ever attained without a measure of exasperation. And even in our little out-of-the-fray southern town we didn't have to go far to be reminded of it. As a matter of fact, the first time Evander and I experienced this harsh fact of life was in our own front yard when we were only four and five years of age.

The Lush, the Law, and Lassie

As usual Chubby and I were outside playing with our favorite dog, a beautiful brown and white collie we had cleverly dubbed "Lassie." She was the perfect playmate, even-tempered, friendly, easygoing with everybody—even strangers. And if that wasn't enough, she could even carry me and Chubby on her back—at the same time!

That memorable day we were rolling around the grass, roughhousing with our friendly canine, when a strange man approached the house. Not thinking too much of it, we went on with our ruckus until we heard a sudden, unexpected noise—a loud, heavy *crrrunch!* coming from just the other side of our yard's sturdy wooden fence. Turning our heads toward the sound, we watched as a teetering, woozy figure slowly emerged from behind the structure. He was a short, squatty fellow with matted blond hair and pale, pudgy fingers that looked painfully swollen. And though he was a safe distance from us, we could easily tell that his tattered clothes reeked of alcohol.

"Hey, you kids," he feebly motioned, "c'mere."

Mom had always told us not to talk to strangers, so Chubby and I just stood there, wide-eyed, mesmerized, too frightened to move. When the drunk saw that we were not budging, he mumbled some profanity under his breath, opened the front gate, and stepped into the yard. Instantly, the usually playful Lassie began to bark and growl at the man. She started pulling violently at her chain as if she wanted to tear the teetering trespasser apart.

Lassie's uncharacteristic outburst soon brought our sister Annette to the screen door. Surprised to see the drunken intruder standing in our yard, she waved him off, yelling, "Get yourself outta here, right now! . . . You hear me, git!"

The man ignored Annette, and instead focused his attention on the other boisterous voice in the yard.

Moving as close to Lassie as the dog's chain would permit, the drunkard started taunting her. Swearing and shaking his fist, he ran toward the animal in a mock charge, then abruptly stopped. He kept up this cruel harassment for a minute or so, all the while advancing ever deeper into our yard. Then, unexpectedly, our playful pet's rage exploded. With a mighty howl, the collie managed to break free of her chain and commenced a charge of her own.

Mustering what little sober mobility he had, the intruder executed a fast but warbling pivot. And letting go a loud string of obscenities, he beat a hasty retreat out our front gate and down the street—with Lassie snarling at his heels.

A few minutes later our panting collie returned, just as calm and easygoing as ever. We laughed about it, reattached her chain, and led Lassie to her favorite spot under the house for a well-deserved bowl of water. Recalling the look of terror on the drunk's face, we were sure that we had seen and heard the last of him.

But an hour later the intruder was back. And this time the lush had the law with him.

The sheriff of Atmore was a tall, lanky fellow with thin, receding brown hair, squinty eyes, a long nose, and an Alabama accent with a decidedly nasal twang. He stood with his arms folded and listened as Annette explained how the drunk had come into our yard uninvited and harassed Lassie.

"She's a good dog," Sis explained. "Lassie was just doin' her job—protectin' Chubby and Lightnin' from this trespasser."

"Well, that's not what the gentleman told me," the sheriff said as he gestured to the teetering man, still reeking of booze. "He says he was just walkin' by and the dog jumped over the fence and tried to bite him."

"He's lyin'," Annette countered, defiantly looking down her nose at the little man.

"Yeah," Chubby echoed, "he wasn't actin' like no gentleman an hour ago when he trespassed on our property and messed with our dog!"

"I've heard enough," the sheriff interrupted, slapping the side of his leg as if punctuating his decision. "Looks like I'm gonna have to shoot your dawg."

Chubby and I looked at each other, neither of us believing what we just heard. We had always been taught that police represented law, order, and justice. The police were our heroes. Whenever we played "Cops and Robbers" there was always a lengthy debate about who was going to play the coveted role of the cop and who would have to endure the stigma of being the bad guy. The police were the ones you called when drunken bums trespassed on your property! But then this sheriff comes along—and not only does he let the intruder get away with his deeds, he even becomes the reeking liar's accomplice! It was everything but right!

The sheriff swaggered to his car and retrieved a black, double-barrel shotgun. As we watched wide-eyed, he began loading it with bullets that looked like missiles. The long barrel of the rifle seemed like a weapon used to bring down an African rhino rather than a friendly little collie. Holding the gun under his arm, he calmly walked past Chubby, then me, and approached the shady spot under the porch where Lassie lay sleeping. It was the place she called home.

Realizing that the sheriff was serious, and obviously calloused to the presence of two impressionable boys, Annette's voice broke the silence, "Chubby, Lightnin', you boys go into the house."

We did as we were told, but once inside we raced straight to the window to see if the sheriff was really going to shoot our favorite playmate. Peering through the glass, we watched the marksman squat down and point the big rifle under the house. From our position just above, we heard Lassie stir and begin to growl—a warning she gave to all intruders. Then she started to bark. Her chain rattled and jangled violently. She wasn't going to cower or whimper. Lassie wasn't going to take it lying down. She was going to go out fighting.

Boom! Boom! The whole house shook from the blast. The rumble sent the squirrels scurrying off to their sanctuaries and scattered Atmore's bluejays up into their treetop retreats. Evander and I could only cling to each other. There was no place for us to hide.

As the terrible sound faded, the sheriff dusted off his hat, spewed out a wad of slimy tobacco, and calmly walked back to his car. Without another word he drove away, and the drunkard, pleased with himself, staggered off down the street.

When the yard was finally empty, Chubby ran out onto the porch. I reluctantly followed. Under the edge of the steps we could see Lassie's blood forming tributaries of dark maroon in the dirt. Evander hurried down the stairs and around to the raised side of the porch. Dropping to his knees he looked into the darkness.

Through his tears he focused on a shaft of light that shone through a crack in the porch floor. Its thin illumination revealed a shriveled, mangled mass of fur, riddled mercilessly with buckshot.

There was no consoling us, although Annette tried. Nothing could be said that could justify this act of "justice."

When our two elder brothers got home from work and learned of Lassie's death, their grief was equally intense. Though thoroughly enraged, James, the oldest of the Holyfield boys, took the news quietly. His stoic, no-nonsense personality would not allow him to vent his anger. Instead he retreated to the back porch and stared out into space; only the subtle trembling of his tall, muscular frame gave away his frustration. As a black teenager in a small, southern town, James was already familiar with the struggle. But despite this experienced perspective, he could no more make sense of the sheriff's deed than the two youngsters who had witnessed the act firsthand.

The second oldest boy, Willie, was likewise dazed by the news, but his emotions were not as restrained. Being an artist, one who expresses himself with his hands, Willie wasn't shy about displaying his feelings. Grabbing up a shovel, he wandered outside and turned the gardener's tool into a sculptor's pick; with tears in his eyes he chiseled away a portion of our backyard and carved out of the earth a place of honor for our playmate. He and James then lovingly wrapped Lassie in one of Grandmother's handmade quilts and respectfully lowered the animal into the ground.

Laying Lassie to rest was a rite of passage for the four Holyfield boys. The women of our clan understood. This male ritual initiated each of us into the real world. As we lowered our playmate into the ground, a deeper level of understanding came to each of us, from big brother James down to little Evander. Standing around the open grave, holding hands, we each experienced the numb feeling that comes with the admission of helplessness. That day we buried our innocence along with our friend.

The despair on Chubby's face as he stood over Lassie's grave those years ago contrasted with the air of assurance I now witnessed in his eyes. From across that loud, crowded dressing room I saw no evidence of childhood helplessness—only the confidence that comes from experience.

That early training camp called Atmore was a hard but effective teacher. It taught Chubby the importance of enduring the struggle of conflict. He learned early on that opposition only has two alternatives: It can make the strong stronger or the weak weaker. And avoiding the experience only prolongs the inevitable. Our childhood in

Atmore was long ago and far away, but its lessons had remained as current as the clock on the wall in that dressing room in 1993.

"Fifteen minutes!" a strong voice bellowed from just outside the dressing room's open door. "Fifteen minutes to the bell. Let's go!" With that boisterous cue the meandering crowd of well-wishers began to pour out of the door and into the hallway, giving the boxer elbow room to assemble his entourage.

Taking part in that procession is another male ritual. This walk from the dressing room to the ring is a time-honored ceremony that reinforces the team's collective resolve to face the battle. Unlike the ritual around Lassie's grave, this observance does not acknowledge the frailties of our humanity. Instead it declares to all who observe: Our side has trained well to overcome these physical limitations. "Team Holyfield" was ready, confident, and able to face the inevitable questions that arise with all confrontations: Who is the weaker? Who is the stronger? Which of the two is willing to endure the struggle long enough to discover the truth?

As our caravan advanced through the dark hallway, nearing the entrance to the coliseum itself, the familiar square shape of the boxing ring came into view. Through the parade of bobbing heads, the distant, illuminated platform looked like the proverbial light at the end of the tunnel. Bright shafts of smoky brilliance flooded the raised, roped-off stage. Its dramatic image not only dominated the darkened assembly, it also triggered within me the image of another hallway and the familiar square shape of the table that once dominated our kitchen in Atmore. It was there, at that table, that little Chubby and I first discovered how to march into the Ring of Life with confidence.

As sure as Lassie's tragedy introduced us to the harsh realities of this world, those midnight trips to the kitchen opened us up to a world that far surpasses the most tangible reality.

The Man in the Kitchen

Being the two youngest of such a large brood, Evander and I not only played together during the day, we even spent our nights together, sleeping in the same bed. Chubby usually slept with his head at the foot of the berth, and I took the opposite approach. The reason for this arrangement seemed logical at the time: If either of us had a bad dream, we each had a pair of feet to grab onto. (Well, for a four-year-old and a five-year-old it was a stroke of genius!) Suffice it to say, the tag team of Chubby and Lightning was rarely apart. In fact, if one of us woke up in the middle of the night to go to the bathroom, he would wake the other. And together we would hold hands and walk down the hallway, which Mama kept lit with the kitchen light.

On one of these nightly treks, we were just leaving the bathroom and were about to turn back down the hall when Evander thought he saw someone in the kitchen. It was late, around midnight. Everyone in the house should have been asleep.

We turned and nodded to each other, as if affirming our mutual curiosity. Then slowly, carefully, we took hold of each other's hand and inched our way into the large, well-lit room.

As we crossed the threshold into the kitchen our eyes grew as wide as saucers. Standing next to the table was a man!—a large, black, bald-headed man! To a five-year-old everything seems big, but by any standard this guy was tall! From a lofty height that seemed somewhere near the ceiling, he looked down at us and smiled. Although we can't recall the color of his eyes, we do remember standing for a long moment just staring at this fellow, and he at us.

The stranger spoke, but not in the normal, conventional way. Although Chubby and I never recall hearing his voice, we eventually struck up a conversation with him, but being only four and five years old, we didn't have a whole lot to say. Still, we must have made a good impression on the man, because after several minutes of chatting the smiling figure came close to us and extended his hands over our heads. He then gently touched the tops.

After this physical contact we scurried out of the room, ran to our mother's bedside, and started babbling on about "the man in the kitchen."

Of course Mama, being bone-tired from a long day at work, simply rolled over and mumbled, "Okay, there's a man in the kitchen. . . . That's nice. You two go back to sleep. Go on now. . . . Back to bed."

And, as if nothing out of the ordinary had just occurred, we scampered back down the hall, jumped into bed, and naturally fell asleep.

Every night for about a week this strange scenario was repeated. Around midnight Evander and I would fearlessly hop out of bed, walk down the hallway, and have a chat with the tall, dark man in the kitchen. Afterward we would go to Mom's room, wake her up, and try to tell her about it. The nightly game apparently began to wear down her patience, because finally one evening she let us have it.

"Why do you two come in here every night talking about some man in the kitchen? There ain't no man in there! You two better stop this and get back to bed before I get up and whip the both of you."

That's all we needed to hear. In a flash we were in our bed with the blankets up over our heads. No sooner had we settled under the covers than a pleasant hush fell over the house. Our brothers, sisters, mom, and grandmother had long since retreated to their respective rooms, and all of the lights were off, except of course the one in the kitchen, which lit the hallway. In fact it was so quiet we heard Mom when she eventually got up from her bed and walked down the hall. We heard the refrigerator door open, then close. Then, out of no-where, there came the sudden high-pitched sound of a glass crashing on the floor, accompanied by the bone-chilling shrill of a woman's scream.

Instantly our serene home turned into a madhouse. In simultaneous chaos all of the bedroom doors flew open and a confusing echo of voices reverberated through the hall. After a few disorienting seconds my entire half-dressed family was standing in the kitchen, wide-eyed and out of breath, each trying to avoid stepping in the white puddle of milk and broken glass splattered on the floor. Our collective stare was focused on Mama. She was trembling. Frantically pointing toward the sink, she stammered, "A man . . . a m-m-man!"

"Mama, nobody's there," Eloise reassured. But Mom was not convinced.

Still shaking, she eased herself down into a chair at the kitchen table and tried to regain her composure. The family, both shocked and curious, gathered around her and began asking the most obvious question: "What happened?"

Mama then pointed to her two youngest and attempted to explain. "Chubby and Lightnin' have been wakin' me up every night, talkin' about some man in the kitchen. I'd tell them to go to bed 'cause there wasn't no man.

"I lock the back door every night. So there's no way anyone could get in here. Then tonight," she paused and inhaled a deep, calming breath, "they came to me again. Since they woke me up, I decided to get something to drink. I went to the refrigerator," she gestured around the room, reliving the moment, "poured me a glass of milk, and sat down right here. When I looked up I-I saw th-this man, a tall, dark, bald-headed man s-s-smiling at me. Ain't no-no one suppose to be in this house! I started screaming a-a-and he just . . . v-vanished!"

As if on cue the entire family turned their attention on me and Evander. A flurry of questions followed. We answered each one as best we could, and passed along every detail possible about the stranger. However somewhere in the middle of this kitchen-table inquisition, a soft, but feisty voice broke through the clamor and brought the Q & A to an abrupt halt, "The man was an angel from God."

Everyone turned toward the speaker, dumbstruck. Rolling up to the table in her wheelchair, Grandmother Hatton continued, "When the angel extended his hands and touched the boys lightly on the head, he was anointin' 'em, blessing 'em with God's gifts."

Another hush fell over the house. Everyone looked at Mama, then at me and Chubby, then down at the shattered glass of milk. It was obvious to every Holyfield around the table that something out of the ordinary had happened.

At the time of Grandmother's great pronouncement neither Chubby nor I understood what "gifts" meant. In fact, for a long time we thought we had been blessed with the ability to stay in trouble with her.

It seemed that from that night on, Grandmama was constantly correcting us, pushing us to improve. Like the boxing coaches Evander would later encounter, Grandmother was a stern disciplinarian. She took us to task for the most insignificant transgression. Each time she disciplined us, she would first quote an appropriate portion of the Bible, both chapter and verse, then pinch us on the arm for "the seeds we'd sown." Pearlie Beatrice Hatton may have been in a wheelchair, but she was determined to do everything she could to get us ready for our "special work."

All grandmothers feel that their offspring will attain some measure of greatness. But after that "man" visited the kitchen, our God-fearing grandmama made it her special responsibility to coach us on how to survive inside this roped-off ring called life.

"All things work for good, even the bad things," she would say in her southern drawl. "God will not put upon you more than you can bear. He'll never put you in a place where you can't excel. Things may not always go your way, but if you'll trust Him, and keep on—

no matter what—He'll give you the strength ya need. He has His reasons. And in His good time He'll turn things around for His glory, and your improvement. You boys can do anything! Because greater is He that is in you, than he that is in the world . . ."

The man in the kitchen visited us a few more times, but in contrast to Grandma's memorable instruction, neither Chubby nor I can consciously recall the things he told us. All I know is that this mysterious "man" made a series of unexplainable visits to our Alabama kitchen. Doing so he gave two ordinary boys an introduction to the improbable and the overwhelming confidence to attempt the extraordinary. That is, with a little help from Grandma Hatton . . . and God. . . .

The Final Gauntlet

Like the hallway to our Atmore kitchen, the corridor through which the Holyfield entourage paraded also emptied into a large, well-lit room: the coliseum itself. The instant our procession entered the arena the entire place exploded in a near-deafening crescendo of mayhem. The scene was a chaotic mixture of jubilant fans cheering, jumping, applauding, and yelling, "Holy! Holy! Holyfield!"

Making our way down to the ring through the middle of this massive demonstration was like running a gauntlet of your best friends, each wanting to slap you on the back and shake your hand. But this clamor and commotion never flustered the boxer. As in every fight, Chubby's attention was focused straight ahead. His thoughts were centered on the reflected white square of the boxing ring.

Finally we reached the raised stage. In that moment I became aware of the adrenaline pumping through my heart, causing it to beat wildly within my chest. The reality of the moment had finally broken through to my reason. In the middle of this mayhem I suddenly realized that my little brother was about to step through the ropes of a situation from which he could not retreat. And there was nothing I could do about it.

Evander had faced Riddick Bowe before. During the course of those battles both men had experienced the thrill of victory, and they had both known the agony of defeat. But this time around, their match was for something far more valuable than a prestigious title and a gem-studded belt.

Considering these things, I felt as if I were standing once more at the window, waiting for the sheriff to fire off those inevitable shots. And in that instant I revisited the numbness that comes with the admission of helplessness.

Then, through the ropes, I caught a glimpse of Evander's already perspiring face. It was that same expression, one that often appeared when he was off in "the prayer closet." His expression and its calming affects ignited within me that old, overwhelming confidence to attempt the extraordinary.

As he took off his robe and flexed his well-trained muscles I couldn't hold back my smile. I knew that the bell for round one was about to ring and that there was going to be a struggle. But despite my trepidation that trouble could easily stumble into the front yard of our hopes, I knew that Chubby and I had both been introduced to the improbable: The notion that God hears and answers prayers. Whatever the outcome, I was confident that Evander "Real Deal" Holyfield, could—and would—go the distance. And as usual I had a ringside seat.

CHAPTER 2

FROM ATMORE TO ATLANTA

Life is an unpredictable series of endings and beginnings. The same could be said for our childhood in Atmore. On the whole, that little Alabama town was a wonderful place to begin life. But shortly after we buried Lassie, Mom packed up Grandmother and all of us kids and moved us out of Atmore, back to Atlanta. I say "back to Atlanta" because our family shares its history with that old Georgia city. Not only is it Mother's birthplace, it's also the native home of all our brothers and sisters, except for Willie, me, and Evander.

In Atlanta, thirteen years before, the marriage of Joseph and Annie Holyfield had ended. After they divorced, he moved on to Michigan and began again. Soon afterward Mama received a letter from her Alabama relatives saying that her mother was very sick, possibly near death. So she packed up the kids and came to Atmore, to Grandmother Hatton's aid.

The matriarch of our family had suffered a mild stroke. The crisis was intense, but it didn't last for long. Pearlie Beatrice Hatton was a strong, determined, spiritual woman. With Mama's care, Grandma's constitution steadily improved. Eventually, her health stabilized to such a remarkable degree that she ended up taking care of all of us, especially after Mom went to work.

It was back during these "Atmore days" that Mother met Ison Coley, Chubby's father. Mom described him as a robust, dark-skinned, gentle man. A lumberjack by trade, he hauled the big timber for the local mills. He and Mom made plans to marry, but it just wasn't meant to be. An irreconcilable dispute erupted between them, bringing their relationship to a sudden, unexpected end.

Beginnings and endings, they are the only predictable constants of life. And moving from Atmore back to Atlanta was definitely a fresh start for us all.

It began with the family's arrival at our eldest sister's home. Joe Ann's four-bedroom house, in the southeastern suburb of Summerhill, was already occupied by five residents: Joe Ann, her husband, Joe, and their three children. With our appearance at their front door, the population of 275 Connally Street rose dramatically: Added were Grandmother, Mom, Eloise, James, Priscilla, Annette, Willie, me, and little Evander, for a grand total of fourteen! It was a little crowded, but there were no complaints; everything was different, exciting, and new. Our "back to Atlanta chapter" was just beginning.

Everyone in our family worked. We were taught early on that a job is not just a paycheck, it's a privilege. People who earned a living deserved respect, no matter how menial their task. Our mother's tireless example showed us that sense of dignity. Growing up with that kind of work ethic, it didn't take long for the Holyfields to carve out their own, enterprising niche in the community.

Joe Ann McCoy, our married sister, who never left Atlanta, worked at Southern Bell Telephone. The second oldest, Eloise, quickly found a position with the Job Corps. James and Willie, the oldest of the boys, were able to secure work in construction, while Priscilla and Annette got jobs at Atlanta's famous Varsity Restaurant. Mom, who had worked for years as the head cook at a restaurant in Atmore, had no trouble filling the role of chef at Peachtree Street's Henry Grady Cafeteria (today the site of Westin Peachtree Plaza). The only family members exempt from this duty were the babies of the bunch: Anthony, Angela, and Alisa (Joe Ann's kids). And of course, Lightning, age six, and five-year-old Chubby.

With such a full house, mornings on Connally Street were, in a word, "busy." Evander and I would often wake to the sound of laughter and the clanking of breakfast dishes in the kitchen. All the working folk would be crowded around the table drinking coffee and chattering about the latest news, their jobs, or what they hoped to accomplish that day. The vitality of it all was often as rousing as the caffeine in their java.

That energetic, early-morning bustle and chatter fascinated me. I recall wishing Chubby and I could hurry up and "get grown" so we could go to work like everybody else. But after the morning crew left and the house quieted down, those dreams of making a living would always give way to childhood's natural vocation: make-believe. And that occupation kept us young'uns (and our keeper) very busy.

Hide and Seek

Our new neighborhood in Summerhill was similar to our old one—only bigger. Back in Atmore we were content to play inside the boundaries of our old fenced-in yard. But now we were in the big city. And it didn't take long for Chubby and me to realize that all of Connally Street was a potential playground!

The neighborhood was enormous, and it was swarming with kids! The recreational possibilities in such a place were mind-boggling: football, cops and robbers, basketball, hide and seek. To our small-town eyes it seemed as if we had stumbled onto utopia! Then Grandmother's familiar voice issued a command that brought us partway back to reality. "Stay in the front yard and play. Don't go down the street. I can't see what you two are gettin' into down there."

It was torture. From the boundary of our front yard Chubby and I could plainly see other kids having fun. In fact, a group of them were so close, we could hear their laughter and painfully observe their preparations for a game of hide and seek.

From my vantage point I could see the large tree, designated as home base, and the boy who was "the seeker." Positioning himself so the wide trunk stood between him and those who were hiding, the seeker closed his eyes and began to count out loud, reciting a melodic verse, "Last night . . . the night before . . . twenty-five rifles at my door . . . I got up . . . I let them in . . . I hit them in the head with a rollin' pin . . . Five . . . Ten . . . Fifteen . . . Twenty . . ."

Standing on the sidelines we watched as the kids scattered in a frantic search for a hiding place. Some chose obvious locations behind a car or another tree. A few selections were pretty ingenious: a discarded cardboard box sitting out in plain view, the uncovered bed of an old, dilapidated truck. By the time the boy called out, "Ready or not, here I come!" Chubby and I knew the location of all the seeker's prey. And we managed to squeeze a little fun out of the advantage. As the seeker stalked his victims, one of us occasionally called out, "You're getting hot!" or "Brrrrrr, you're cold!" Eventually, however, everyone either made it back to home base or was tagged before reaching the tree. And the last one caught became the designated seeker the next time around.

This got old after a couple of games. Having been relegated to spectator status by Grandmother's command, we were getting a little restless. The kids—and all that fun—were so close, yet so far, far away. . . .

Stay in the front yard and play. . . . Don't go down the street. I could see it in Chubby's eyes; like me, he was aching to get in on the action.

It's amazing how we can talk ourselves into doing things we know we shouldn't. If you want to do something badly enough, the things you must do to reach that goal never seem to be so bad—at least at the moment. Such was the case with Chubby and Lightning.

Each of us knew the consequences of disobeying Grandmother. Yet standing there, within our yard's boundary-line, watching others have fun, we were already suffering unusual punishment without cause! If we were going to be punished, we might as well do something to deserve it. We weighed the sting of Grandmother's pinch against the pleasure of participation, and our mutual decision took us . . . across the line.

We figured we could go down the street and play for a while. Grandmother rarely checked on us. She'd never know. The plan was simple: We'd do all of our hiding close by, so when Grandmother called us we could run back and reappear from around the side of the house. This little ruse would give her the impression that we hadn't left the yard. The scheme was foolproof. What could go wrong?

The next hour or so went by like a flash. Chubby and I really got caught up in the action. Being the last one discovered after playing countless games, it was now finally my turn to be the seeker. So I leaned my head against the home base tree, closed my eyes, and began the melodic verse, "Last night . . . the night before . . . twenty-five rifles at my door. . . ." I was just about to reach 'eighty-five' in my count when a faint, sudden sound stopped me cold.

"Chub-bee! . . . Light-nin'!"

Instantly my eyes flew open and I frantically scanned the forbidden landscape for Evander. Of course, agile little brother was already hidden. Moving out from behind the tree I called to him, "Chubby, Grandmother's callin'! We need to get home—now!"

Not a sound. No movement at all. The neighborhood street was suddenly deserted. No doubt everyone, including little brother, thought my actions were some slick trick to expose the hideouts of the gullible.

"Chub-bee! Light-nin'!" Again, the wind carried the faint, familiar voice down the street. I couldn't go home without him. How would I explain his absence? That's when the reality of the moment hit me. We were in big trouble.

"Chub-bee! Light-nin'!"

If time flies when you're having fun, then moments like this could arguably be measured in years. Finally, thankfully, one of the kids convinced Evander that Grandmother was really calling. And when that news connected with Chubby's brain, he bolted from his hideaway. The two of us then raced back to the violated boundary of our yard.

On the front porch sat Grandmother, the ultimate seeker. Obviously, plenty had gone wrong with our plan. She had discovered where we had been hiding. And though she was confined to a wheelchair, she managed to tag both of us before we reached home base.

"You two get in this house! Didn't I tell you to stay in the front yard?"

"Yes ma'am," we answered in unison, with a tone of humility that blatantly solicited mercy.

Pointing to the living room sofa she declared, "You two have been disobedient." She then shifted her weight in the wheelchair, and from her side she retrieved an old book. Half of the front cover was torn off. Its crumpled pages were marked up with scribbles in the margins, and entire passages were underlined in dark, black ink. That old Bible was as much a part of Grandmother as her wheelchair, but its pages took her to places where no earthly wheels could ever go. As we took our place on the sofa, we both knew that she intended to show us the error of our ways in hopes that one day we too might discover those heavenly places.

"Exodus twenty and twelve says," she began, leaning forward in her chair, " 'Honour thy father and thy mother: that thy days may be long upon the land which the Lord thy God giveth.' " Grandmother was just getting warmed up. By the time she hit her stride, she had explained all of the ways to honor one's parents—including grandparents. Then she turned to dishonor. "And the gravest of these is blatant disobedience!"

Sitting there listening to her lecture, my six-year-old mind began to wander. Secretly I wished that the sermon part of our chastisement would conclude. I wanted to get my pinch over with so I could go back outside and play. As the minutes ticked by, this secret notion grew. Finally, when I saw that Grandmother was nearing the end, I scooted up to the edge of the sofa, ahead of Evander, and volunteered to receive my correction first. Naturally I wasn't looking forward to it. Grandma's arm pinches were painful and intense, but at least they were over with quickly. So I offered my arm and prepared myself for the inevitable. But like my first foolproof plan, this one didn't turn out as expected either.

I felt Grandmother's left hand take hold of me. Then out of the corner of my eye I saw her pick up something. A long, thin, leaf-stripped offshoot from one of the bushes in the yard. Mama's switch! Mother kept it around the house for special occasions. And as Grandmother raised her right arm high I realized this was one of them.

For a woman past sixty, sitting in a wheelchair, she wielded that switch with the precision of an orchestra director's baton. The music she conducted was a stinging, repetitive chorus, driving home the basic themes of honesty, respect, and the harsh harmony of actions and consequences. Her painful music made me dance all around that wheelchair. And I thought the crescendo would never end.

Then it was Evander's turn. Grabbing onto him with a vise grip, she pursued him with her switch. No matter how he turned and twisted, the weapon found its mark. Although the wheelchair was anchored, it swayed and rocked as Chubby pulled and bucked. It was a game of tug-of-war between them; Evander tugging, determined to get free, and Grandmother firmly entrenched in a full-scale war against that rebellious nature common to every child of Adam.

Through discipline our Grandmother Hatton made sure that we would remember our disobedience so we would never trivialize our transgressions. Whenever a boundary was set for us, she wanted to make sure that we thought twice before crossing the line. Over the years, no matter what games we played, no matter how far Chubby and I wandered off into forbidden territory, Grandmother's persistent discipline and consistent discipling always succeeded in calling us back to home base.

Indelible Image

The strict discipline Grandmother introduced into our family not only brought order to the crowded chaos, it helped to mold the emerging characters and talents that were budding throughout the house. Among the most obvious of these talented characters was our older brother, Willie Holyfield.

"Bobo," as we called him, was the artist of the family. Without any formal training, he could pick up a pencil and transform a blank sheet of paper into the graphite rendering of a recognizable face. With well-placed lines and subtle shading he brought life to the remembered image of a friend or the detailed landscape of places that existed only in his imagination.

In those early days of our "Atlanta chapter," Bobo displayed a wide range of abilities from painting to braiding hair to sculpting. Using a pocket knife, a file, and an old piece of firewood, Willie could instinctively cut, carve, chip, and shave until the image of a squirrel found its way through the shards of flying bark. Willie's talent and potential were obvious and abundant; but sadly, discipline was not a part of the package.

Grandmother would often warn us that the abilities we each possessed must be used and developed prudently. "God didn't give you all these gifts so you could sit on them and be lazy," she'd say. "He expects you to use your time wisely and develop them to His glory. He gave the gifts to you, but it's up to you to do the polishing. And every day that you don't polish your talent, you lose a piece of it."

Bobo did many things with his talent, but polishing his gift was not one of them. Over the years he never attended any public art classes nor did he ever privately study the fundamentals of his craft. To him his gift was an inborn instinct, a natural commodity to turn on and off at his convenience.

Eventually, just as Grandmother warned, Bobo's gift slowly slipped away. He never realized he was losing it, until it was too late. The harsh lessons Willie learned had an effect on us all. His unpolished gift is a "stilled life" that hangs in the gallery of our family's memory. Its indelible image left its impression on everyone, especially Evander.

The combination of Grandmother's warning and Bobo's example motivated young Chubby. It stirred up his awareness for personal excellence and his need for discipline. And that redirected sense of order helped his own, obviously budding, talents to blossom.

The Warren Memorial Boy's Club

The first real inkling of Chubby's athletic gifts came in 1968, when Evander was six. By then we were both enrolled in Atlanta's E. P. Johnson Elementary. Usually, after school we would spend the afternoon (and our excess energy) at the corner of Connally and Georgia Avenue, where "The Church At Heart" held an arts and crafts program for neighborhood kids. But one memorable afternoon, after the last bell, classmate Michael Brown asked Chubby if he wanted to go with him to the Boy's Club.

Now, the Warren Memorial Boy's Club was the place to be if you were athletic, adolescent, and of course, a boy. So naturally Evander said, "Yeah!"

There was just one small problem; to get in, he had to be a member. The solution? A simple, annual registration fee of fifty cents. But that solution, in turn, led to another problem: Evander had to get both the necessary permission and the money from Mother.

"I don't know anything about this boy's club," Mother said skeptically when Evander and Michael came calling. "Who runs this place? Who would be supervising you?"

Michael, a veteran member of the institution, capably answered all of her questions, and even suggested that she talk to his mother. She had once voiced the same concerns.

Mom was still hesitant. Then Michael mentioned something that seemed to catch her attention. "Along with their sports, art, and music programs, the Boy's Club offers a Bible study, every Saturday morning." That was the clincher.

Mama smiled, and with a little twinkle in her eye, she gave both Chubby and me her permission. And the required twelve bucks.

Soon a white van sporting a blue-lettered logo, "Warren Memorial Boy's Club," picked us up on the corner of Connally and Georgia, near our church. Upon arrival we discovered the place was everything Michael said it was, and more. The two-story structure housed an indoor Olympic-size pool, an NBA regulation basketball court, a boxing ring, a library, a woodwork shop, an arts and crafts area, a game room packed with pool tables, hockey tables, shuffleboard, pinball machines, and a music room for choral and instrument practice. Their outdoor facilities were equally impressive: a regulation-size baseball diamond and a football field that doubled as a soccer court.

If we once thought utopia was our Summerhill neighborhood, we were certain this enormous place was heaven!

At the entrance there was an information/registration desk where everyone was required to sign in. There sat a stern white lady named Mrs. Hawkins. She greeted us with a smile as warm as sunshine. But we soon learned that to disobey one of her orders, "Boys, stop running in the hallway. . . . Don't wrestle on the steps. . . . No foul language," brought swift and immediate reprisal. She had the agility of a linebacker, and if you tried to run away, she would track you down and put a switch on you. Mrs. Hawkins had a partner, Mrs. Hornsby, who assisted her in discipling the boys of the Boy's Club; we referred to them as the tag team. Mrs. Hawkins played the role of no-nonsense registrar, and Mrs. Hornsby was the quiet, gentle one who placed salve and bandages on our wounded egos. However, there was so much to do at the club you seldom had time to get into trouble.

In the beginning Evander and I experimented and signed up for a lot of different things: baseball, basketball, soccer. But initially, the one activity that captured Evander's imagination was football.

We started out playing on Coach Alex Stone's 65-pound team. Chubby played offensive fullback and middle linebacker on defense. I played tackle and defensive cornerback. It didn't take long for the cream of Evander's natural ability to rise to the top.

I recall several games where the team would be in a huddle after a particular play, and our coach would send in a play from the sideline to our quarterback. The quarterback would be in the center on one knee, breathing hard, and he'd say, "Okay, we gonna run a 3–4 trap, fake the halfback, give to the fullback on 3–24. Got it?"

That play meant that we were going to pretend to give the ball to the halfback when in actuality we were going to give it to Evander, our fullback. Once Evander got the ball he was going to run through the third and fourth hole, which would be created by our guard and myself.

Now that was the way the play was supposed to go. But Evander began improvising. When the quarterback said, "Three twenty-four," the guard and I would attempt to create an open path through the third and fourth hole and the quarterback would fake the ball to the halfback, then give it to Evander. Once Evander received the ball he would blaze his own path if none was open.

Early on, he was averaging about three hundred yards and four touchdowns a game. And when it came to defense, he quickly topped the list with the most sacks and single tackles. Every year Chubby easily won the Boy's Club trophy for Most Valuable Player—for both offense and defense.

Evander was so fast as a kid that once he had the ball he would dash toward the sideline and simply scamper around the opposing team's defenses. The word in the football community got around equally as fast: "Don't let number 34 beat you around the corner. If Holyfield gets there first, he's gonna score." Chubby could turn that corner 90 percent of the time. And nine out of ten of those occasions he'd cross the goal line.

Often, when the opposition managed to pursue him, he would instinctively cut back against the grain, charge up the middle, then head for the opposite sideline, and again, score. Whether he was playing offense or defense, baseball, basketball, or soccer, Evander was feared, respected, and admired by his peers.

He was, and remains, a natural born athlete. And over time he learned how to discipline and polish his talent. He was a fanatic about practice, constantly setting goals for himself and breaking them. Then he'd set even higher ones—and ultimately surpass them as well.

One of his earliest childhood aspirations was to play for the Atlanta Falcons. Evander was more than just a fan; he was obsessed with the team, especially number 43, Dave Hamilton. Evander wanted not only to emulate him but one day actually to *be* him. Such adolescent enthusiasm taught Chubby how to focus on his goals.

Our family actually thought for many years that Evander was destined to be a professional football player. But as we've come to learn, life is an unpredictable series of endings and beginnings. And one chance encounter with the right person can change everything.

I Wanna Hit That Speed Bag!

There is nothing more alluring than the forbidden. This holds doubly true for curious eight-year-olds called "Chubby." Being involved in so many activities, he naturally knew his way around the Boy's Club. One area of the facility was understood to be "off-limits." At the far end of the gymnasium, behind the basketball court, there was a section literally fenced off from the regular membership. It had the distinct air of being "exclusive." The only people allowed to pass through the gate were the Warren Memorial Boxing Team.

The restricted area and its equipment seemed unfamiliar yet strangely compelling to Chubby. A heavy dark-brown leather bag hung from the ceiling, and a smaller one dangled oddly from what looked to be an old basketball backboard. Off to one side was a raised square platform supporting four corner posts; and attached to the posts were ropes that completely enclosed the square. Evander was mesmerized by it all.

Often, after enduring an intense football practice, Chubby would come to the fence and stare through the mesh at the chosen few. He would watch as perspiring bodies danced around inside the roped-off square. And he'd wrinkle his nose with wonder at the sight of normal people throwing punches at shadows. He'd listen to the steady thud of gloves as they repeatedly punched the heavy leather bag, and he'd watch in awe as a pair of quick hands coaxed the dangling speed bag to sing.

Eventually the allure of it all got the best of him. That day he stepped through the forbidden portal, like a man on a mission. His eyes were focused on the dangling speed bag, and as he approached it, he balled up his right hand into a fist. Mimicking the same energy he had observed, Evander propelled his eight-year-old arm toward the bag . . . and missed.

"Hey, you—kid! Get outta here!" The sudden gruff voice of an old man echoed through the gym. It was Carter Morgan, the short, pudgy, white boxing coach.

Pointing up to the dangling, undisturbed bag, Evander shouted back, "I wanna hit it!"

Shaking his head with a hint of a grin, Morgan slowly walked up to Chubby and gazed down at his small, stocky frame. "Don't hit the speed bag." Then motioning the boy to follow, he pointed off in the corner; "There, try that big one."

Evander walked up to the heavy, brown-leather monster suspended from the ceiling and once more cocked back his arm. Letting loose his best no-holds-barred jab, his bare fingers smashed against the worn leather, and immediately an explosion of pain shot up his arm. The old coach couldn't help but laugh, accentuating the fifty years' worth of lines in his ruddy face.

For a moment Chubby rubbed his knuckles, trying his best to ignore the sting. Then approaching Morgan and employing a good measure of bravado, little brother boldly announced, "Mr. Morgan, I wanna join the boxing team."

The coach slowly ran a hand through his receding, reddish-gray hair, and looked Evander dead in the eye, "Young'un, ya gotta be real tough to be on the boxing team." He then turned and walked away.

Rubbing his bruised knuckles, Chubby took note of Morgan's words, and vowed to himself, "I'm gonna prove to him that I'm tough enough. I *am* gonna make the team!"

CHAPTER 3

THE HEART OF THE FAMILY

O nly one Holyfield is able to match Evander's tenacity, discipline, and dedication to hard work: our mother, Annie Laura Holyfield. While Chubby's talents are obvious, Mother's gifts have always been subtle. Yet her formidable diligence has never ceased to be productive.

Since the time we registered our first thoughts, Chubby and I recall Mother leaving for work early and coming home late. Our sister Eloise remembers that before either of us were born, Mom, a restaurant cook, started at 10:00 A.M. and labored to 10:00 P.M., six days a week, Monday through Saturday. After we were born she changed her hours to work from 6:00 A.M. to 6:00 P.M. so that, as Eloise put it, "she could spend more time watching you two grow up."

Back in our Atmore days she didn't own a car and there were no buses. So Mom had to walk an average of forty-five minutes to the restaurant every day—through rain, snow, sleet, and sweltering heat. Although the pace was tough, Mother never complained. In fact once she clocked out and began that long trek home, she would often start humming. Those muffled, muted tones would eventually build in volume and intensity, and before long she would accompany her own weary melody with words:

> Just a closer walk with Thee,
> Grant it Jesus is my plea,
> Daily walking close to Thee,
> Let it be, dear Lord, let it be.

Mother was always shy about singing in public—even doing solos in church, yet when she felt the need to express her deepest yearnings, she'd sing. Sometimes early on Sunday morning, the smell of grits, eggs, and bacon would mingle with mother's melodic, mournful cry. The beautiful sound would float through the house and stir everyone out of bed.

> *In my trials, walk with me,*
> *In my sorrows, walk with me,*
> *In my troubles walk with me . . .*
> *I want Jesus to walk with me.*

The way she would bend and caress the notes, you could almost feel the pain and sorrow she sheltered us from. Any listener within earshot became a witness to Mother's unshakable faith in the face of adversity.

I recall asking her once how she managed to work from sunup to sundown, without ever once complaining about the unfairness of it all. She just looked at me with a smile in her eyes. "Son, life ain't always fair, but it's bearable. God ain't gonna put on you more than you can take. Life can be bitter, and it can be sweet, but the secret is to learn how to take that bitterness along with the sweet.

"God Himself said, 'All things work together for good for those who love Him and are called according to His purpose.' When you love people, it ain't hard to rise early and go to bed late, it's a joy.

"Remember the sayin', 'God bless the child that's got his own'? Well, God blesses the child who provides for his own too."

Mama certainly provided for us. Her faith and hard work helped to make our childhood as "sweet" as the sunflower-shaped butter cookies she always packed in our lunch bags. When the bitter time came and she suddenly fell seriously ill, it was a difficult thing for Evander and me to accept. When your thirty-nine-year-old mother has a heart attack, how do you find the good in the bad?

The doctors at Grady Memorial Hospital informed our sister Joe Ann, "Your mother has suffered two heart attacks and three strokes." And after an in-depth analysis they detected "serious blockage of the arteries, and holes to the left ventricle of her heart." The need for surgery was immediate.

The type of operation they were considering was a delicate procedure, which had never been attempted before at Grady Memorial. So a cardiology specialist was brought in from California, a doctor who was considered one of the pioneers in the emerging field of open-heart surgery in the 1960s.

The team of specialists used short segments of vein from mother's leg and constructed a bypass—an alternate highway—around the blockages. That immediately restored the flow of oxygenated blood to her damaged organ. Afterward, the doctor told Joe Ann, "All of the various malfunctions created a force that flattened your mother's heart, causing it to collapse. Along with the bypass, we opened up her heart and filled it with this." In his open palm, he revealed a wad of synthetic material that resembled towelette-tissue wipes.

The doctors had put all of their knowledge into the task. But the most experienced among them could not predict how long the patient would live—or if she would survive at all.

It was a bitter season for the entire Holyfield brood. For three months Mother lay in the intensive care unit fighting for her life. She was constantly in the forefront of our thoughts. Mama was the center of the family. When she fell ill, everyone's life skipped a beat.

It was like our fearful family was collectively standing at that living room window, back in Atmore—each one anxiously hoping that the sheriff would not pull the trigger and take our loved one from us.

How could anyone find the good in all of this bad?

Chubby and I would marvel when we'd overhear the older folk say to each other, "The Death Angel is standing over her bed, desiring to take her from us. But as long as we, the saints of God, are at our post sendin' up intercessory prayers, God's good will shall prevail, for 'the prayers of the righteous availeth much!'"

At our neighborhood church in Summerhill, appropriately called "The Church At Heart," all fifty members were on their knees. Grandmother Hatton herself spearheaded a core group of praying mothers, and these combined, dedicated groups diligently petitioned God on Mama's behalf, as did the whole Church at Heart.

Evander and I remember those services well. We didn't have any pews in that small church so we sat on the cold iron folding chairs. But that was okay because it didn't take long for the atmosphere to heat up to a feverish pitch that caused the most unassuming people to jump up and exclaim, "Hallelujah! Thank You, Jesus!"

The instruments of our church consisted mainly of clapping hands, patting feet, and an old piano that Pastor Gaston's son-in-law coaxed to make beautiful music. And nobody clapped with more rhythm and zest than Grandmother Hatton.

Each Friday and Sunday Grandma Hatton would raise Mama's condition up to the Lord, "Dear Lord Jesus, we ask that You would heal my daughter Annie Laura Holyfield . . ."

Many amens echoed throughout that tiny church.

"Her children need her, Lord. . . ."

The amens became more numerous and rose even louder.

"Take away the grip of the Death Angel . . . and bring her back to us. . . ."

"Amen, Sister. Amen."

"We put this in Your hands, Jesus, and trust that all things work together for good."

Loud shouts of "Amen!" and "Amen!"

After Grandma had prayed fervently for Mom's healing, the pianist would play a rousing rendition of a hymn like "Oh Happy Day." Grandma would punctuate her thanks for Mom's anticipated healing with clapping.

Immediately the whole church would join in, clapping their hands and stomping their feet rhythmically in 4/4 time. Then Grandmother would go between the beats and measures, clapping in 8/4 time one measure, 16/4 time in another, and then back to 4/4 time with everyone else.

Grandma's hand-clapping was a prelude to the introduction of her tambourine, which she kept on the side of her wheelchair with her Bible and her pocketbook. And Grandma did more than just play the tambourine. The instrument became an extension of her hand and her voice. Once she became filled with the Spirit she would bounce the tambourine off her elbow, creating a kind of thud that mingled with the tiny cymbals. Then she would swing it back and forth against the lower portion of her thigh. Occasionally she would even bounce it off her wheelchair.

The piano player would play accompaniment to this one-woman rhythm section. His fingers would run melodies up and down that piano—from the bass clef to the treble. And the lead vocalist would join in, often singing with her eyes closed, swaying from left to right, her voice intoning, "When Jesus died, He wiped my sins away."

And then the twelve-member choir began at the chorus, their voices washing over the congregation in harmony. "Oh happy daaay! Oh happy day!"

Some members of the church raised their hands toward heaven exclaiming, "Thank You, Jesus!" Others sat quietly, tears streaming down their cheeks and smiles on their faces.

Sitting at the center of this foot-stomping worship was a little old lady in a wheelchair, rocking from left to right with her eyes closed, a smile on her face, and faith in her heart. Grandma knew Jesus would hear their prayers.

When the Spirit is moving, you don't say, "It's 11:30 P.M. Time to stop praising God." No, you wait until the Holy Spirit has done His holy work in God's holy house, and you give praise and thanks for His visitation. So on Friday nights it was not unusual for the members of the Church At Heart on Connally Street in Atlanta to leave church after midnight.

Grandmother would always say, "If the sinners can spend all day and all night praising Satan in the clubs, why shouldn't Christians be able to do the same if we are being led by the Holy Spirit?"

At the time Chubby and I couldn't understand all that was happening around us. All we knew was that ninety days without our mother seemed like an unbearable eternity. To Grandmother's credit she must have sensed our apprehension, and she pulled us to her with her strong, loving arms.

"Everything is gonna be alright. Your mama will be home soon. Don't you two fret none, somethin' good is gonna come outta all this. Remember, 'All things work together for good.'"

"Somethin' good is gonna come outta all this?" How? Our once hardworking mother was confined to a potential deathbed. For us kids, it was difficult to understand the concepts of faith, grace, and the power of prayer. But the most difficult to comprehend of these ideas was the notion that all things worked together for good.

"All things?" How does a woman find "the good" in being sentenced to a wheelchair for life? How does a young mother continually find the good in promising relationships gone bad? How does a house full of kids maintain a positive balance in a home without a father—and possibly a mother too?

Then late one evening, while on a trek to the bathroom, Chubby and I heard Grandmother in her room praying. As we moved down the hallway, we paused and listened at her door. The fervency in her voice was electrifying. It had a rhythm to it, like the rise and fall of the ocean. She was reciting her intentions to heaven with such melodic passion that, to us, Grandmother's petitions sounded like singing.

"Lord, let Thy holy will be done . . ."

Looking back on that bitter season through adult eyes, we now see that Grandmother's sacred song was in fact the answer to our long, unexplained question.

Off in a solitude of her own making, Pearlie Hatton shut out the negative chatter of her surrounding world and concentrated on the positive source of her strength. Grandmother was in that "prayer closet" she always talked about, hiding from the world, seeking God.

And that's what Mama was doing on those long walks to work and back—and when she was in the kitchen, bending and caressing those wordless melodies. It was as if her melodic verse was declaring her faith to her troubles.

Over the years my family has discovered that by listening to the directions of God, we can "home in" on the hidden sources of our difficulties. Also, everyone who learns this lesson can, likewise, squeeze a measure of good out of the advantage.

And because of such solitary songs of prayer, Mama came home, just like Grandmother said she would. The crisis was intense, but with care, time, and yes, prayer, our mother Annie's constitution—just like our grandmother Pearlie's—steadily improved.

But she still seemed sad. We didn't know why until we saw a gold-brown envelope lying on the kitchen table.

Uncle Sam's Long Arm of Care

The official letter had been torn open along its side, just nicking the state seal of Georgia, which was printed in the top left corner. Further down the face of the envelope, through a rectangular window, a hint of the correspondence was visible. By its crumpled appearance the documents seemed to have been studied, then hastily stuffed back into the envelope. Across the manilla cover, five words were scribbled in bold, angry print:

RETURN TO SENDER, NOT NEEDED.

Mama's handwriting was recognizable to everyone in the Holyfield family, and so was the implication of the words: Our welfare was Mama's top priority; government welfare was not. The mere notion of turning over her responsibility to a stranger was unthinkable to Mother. She felt there were far more needy folks than us.

The Heart of the Family

Given Mama's tenacity, the postman was not a welcome visitor that summer. Every day he'd drop off a mountain of mail: correspondence from doctors, letters from government agencies—all expressing their concern for her health, along with offers of assistance. Even mother's personal physician mailed her a note, citing the possibility of another heart attack. He forbade Mama to return to work at the Henry Grady Cafeteria, and he told her employer so. The idea of being unable to work, regardless of the reason, went against everything that Mama stood for. She had always told us, "Sons, always maintain your independence by being self-sufficient. Never let anyone rob you of your independence by making you totally dependent upon them for your livelihood. To be totally dependent on others is to be in a position to be totally controlled and manipulated by others." All that this "caring" correspondence managed to do was frustrate Mama and upset the delicate balance of her blood pressure.

Sensing this effect on Mother's disposition, Joe Ann called a family meeting. We looked up to her—not because she stood a full six feet tall but because she, with her large, pretty brown eyes and milk-chocolate complexion, exuded a quiet dignity. Joe Ann rarely spoke, but when she did her gentle words were always carefully chosen and full of wisdom. When she called for a gathering of the Holyfields, we knew the occasion was important. Attendance was mandatory.

This was not an ordinary family meeting; it was a serious conference. We had to devise a plan to remedy the financial slack caused by mother's condition.

The gist of the solution was that everyone was going to pitch in and take on a little extra work. Evander and I even threw in our two cents' worth, which when added together, almost matched the nickel deposit on the bottles we volunteered to collect.

After that family summit, mornings around our house seemed even busier. As always, Chubby and I would awaken to the sound of chattering voices and clanking breakfast dishes. The only difference was that now we had a reason to join the working folk around the table. Although we were the novices at that adult gathering, we felt important. In fact nothing matched the elation of jumping up from the table and declaring proudly, "Can't sit around and talk all day. There's lots a work to do, and we wanna get an early start!"

From midmorning, well into the heat of the summer afternoon,

Chubby and I pounded the hot Georgia asphalt in search of returnable bottles—especially those pale-green ones embossed with the Coca-Cola logo. We explored everywhere. No dumpster was left unturned. We'd find the glass containers along the sidewalk and scattered around the playground. We even went door-to-door, asking our neighbors to load us up with their empties.

At the end of the day, we would haul our bounty down to Mr. Neal's store on the corner and trade the pile of glass for cash. Although we were hot and hungry, Chubby and I would race home with our earnings, proud that we could add an extra four to five dollars to the family budget.

Soon after those scavenger hunts began, we moved out of Joe Ann's house into a place of our own. That miracle of red brick and wood was an unexpected boon for our family. And Evander and I were certain that our bottle money made it all possible.

Life is an unpredictable series of endings and beginnings. And its early lessons have not gone unnoticed by us Holyfields—especially Evander. Although little brother and I have endured some pinches, a few switches, some disappointments and questions, we learned early on the importance of hard work and discipline and the value of faith. Over the years, no matter how many bouts are fought or how much bad is endured, we've always managed to find a measure of "good."

As Evander displays each time he steps into the ring, win or lose there is always a reason to give thanks. Because when we learn from the bad—that's good. But when we're not sure, or we've wandered too far into forbidden territory, there is a way to find the right direction. It is a lesson Chubby and I were taught early on: Simply play hide and seek. Hide away from the world, off in a solitude of your own making, and seek God's voice. Because He's always at home base. And He never gets tired of calling.

CHAPTER 4

THE NOVICE

The new place on Cherokee Avenue was just a five-minute drive from Connally Street. It was slightly smaller than Joe Ann's four-bedroom home, but it had the marked advantage of being less crowded; now there would only be three to a bedroom, instead of four. To us, the place was a sprawling mansion.

Living in such roomy conditions took a little getting used to. It was common practice for Chubby and me to share beds, blankets, and bathrooms. And even under those circumstances we mostly got along with each other; that's what a family does. So it's ironic that it was here, in this "sprawling" environment, that we first learned the concepts of boundaries. That notion was introduced to us by the addition of a strange, new word to our beginner's vocabulary: segregation. We would grow to discover that this word implied an "us versus them" way of thinking.

When we moved into the new neighborhood, we also entered a new school district. And being under its jurisdiction we were required to comply with the Civil Rights Act, just signed by President Lyndon Johnson. The law dictated that Chubby and I transfer from E. P. Johnson Elementary to the newly integrated W. F. Slaton Grade School.

Before we planted one foot in that school, Mama sat us down and told us all about racism—how some people are so ignorant that they hate other people because their skin, religion, or culture may be different. But she gave us a formula for overcoming racism. She said, "Sons, people don't like to talk about racism, but it's a fact of life. And racism is going to be here just as long as people refuse to practice brotherly love the way Jesus taught it. But the best way to overcome racism is to get a good education and be the best in whatever you pursue; even racism has to eventually bow in the presence of excellence."

However, at W. F. Slaton, we never had a racial problem, and we really didn't understand what the commotion was about. All we could figure was that it had something to do with living in close quarters and trying to get along. Such ideas were natural to us. Yet the idea of such "closeness'" seemed to anger others. It was confusing. One fact was obvious, whatever the trouble was, it affected the grown-ups, not the children.

We never thought of our next-door neighbor Timothy as being white, or the kids down the streets as Hispanic; they were just our friends. Kids our age who enjoyed baseball and football, like us. They were companions who shared our toys and even the confusion of those crazy days. None of us were ever conscious of any color barrier—that is, until society went out of its way to invent it.

At school the segregation law was enforced, but at the Boy's Club the statute was ignored, mainly because it wasn't necessary. As the hub of activity in our multiethnic community, the club had always been integrated. Asians, blacks, Hispanics, whites—you name it and the Boy's Club had it. The only barriers there were the limitations we placed on ourselves.

However, one group at the club was a little choosier than the rest. Coach Carter Morgan's words still echoed in Evander's head: "Young'un, ya gotta be real tough to be on the boxing team." Slowly but surely, the old man's statement was becoming a novice's challenge; a goal to be reached and surpassed.

So Evander began showing up at that fenced-off area of the gym day after day. He'd wait near that dangling speed bag until Carter Morgan noticed him, then he'd repeat his plea, "I wanna hit that bag! I wanna join the boxing team."

At first Morgan's response was still, "Young'un, ya gotta be real tough to be on the boxing team." He'd had many other kids say they wanted to join the team; they'd be exicted for a while, but after a few weeks their interest waned.

Evander was different. Day after day, week after week, he reappeared. "Coach, I wanna join the boxing team." Finally Carter believed that this kid was there for the long haul. He began to work with Evander—even allowing him to work out on the speed bag.

A Pigskin Ball and Leather Mittens

What initially lured Evander into the ring was the attention he received from Carter Morgan. In a way that crusty, freckle-faced coach was the father figure Chubby had always wanted.

Evander enjoyed being around him, earning his trust and approval. He reveled in any activity that gained the coach's favor. He would bang the heavy bag relentlessly and jump rope till his arms and legs were spent. He would spar with the toughest opponent available and lift weights with repetitious abandon. He would do anything just to coax a brief wink of recognition from Carter Morgan.

Although little brother would rather have had a football in his hand, he was willing to put on a pair of gloves instead if it would make Carter Morgan smile. But then again, watching Evander spar, back in those early days, put a grin on everybody's face—on one occasion, even his opponent's.

Usually at the bell, Chubby's small frame would explode out of the corner and attack his rival—head-on. Holding back nothing, employing the full measure of his strength, he would pummel his challenger with an endless series of wild, windmill-like blows. This awkward onslaught would continue nonstop until the bell sounded again—or his flustered adversary surrendered.

At the end of those early matches, when the referee held up Chubby's arm in victory, the challenger would often burst into tears. Seeing another eight-year-old crying tainted Evander's first wins. The idea that he had caused someone else's pain, the notion that he had hurt someone bad enough to make him cry, often made him feel far worse than the loser. Frequently he would leave the ring muttering to himself, "Why am I doing this?"

His frustration soon began to affect his performance. Before a match Chubby would experience the same uncomfortable butterflies that everyone gets in face-to-face competition. But then, during the fight itself, that natural apprehension would escalate. Not only would he be cautious of his opponent injuring him, but gradually, Evander also began to dread the notion of actually hurting his opponent. This anxiety, along with his racing adrenaline, would knot together as he waited for the referee's decision. If he lost, he would be devastated. But if he won, his opponent's tears would make him feel even worse.

This inner torture haunted Evander, and thoughts of quitting invaded his mind. Then he'd see Coach Morgan's elation when the referee raised Evander's arm in victory, and the apprehension would ebb, at least for the moment. Only to be rekindled anew at the opening bell of his next fight.

Chubby carefully evaluated the situation. Utilizing eight-year-old rationale, he noted that his challengers usually cried when he hit them in the face. So, for his own conscience's sake, little brother decided, "I won't do that anymore." At this age, the kids' gloves are padded like pillows, and the kids wear headgear. So they cried more out of frustration and humiliation than pain.

In the next match Evander was pitted against one of the cry-babies. When the bell rang Chubby jumped out of his corner and then proceeded to land his gloves everywhere allowable: the chest, shoulders, the midsection—everywhere except the face. His challenger soon began to rack up points, for he wasn't as selective as Chubby.

This charade went on for two full rounds before Coach Morgan finally stooped down into Evander's perspiring face and barked, "Go to the head! Young'un, why don't you go for the head!?"

"Coach, if I hit 'im in the face, he's gonna cry!"

Catching Chubby's flailing gloves between his large hands, Morgan secured his student's full attention, then grunted, "Kid, they don't cry because you hit them in the face. They cry because you win, and they don't! Look at him over there," the coach gestured across the canvas to the opponent's corner. "He's smiling at ya'. He's laughing 'cause he's outscored you for two rounds. What'r ya gonna do about it?"

When the bell rang again, Chubby the human windmill burst into the center of the ring and commenced swinging so many punches at his opponent's smiling face that the challenger could not stay on his feet. Finally, after the smiler fell—twice—the ref stopped the contest and raised Chubby's arm high in the air. His opponent was too dazed to cry. And Coach Morgan was too pleased to hide his approving grin.

After that, Evander became a two-sport athlete. Although football remained his first love, something about boxing, and that cantankerous old coach, kept him climbing back into the ring.

Admittedly, at eight years old he was a novice at both efforts: a small bundle of raw energy on the football field and a gawky windmill inside the ropes. Nevertheless, he persevered. Combining the benefits of time and discipline, Chubby diligently pushed himself to polish his natural athletic abilities. Under Coach Morgan's tutelage Evander never lost a match between the ages of eight and eleven. He was determined not to let his talent slip away.

During these grade school days, the coach must have sensed his student's lack of fatherly influence, for gradually Carter made the uncharacteristic effort to be Evander's pal. When he would show up at the Boy's Club, Morgan would go out of his way to send him on "special errands." At one point this seemingly unfeeling old coach even let Evander carry his car keys. A small gesture, but the kind of thing a father would do to instill a sense of value in a son. Morgan wanted Chubby to know that he considered his boxer to be an asset both in the ring and outside the ropes.

The old coach knew Evander was a member of that rare, infrequent breed of fighter that comes around about as often as Halley's Comet. Morgan recognized in Chubby "that certain something," which has yet to be explained, and he never tried. The old coach was a man of few words. However, there was one memorable occasion when he let his guard down and spoke his mind.

The episode occurred just after Evander had defeated an exceptionally tough junior division opponent. As everyone gathered around him, congratulating him on a job well done, an extremely pleased Coach Morgan embraced his student and uttered a collection of words that Evander has never forgotten.

"Young'un, one day you're gonna be champ of the world!"

That night Evander came home elated. He cherished the words and repeated them over and over. He believed the sentiment totally, wholeheartedly. Why? Because Mr. Morgan said so!

That collection of words bounced around the back of Chubby's mind all through grade school and junior high. And over the next few formative years, he successfully juggled his elementary and junior high school notebooks with a pigskin ball and a pair of large, leather gloves. Although he continued to entertain visions of an Atlanta Falcons jersey, Evander found increasing pleasure in shoving his growing hands into a pair of Morgan's lace-up mittens.

Yes, Chubby grew—but not enough. Although each progressive season saw him rack up an impressive list of alternating TDs and KOs, one looming obstacle constantly dogged his athletic progress: his small frame.

As the old saying goes, "People judge a book by its cover," and in Chubby's case, "an athlete by his size." Despite his natural ability, Evander's less-than-average size continually categorized him as a "novelty." Few considered him more than a curious munchkin with surprising energy. In the eyes of his world, Chubby's "pocketbook cover" did little to suggest the "great American blockbuster" he would eventually become.

Throughout grade school Evander's small size made his big

dream of pro ball seem even more enormous. But that looming obstacle didn't stop him. If anything, it made him try harder.

Life Lessons and Love Lost

As every football-fantasizing teenager knows, the surest method of attracting the pros is to rack up an impressive performance record in both high school and college ball. Such was Evander's intent when he suited up for tryouts with the Fulton High School Red Birds. He was certain that the league's wings would eventually carry him up to the lofty heights of the Atlanta Falcons. But that teenage vision was not shared by his evaluating coaches. In fact the longer they studied Chubby's small 110 pounds, the more they envisioned him to be a novice, a Boy's Club amateur.

Displaying their silver whistles about their necks like a badge of authority, his judges ran Evander through a gauntlet of demanding drills and hard-hitting plays. Chubby's past athletic adventures seemed of little consequence. Chirping out commands using short, high-pitched blasts from their whistles, the Red Birds put him through their punishing wringer.

Eventually, by sheer sweat and determination, Chubby managed to convince the coach and staff that his small frame carried a big heart. His consistent performance illustrated to his surprised judges that he was indeed qualified to wear the team's red wings. However, being qualified for a task and actually being allowed to do the job are two different things: Evander made the team, but he rarely made the field!

He would dutifully suit up for every practice. And each weekend of pigskin season he would don his Red Wing jersey and psych himself up for the game. But more often than not, the only thing he fired up on those cool Georgia nights was his own benchwarming backside.

It was agony for him to sit and watch his companions slug it out on the field. Every time the ball was snapped, he would focus his attention on the action and mentally put himself on the line of scrimmage. From his sideline vantage point he studied the other team's strengths and analyzed their weaknesses, especially the middle linebacker, the position he coveted. Evander was determined to be prepared for that long-awaited moment when the coach would give him the nod.

In a way Evander's predicament was much like Mama's. Her doctor's evaluation kept her at home, sidelined. Every morning she suited up hoping for the chance to get back in the game. Both Chubby and Mama were ready, willing, and anxious to get their long-awaited nod to take the field, but others thought they lacked the proper heart to do the job they loved.

The football season was more than half over when Chubby finally stood up during an afternoon practice. "Coach . . . Coach!" he called out, rubbing his warm, slightly numb backside. "Let me try the middle linebacker spot."

Looking over his shoulder the man with the whistle responded, "Holyfield, how many times do I have to say it? You're not big enough for that position. Those guys weigh 190 pounds or more! They'll walk right over you. Stick to cornerback."

Undaunted, Evander picked up his helmet and moved toward the field. "The next play, put me in as middle linebacker."

"Holyfield, I told you—!"

"If I stop the runner, I get to play the position," Chubby interrupted, putting on his helmet. "If he gets past me, I'll settle for cornerback."

The coach stood silent for a moment, fuming. Then, after a couple of heavy heaves from his chest, he gave a quick nod toward the field. Evander trotted out to the line of scrimmage.

Taking his coveted position, Chubby readied himself for the test. The opposing quarterback stepped in place behind the center and began his count, "Three-fourteen! Three-twenty-five! Hut! . . . Hut!" He snapped the ball, and the players went into action.

Watching the runners in the backfield, Evander tried to determine which one the quarterback would target. First, there was a fake to the smaller of the two halfbacks. Then, the ball shot into the air, and as it descended Chubby zeroed in on its destination: a burly mountain heading straight for him!

When the fullback crossed the line of scrimmage, he was met by 110 pounds of solid determination. And with a heavy thud, reminiscent of a ball bat striking a side of beef, the runner was stopped cold in his tracks.

"Whoa!" a collective yell erupted from the sidelines. "Did you see that! Who made that tackle?"

As he left the field, Evander got a smattering of applause and back slaps, but the only response that really counted was that from the man with the whistle.

"Good hit, kid. Have a seat."

Maybe the hit wasn't good enough for the coach. Maybe he thought it was just luck. Whatever the case, even after making the hit of the day, Chubby saw very little game time. And he wasn't happy. The more he warmed the bench, the colder he grew toward football.

Then one afternoon Evander told Mama he had decided to quit. He knew that she, better than anyone else, would understand.

"You're gonna what?"

"I'm gonna quit, Mama."

"Quit football? Why?"

"I've tried! I can't do it no more. I go to practice. I go to the games. I give it everything I got—but it's not enough.

"I wanted to go to the pros, but they tell me I'm too small. They keep me on the bench. It's a waste o' time."

As Evander paced back and forth, Mama sat for a moment and thought. Staring off at nothing in particular, her eyes were soon drawn toward a glistening gold object across the room. One of Chubby's trophies reflected the light of the afternoon sun. Her eyes moved from that statuette to the one next to it. Then to the next. Close to fifty awards lined that wall—citations and souvenirs, all heralding the multiple athletic talents of Evander Holyfield. She turned her gaze back toward her son.

"You'll never know what will happen if you don't finish what you start. You gotta wait for your opportunity. Ya gots to keep on keepin' on till it comes. When it does, grab it, and don't let go!

"There's always gonna be people attemptin' to pre-judge you by your size or some outward thing. It's not fair, and I know it. Just remember, man may look at the outward appearance, but God judges the heart."

Gesturing to her own surgery-scarred bosom, Annie Holyfield all but whispered, "It's what's inside you that matters. It's what's in here that counts. Don't you quit; I didn't raise no quitters. Find the good in the bad. Finish out the season. Strive for excellence. Work just as hard at practice as if you were playin' in every game, so that when that opportunity comes you'll be prepared to grab it, and hold on tight!"

Evander did what he was told. Although he wasn't a happy

camper those last few weeks, he stuck it out. He never missed a practice. And each Friday night he would take his place on the bench fully padded, with helmet in hand, as if he were actually going to play.

The "good" that Mama spoke of finally revealed itself during the fourth quarter of Fulton High's last game of the season. The Red Birds were leading, and the tension on field was as visible as the players' hot breath in the cool night air. Both sides were taking their positions for the kickoff when the coach pointed to Evander, "You're in."

In an almost dreamlike state, Chubby's well-trained body shifted to automatic. He could feel the points of his cleats sinking into the grass turf but was barely conscious of his hands pulling the helmet over his head. As he eagerly took his place on the field, the choir of yelling fans faded, and Mama's whispered words rooted him on, like a private, personal cheer: "When opportunity comes, grab it! Grab it and hold on tight!"

And that's exactly what he did.

On the third play Evander watched as the opposing quarterback feigned a handoff to the fullback and then turned to pitch the ball back to the halfback. Digging his toes into the turf, Evander darted to the left end. When he started, he was a step and a half behind, but the small defensive back picked up the difference by sheer determination. The halfback met the scrimmage line at the same moment he felt Evander's shoulder pads crashing into his legs. Evander held the wily back to no yardage gained.

On the opposing team's next possession, a fullback came barreling through the Fulton High line. He looked a head taller and half-a-kid heavier than Evander, but Chubby put his head down, wrapped his hands around the fullback's legs, and wrestled the bigger player down.

The stands roared their approval. Where had this kid been? It was as if Evander had claimed his portion of the football field and nobody, *nobody*, was going to trepass. The rest of the quarter showed the same scenario: backs charging through the Fulton High line or around the Fulton High ends, only to be met by a small but determined Evander Holyfield.

"Good job," the coach offered, slapping Chubby's shoulder pads approvingly. "I didn't know you could play that well. See ya next season, kid."

The sentiment was genuine, but the timing was off—about a

full season. Evander was grateful for the chance to publicly prove himself, but the thought of warming the bench for another year left him cold.

Football season passed, and as fall turned to winter, Evander's longtime dream of joining the Atlanta Falcons likewise iced over. Football had inspired him to get out of bed each morning, and its weary pursuit helped him to sleep each night. The dream of wearing that Falcon jersey was the original motivation behind all of Chubby's athletic endeavors. Letting go of that aspiration wasn't easy, but it was necessary.

Whether it's football or the beau next door, letting go of a first love is among the highest hurdles life puts in your path. Nevertheless, it is an experience every novice must endure if the rank of maturity is to be reached. The self-examination that inevitably follows creates wisdom. It is an ancient rite of passage that transforms suffering into strength, and misfortune into advantage. It is nature's way of harvesting the good out of the bad.

One recurring thought knocked the chill off Evander's disappointment: the Boy's Club boxing ring and the feeling of slipping his hands into a pair of Coach Morgan's leather mittens. Virtually overnight, the idea of dancing around a twenty-nine-foot circle with fists perpetually raised at eye level became appealing. The thought of pounding away at a face-to-face opponent who is likewise pounding back, for twelve three-minute rounds, suddenly seemed inviting. It was a contest Evander realized he could handle—despite his size. It was a challenge he knew he could meet, in spite of his volume. Boxing began to take the shape of a realistic goal, worthy of his aspiration. Besides, the spark of a new challenge was just the thing to melt away the cold disappointment of a lost love.

CHAPTER 5

THE SWEET SCIENCE OF BOXING

Carter Morgan's brand of coaching was a rare blend of tyrant, teacher, and understanding friend. A serious man, he often appeared to the uninitiated as overbearing and grouchy, but that was just his way of weeding out the fainthearted, fickle folk who refused to take the time to improve. His familiar motto, "There's no tomorrow," summed up his entire philosophy. The sixty-plus-year-old Morgan was not about to spend a moment on anything or anybody he thought a waste. Every boxer on his Boy's Club team knew it. And no one understood that message better than Evander.

In the gym, Coach Morgan could see that same stubborn resolve in every ripple of Chubby's developing muscles. His student was no longer a mesmerized child, shifting his adolescent attention from baseball to football to boxing. The boy was now sixteen, fit, and focused on one single goal. It was plain to Morgan that his prodigal fighter had not returned simply to learn "the tricks" of the trade. Evander had come back to learn the trade itself—the sweet science of boxing.

The two men took to the challenge with equal gusto. The gruff, often demanding coach wasted little time in pushing Evander to his limits—and beyond. Morgan forced the teenager through a daily regimen of torturous incremental steps, the kind of regimen that creates warriors.

The first goal Coach Morgan set for his protégé was the introductory class of the Southeastern Boxing Division. Evander's first ranking fight was to be for the ironic regional title "novice." To me, the ranking's one-word title did not seem an appropriate description of my brother's range of experience. But it was one of those paradoxical signposts that mark the ongoing "endings and beginnings" of life.

Although Chubby had secured the title of novice in the Southeastern Boxing Amateur Division, he was a long way from becoming the sport's celebrated "Real Deal." He still had to climb through the more advanced divisions. Next was the open level. He possessed the natural physical talent and the drive to succeed, but he lacked the wisdom that comes with experience and the conditioning of genuine competition.

Now the eternal ring of Coach Morgan's words, "One day you're gonna be champ of the world!" drove Evander to rise before dawn and will one foot in front of the other.

"Hey, Bernard! Saw that crazy brother of yours this mornin'," the kids at school would often snicker as we'd pass in the hallway, "Around 6 A.M. he was runnin' down the street throwin' punches at invisible people. What's the deal?"

Like any average high schooler, Evander wanted the approval and recognition of his peers, but displays of encouragement rarely occurred. Back in the late 1970s, boxing was considered a nontraditional sport. Many years would pass before it finally reached the "A list" of extracurricular school activities. Evander often seemed like the outside person of some inside joke. So, more often than not, he kept his dreams to himself, leaving his friends to scratch their befuddled heads.

What our classmates didn't understand was that Evander was not the average teenager. He was now totally focused on one overwhelming ambition. And he was determined to endure all of the difficult steps necessary to reach it, whether his peers understood him or not.

Chubby was past the stage of pushing himself to gain a compliment from his coach. He was now plunging headfirst, deep into the disciplines of the fight game. And Coach Morgan's eagle eye was still watching . . . and waiting.

Signs of Maturity

Despite his low profile around school, Evander was gaining some recognition in the local boxing community. His bouts—from his early days up through his novice ranking and just beyond—had mainly been one-sided affairs in Chubby's favor. That consistency, along with his energetic performances, quickly singled him out as the up-and-coming amateur to watch. Ultimately, all of this attention made his next official challenge, the Open Division, more demanding, both professionally and personally.

Upon reaching this pivotal category, a fighter is considered to have achieved such a level of maturity that he is no longer matched up by age but by weight, thereby testing not only his skill but also his physical strength. The Open Division separates the men from the boys. It determines whether a boxer sinks or swims.

As he climbed through the ropes for his initial match, Evander knew his performance would be appraised, at least in part, by his size, as in his bench-sitting football days. He knew this worry would cloud his concentration, so he got off by himself and slipped into that private solitude of his own making. There, he hid away from the world and sought the strength and direction of God.

When the bell rang for the first round, Evander shot out of his corner with a focused determination that was rare even for him. After letting loose a flurry of body jabs, he cocked back his right arm and put all of his 147 pounds behind the swing. It only took a millisecond for the gloved hand to fly through the air and strike his rival's surprised, unprepared jaw. But with its impact, a sound similar to a *swack!* emanated from the ring and echoed throughout the gym. That reverberation was immediately followed by a groan, and the thud of Chubby's pound-for-pound opponent hitting the canvas.

That first Open Division match went down in the books as sixteen-year-old Evander Holyfield's first confirmed knockout. An action that everyone took as a sign of maturity. This deed generated that extra measure of attention. And that increased recognition carried Evander to a higher level; he was finally getting a peek at his own undiscovered power.

The next few bouts took Evander on the ride of his life. With seemingly effortless precision he breezed his way through a series of pubescent, warrior wanna-bes. In short order, he found himself on the roster of contenders for the Open Division's semi-finals.

An Unfamiliar Tug

His initial assignment in this contest was to make quick work of a young hopeful named Jackie Winters. By all appearances the task seemed no more difficult than the routine bouts he had faced up to that point. Gazing across the ring, sizing up his opponent,

Evander estimated that the lad was no bigger than himself. In his eyes, Winter's manner appeared nervous and insecure. Recognizing this, Evander concluded that their bout would be nothing more than a good warm-up.

The official scoring of rounds one and two confirmed Chubby's confidence. Young Winters held his ground, but it was Holyfield who racked up the points. As anticipated, everything was going Evander's way. Then, in the blink of an eye, without any warning, he felt the sudden, painful brunt of an anvil crash against the side of his head. With that impact, the abrupt tug of gravity pulled him straight down. He was in the grips of an uncontrollable free fall.

The ring elevated. And as the textured pattern of the canvas grew increasingly larger, Evander's dazed mind wondered how he was going to get up again.

The seconds ticked by with every slow-motion down-stroke of the ref's arm, and Carter Morgan sprang toward the ropes. With his eyes focused on Evander, the old coach released a bellow: "Get up, young'un! Show 'em your stuff! Get ya gloves up! There's no tomorrow, kid! *Get up!*" Wringing a towel between his fists, the coach stared anxiously down at the canvas, his wide eyes watching and waiting for some confirmation that his boxer was still in the fight.

Disoriented, his head a clutter of muffled sounds and bright stars, Evander felt as though he were still plummeting toward certain destruction.

"Get up, young'un! Get up!"

The familiar voice seemed far above him, but it slowly stirred his numbed senses, and after another slow-motion moment he began to move. The action was tentative at first, more of instinct than design, but his strength soon returned. And with a burst of energy that seemed to come from deep within, Chubby spread his strong arms and pushed himself up onto his legs.

But before he could reach his full height, Jackie Winters attacked again.

Bracing himself for the oncoming charge, Evander spontaneously threw up his arms, and after a blurred second, the two contenders were wrapped together in an equally binding clinch.

With his hands confined, Evander's dazed reason devised an impromptu counterattack to break the deadlock: he spit out his mouthpiece and took a bite out of Winter's shoulder. The wounded fighter pulled back in pain, letting loose his grip—and a yelp that echoed in unison with the clang of the bell.

Hearing that welcome sound, Evander exhaled a long sigh of relief and slowly shuffled back to his corner. Dropping his tired frame down on the stool, he could not bring himself to look up into Coach Morgan's eyes.

At that painful moment, the coach's words, "Young'un, one day you're gonna be champ of the world!" seemed very unlikely. Evander was embarrassed, hurt, and disappointed. That Winters kid was tougher than he looked; and the reality of that fact struck Evander harder than Jackie's surprising swing.

Sitting on that stool Evander reminded himself that he was guilty of the very thing that he disliked most in others: He had judged a book by its deceptive cover. It was a painful, arrogant, stupid error.

As Morgan tended to Evander's bruises, he could sense the wheels of his student's mind turning. Seeing Evander's bloodshot eyes staring off in thought, the coach realized that his fighter's unexpected free fall had done him some good.

"What's done is done, young'un!" the old coach grunted down at the meditating boxer. "Stop thinkin' 'bout the past and get your head outta the future. All that matters is *here! Now!* The next round! There's no tomorrow!

"If ya don't believe in yourself, what your eyes tell ya *won't* matter. And if ya got the faith, what your eyes tell ya *don't* matter. Get ya gloves up. Get in there. . . . Finish it!"

With a firm nod of his clearing head, Evander popped in his mouthpiece and jumped to his feet. Dancing in place, he waited for the bell. And as its high-pitched shrill ring filled the gym, he strolled to the center of the ring and waited for Winters. It was just the confirmation Morgan's eye was looking for. The youngster was learning.

The rest of the bout was a blur of flailing arms and wounded pride as both young boxers fought to come out on top. As Morgan urged him, Evander kept his mind on the bout. The grogginess that clouded his thinking was a new sensation, but Evander fought through with courage and tenacity.

That night Chubby managed to retire with an equal measure of consternation and consolation. The Open Division bout with Jackie

Winters left Chubby with a painful (but minor) head concussion, a bruised but improved resolve, and a split-decision victory to his surprisingly fit contender.

The injury and knockdown, however, would pay long-term dividends. Evander won the bout the hard way and learned that a knockdown didn't automatically take him out. He could fight through the surprise, confusion, pain, and fear. Evander Holyfield would eventually be known as the boxer who just wouldn't give up. I believe that the seed of this character trait was planted that night, in the ring with Jackie Winters.

Until that evening, Evander had never viewed a boxing ring from the abyss-like depths of the canvas. Being at eye level with his competitor's tightly laced hightops was not an experience he cared to repeat. The episode was humiliating, disappointing, and yet enlightening. It was one of those necessary incremental steps that readies a boxer for the next time. As were the next years of losses.

The Loss Column

Only four of us were now living at home: Mama, Grandma, Evander, and me—and I had one foot out the door. Just about the time Evander was wrestling with the Amateur Boxing Open Division, I was graduating high school and packing my bags for the United States Signal Corps. Although the family was sad to see me go, they were proud of my decision. They knew that, for me, enlisting in the service was the right choice. It was what I wanted. Still, leaving home was difficult—not only for me but for my brother too.

We were the Dynamic Duo, the Two Musketeers, the tag team of Chubby and Lightnin'! Until the day I threw a duffle bag over my shoulder and walked out the front door, neither of us could remember a time when we were apart.

We had shared the awe of those strange nights with the "man" in the kitchen, we had witnessed the horror of Lassie's murder, we had created countless adventures in our own backyard, and we had discovered the endless possibilities of the Boy's Club. As a team we had scavenged for bottles, and as brothers we had shared the bounty. We learned about the bad. And sitting side by side at Grandmother Hatton's feet, we discovered how to find the good.

Those mutual memories would never be lost. But now it was time we each moved on and readied ourselves for the next phase of our individual lives. When I walked out that door, it was the beginning of our first solo adventures.

Upon trading in our small house for a crowded barrack, I was swiftly introduced to a whole new world. It was exciting, scary, and a little lonely. But in the time it takes to blow reveille, my attentions turned from home and family to a more pressing matter: surviving boot camp.

Evander, on the other hand, had a more difficult time with the transition. He had never lived in a room by himself, and the sudden change made the small dwelling seem like an empty stadium. After a few months of this solitude he began to entertain thoughts of his own front-door exodus.

Often, during his early-morning runs, as his feet pounded the pavement, his imagination would likewise run free, exercising his dreams of independence. And like any teenager on the verge of adulthood, his pulse would quicken at the very thought of having "a place of his own."

Nevertheless, Evander was not the type to throw caution to the wind. Just as sure as his morning runs were governed by the boundary of physical fatigue, his daydreams were controlled by the limitations of reality.

Although he contemplated leaving, Evander was conscious of the hurdles that stood in his way. His desired independence was a luxury that was dependent upon money, and he was all too aware that he had yet to save up enough for a couple months' rent. Between school, training, and his weekend boxing matches, he could only make time for occasional odd jobs. And those part-time efforts amounted to just slightly more than the bottle money we used to scavenge as kids.

In Evander's practical mind, the obstacle of money was a hard one to overcome, but it was not as difficult to get around as Mama. Annie Holyfield was the border guard of the family, dedicated to monitoring all departures through our front door. Chubby knew that even if he had the money, he could never leave the house until he displayed the proper credentials to Mother: a high school diploma. He knew that he would have to occupy the enormous solitude of our small bedroom for another two semesters.

This teenage trial, taken at face value, may seem a bit trivial. But Evander's uneasy solitude was the backdrop for the struggles he would soon experience in the ring. Up to that point in his amateur boxing career, his stats did not display a single digit in the loss column. Although he had experienced a few close calls, each time the final bell rang, the ref raised his arm into the air. He had yet to learn the meaning of the old adage, "For something to be born, for something to live, something must die."

It was an important lesson, as necessary to his development as the strain of an extra bench-press rep. This measure of wisdom was introduced to him through the gloves of a young boxer from Rockdale County, Cecil Collins.

Solitary Adventure

At first glance, there was nothing about the Holyfield-Collins fight that suggested the occurrence of anything out of the ordinary. As with every Boy's Club match, the gymnasium floor was adorned with sixty-odd folding chairs surrounding the raised, roped-in ring. The chairs themselves were occupied by the usual mix of family, friends, and fanatic fight fans. And as always, in anticipation of the bell, the atmosphere was awash with a collective anxiety.

Evander climbed through the ropes decked out in full warrior regalia: dark trunks, lightweight lace-up shoes, the required protective leather helmet, and his old Boy's Club tank-top boasting the insignia "Carter Morgan Boxing Team." Appearing self-assured, he swaggered about in his corner, occasionally glancing over at his adversary with a subtle, curious glint.

Like Winters before him, Cecil Collins bore little resemblance to a tough opponent. Nevertheless, Evander remained inwardly cautious; he had learned that lesson, the hard way. Never again would he take anything, or anyone, at face value. Still, the subconscious whisper of his undefeated record kept Evander's confidence high and his bravado obvious.

At the bell, the two went at each other with the zeal one might expect from teenagers. At first they toyed and tested the boundary of one another's agility. Then they began to dance around the ring like a bashful couple on prom night. They weaved and bobbed in a textbook two-step of offensive action and defensive reaction. The exchanges between them were so uniform, so balanced, the judges' scoring was virtually even. It was turning into a match in every sense of the word.

Feeling a little flustered by the deadlock, Evander decided to turn up the heat. In classic Holyfield fashion, he maneuvered himself inside Collins's defenses. And when the opportunity presented itself, Evander let loose a roundhouse punch that sent Collins reeling.

Pleased with himself, Evander paused for a moment to admire his handiwork. But before he knew it, Collins reeled himself back around and hooked Evander under the chin with a roundhouse of his own.

Evander returned to his corner, shocked and dazed. He was used to hitting kids who didn't hit back. As a young boy Evander had been called "One Punch Holyfield" because several of his bouts were decided after he threw one hard blow.

Evander complained to Morgan, "Coach, I hit him and he hit me back!"

"Yeah . . . well welcome to boxing, Evander," Morgan replied. "Now, are you going to get him?"

Evander's shocked face didn't display the confidence that Morgan was looking for, so the coach tried another tactic. "Look, you gonna let that white boy beat you? Go in there and beat him up!"

Evander charged toward his adversary like a steamroller as the next round began. He slipped in a shot to Collins's ribs. Collins returned the favor. Evander let go another salvo. Again Collins countered with one of his own.

For what seemed like an eternity the two traded blow for blow— and racked up point for point. Finally Evander's pent-up frustration involuntarily exploded. He wrapped his muscular arms around Collins's midsection and picked him straight up off the canvas. Then with a mighty heave, he tossed him across the ring like a sack of potatoes.

The referee raced over to the two combatants and pulled Evander away. "Disqualified!" he yelled, raising Collins's arms in victory.

As Evander returned to his corner, Morgan screamed, "What did you think you were doing?!"

"Coach, you told me to beat him up so I was trying to beat him up!"

"You—" Morgan's angry face broke into a smile. He *had* told Evander to beat him up. Next time he'd choose his words a little more carefully.

Armed with this resolve, Morgan and Evander scheduled a second match between Holyfield and Collins.

In preparation for the rematch, Evander pushed himself physically, keeping in mind that loss column on his record. He was resolved to wipe clean the smudges that tainted his reputation.

This bout started like the first one. Evander and Collins both clashed in the center of the ring and kept swinging until the round was over. Neither fighter moved much; instead there was a dizzying whirl of arms as each seemed equally determined to land more punches than the opponent.

The bout continued with almost no style except stand-and-punch. When the final bell of that second match echoed through the gym, the judges again awarded the bout to Collins. As the ref once more raised young Cecil's arm into the air, Evander's balloon burst. Like the crybaby opponents of his childhood, Evander found it was his turn to weep. Once more Collins had won.

Although Carter Morgan was just as disappointed as Evander, he did not waste any time offering his student compassion. Self-pity was the cause of the whole fiasco, the old man knew. Like any good coach, Morgan could see that Evander's attention had been focused on himself, on his reputation, not on the fight. What his young boxer needed was provocation, not consolation.

"Young'un, nothin' in this world is free," Morgan's gravelly voice declared. "If you want somethin', it's gonna cost ya. And if you want it bad enough, you'll pay. Ya want Collins? Ya gonna have ta work for it. If ya pay the price, you'll earn the prize."

Evander heard the coach's words, but he didn't know how he could possibly give any more. He felt stuck, stranded in a kind of limbo. He was restricted from leaving home until he earned a high school diploma, and he was confined to the Open Division until he achieved a win over Cecil Collins. If that wasn't enough, he knew that no one could get him out of this mess but himself.

Listening to the old coach's provoking words, Evander grasped the underlying truth all too well. Only he could pay the price to earn the prize. His one-punch-victory days were over. He was almost a man. The Age of Struggle had begun. Yet of all the obstacles blocking his way, the most devastating to Evander's forward motion was himself.

Solitary Refinement

A funny thing about us humans—we often want to avoid experiencing the very thing that can improve us. We go to the greatest lengths to escape discomfort, even when we know the aggravation can bring about our good. Ask any sick child who's balked at bad-tasting medicine.

In order for Evander to one day become "champ of the world," as Morgan once declared, my brother would first have to become the champion of something far more difficult. He would have to endure the struggle of conquering himself.

If the difficulties of our childhood were any indication of his ability to meet this ordeal, Evander was ready. Everything you do prepares you for everything you will do. Chubby had been "a struggler-in-training" since the day he was born.

It's been said that a child who struggles to life through the portal of its mother's birth canal lives an average of five years longer than an infant who enters this world by way of caesarian. There is something about the labor of natural birth that instills "life" in the participant. Adds quality and quantity to the individual's existence.

That initial fight to reach the light at the end of the tunnel teaches us, early on, that we are capable of traversing all of the gauntlets of this existence. The prebirth struggle is intended to be the first of many "life workouts" to build up our strength and teach us the lessons we must learn.

In the end, these grapples with life prepare us for our inevitable journey through that final tunnel, toward the bright, white light of God's eternal life. In other words, everything you do is preparation for everything you will ultimately do . . . and become.

However, in order for something to be born, for life to flourish, something must die. It is an undisputed law of nature that can be found in every facet of life: A seed must first fall to the ground and be buried, before a mighty oak can bud. It is even true in the conception of a human being. Male sperm must first struggle through a biological gauntlet and die in order for one to reach the female's egg and fertilize life. Discovering this law would mark the genesis of Evander's own, personal struggle.

Gauntlet of Struggle

Evander's next obvious step was a third match with Cecil Collins. To that end, he and Coach Morgan dedicated their combined assets of strength and experience. Through diligence, discipline, and plain hard work they forged an unspoken alliance that tolerated nothing less than a mutual, 100 percent team effort.

Every afternoon after school Evander donned his gloves and leather helmet. He energetically attacked whatever assignment Morgan put before him. He bludgeoned the heavy bag and sparred with his teammates with equal rage, each target the face of Cecil Collins.

The coach's devotion was similarly intense. With the zeal of a fanatic, the old man pushed and prodded Evander to ever-higher degrees of excellence. With a wrinkled brow, Morgan studied his boxer's balance and coordination. He scrutinized the mechanics of Evander's physical attacks and mental defenses. And with the hair-splitting detail of a ringside judge, the coach magnified every flaw until Evander exercised it into an asset. Together, the two were a well-oiled machine constantly striving for perfection.

Their strenuous workouts continued relentlessly, but with each passing session Evander began to detect signs of impatience on Morgan's part. After grunting out a command or pointing out a flaw, the old man would inhale a number of short, staccato breaths as if flustered, and walk away. And with increasing frequency, when he should have been watching Evander's form, Morgan would sit off by himself with his eyes shut tight, as if in deep thought.

Taking note of the coach's behavior, Evander pushed himself even harder. Although he had the physique of a man, his need for a father's praise still existed. It compelled him to do even more. Ironically Morgan's sporadic displays of indifference did almost as much to improve his fighter as his undivided attention would have. Yet, whether or not Morgan's actions were deliberate, or Evander's assessment of those actions was correct, the interplay of these variables served to increase the pace of the training.

Sustaining this regimen was difficult. Early-morning runs, followed by a full day of high school studies, homework, and a long evening of physical training—Evander's schedule was excruciating. And at the end of the day, even after such a workout, his body could barely rest, for his mind continued to spar with his problems.

Late at night, in the solitude of his room, he saw the referee lifting Collins's arm in the air and heard the echo of Morgan's goading words, "Young'un, nothin' in this world is free. If you want somethin' it's gonna cost ya."

In that small bedroom we once shared, Evander's exasperation became a kind of insomnia, keeping his mind wide awake, replaying his defeats and unanswered questions. "Why can't I get past this? What am I doing wrong? What more can I possibly do?" Over and over he rewound his memory, scrounging for clues. And finding no shred of exterior evidence to account for his anxiety, Evander reluctantly turned his search inward.

It is a scary, desolate feeling when there is no other option left but self-examination. Reaching this impasse can be closely akin to solitary confinement. Yet if the choice is made to face the mirror that hangs in that inner cell of self, the moment of struggle can be magic.

It is in that instant that the light at the end of the tunnel appears and the prison door is unlatched. For us Holyfields, such introspective times bring to mind the Bible stories that Grandmother Hatton recounted to us as children. Knowing this, it is safe to say that somewhere in Evander's solitary struggle he recalled his favorite fighter from that tattered book and compared him to the image he saw in his mirror.

Shadow Boxing

One warrior Grandma used to tell us about was a teenager who once voluntarily climbed into the ring with an adversary nearly three times his size. In that long-ago skirmish, which Grandma used to detail with all of the flair of a ringside commentator, the boy David found himself eye-to-knee with the giant Goliath.

Although he knew that the stakes were life and death, David gave little thought to his own safety, even declining the king's offer of his personal armor. Instead, he discarded his fears, along with the bulky breastplate, and focused his full attention on his task. As family, friends, and his entire nation looked on, the young'un summoned the true source of his strength and knocked out his opponent with a single, well-placed stone from a slingshot.

Considering that Evander had already lost twice to his Goliath, David's strategy was worth looking into. This Old Testament teenager had not only ignored his opponent's intimidating words, he had blocked out his own army's advice. He neither judged Goliath by his intimidating size nor considered his own lack of size. Instead, like Mama and Grandma, David played hide and seek.

On that open battlefield, the young warrior hid away from the terrifying images of his world, and even from himself. Subconsciously, he shut out the chatter of the exterior world and sought the inward strength and direction of God. He knew that his experience, along with God's direction, was more than enough to win the day. And with the confidence of that unhindered focus, David adjusted his aim and caught a giant right between the eyes!

Emulating this young warrior's character, Evander began the long evolution of personal solitary refinement. He recognized that he had to bury within himself the very thing that David also had to suppress: the mind-cluttering emotions and egotistical fears of his self importance.

It was a struggle.

Peering reluctantly into the mirror of self-examination, Chubby faced the shadowy reflections of his pride, his fear, his needs, his desires, and his selfish will. They stood in two facing lines in classic gauntlet formation. Evander would have to fight his way through the ranks of his own selfishness.

It was a long bout. It went on for weeks. Evander was relentlessly punched, shoved, and restrained by the shadows of his own nature. But he stuck with it, gaining points on sheer determination.

Every morning he would run, go to classes, do his homework, and endure the nightly sparring sessions with his ambitious teammates and seemingly weary coach. But he persevered, shadow-boxing his way past his pride.

In the seclusion of his room, Evander hid away from both the world and himself. Burying his self-importance, he slipped off into his own private prayer closet. There, in that spiritual solitude, Evander gradually learned how to listen with the "ear of the soul," the heart. The dialogue that takes place in that intangible inner dimension is as unexplainable as our conversations with the man in the kitchen. Nevertheless the impact of such spiritual exchanges affected Evander deeply (and continue to do so), both in and outside of the ring.

Slowly his bravado was torn apart, and what developed in its place was stronger and wiser. In time he was both ready and eager to confront his Goliath again. But no longer was his zeal fueled by heady self-importance. No longer would Evander Holyfield step into the ring haughty. From this time forward he resolved to be humble.

Coach Morgan's "champ" was on the verge of conception. He had managed to box his way through the shadows of his nature. He had begun the long process of listening to his heart and daily burying his self-importance.

The lesson was learned. But the struggle was far from over.

CHAPTER 6

THE 90 PERCENT EDGE

The third and final confrontation between Evander and Cecil Collins is significant not because of what happened inside the ring but because of what *didn't* occur there. . . .

At the first round bell, the two teenagers met in the center of the canvas and began their inquisitive promenade. Staring into each other's eyes over the tops of their raised gloves, each reflected on what the other might have learned from their previous encounter. Simultaneously reading the other's body language, looking for that momentary breach in defense, the two weaved and bobbed, balancing their muscular frames on their dancing feet.

When two opponents are so evenly paired that neither one can be judged the dominant force, the match must be appraised on a deeper level. Such a contest becomes a sparring of spirits. And measuring the boxers' performance using the ruler of inner strength, the dominant contestant was obvious. This time around, Collins was the cocky one. Having beaten Evander twice, Cecil no doubt considered himself to be a giant in the ring. And the mental image of his perceived self-importance put him at ease.

Evander, on the other hand, was alert. Although his ego still whispered reminders of those marks etched in his loss column, he refused to listen. He had discovered that the only thing anxiety can alter is a person's positive attitude. And he was determined not to let anything cloud his resolve.

Having shadowboxed his way through the gauntlet of his own fears, Evander was not about to let anything, or anyone, deter him from the goals that he and Coach Morgan had set, especially not Cecil Collins.

That night in the ring, for a single instant, both boxers shared a common image: Collins saw himself as a giant. Evander saw him as just another teetering Goliath. Yet pound for pound, blow for blow, neither one appeared to grasp the pivotal advantage. Once again their confrontation might end in a dead-even match.

Three grueling rounds later, the well-matched, perspiring amateurs connected with their last blows and retired to their respective corners. On the surface, there was little indication of the outcome. Each boxer had exhausted both his energy and the wealth of his experience in the struggle. The judges would have to look deeper than the Open Division rule book to determine whether the bout was a draw, a split decision, or a decisive win.

After much deliberation the match was finally measured using the ruler of inner strength, which in boxing terms is called "heart." Considered to be the most improved of the two contestants, having fought his way back from two devastating losses, the added mark in the win column was awarded to Evander. The goals he and Coach Morgan had set were finally once again in sight.

This final bout with Cecil Collins is noteworthy because of what Evander did not do in the ring. For the first time he didn't listen to his selfish fears. He didn't lose his head, or let his mind wander from the task at hand. Instead he allowed himself to be guided by his inner strength, the ear of the soul: his heart.

Because he did not let himself get in the way, Evander stumbled across the fight formula, which he still follows today: 10 percent physical and 90 percent spiritual. Apply yourself in this fashion and there is no battle that cannot be won.

Evander did not allow his selfish fears to hinder the effects of that 90 percent edge, so he managed to topple his Goliath. And he learned a lifelong lesson. Even today, Evander frequently makes mention of Cecil Collins during his talks to predominantly black schools.

"You can't judge by skin color," he says. "You can't tell just by looking at someone how tough they are. If you take a person for granted, he's likely to shock you. My arms were bigger than Cecil's. His skin was white. His eyes were a little bit crossed. I thought, *This is gonna be easy,* and he beat me twice.

"Over and over I've found that the guys I thought looked really tough weren't so bad, but the guys I thought wouldn't be a problem proved to be my toughest bouts. You can't judge anybody by appearance. Everybody deserves respect, regardless of what they look like or the color of their skin. They could be a good friend or coworker someday."

Evander had learned his lesson, and as the judges' decision was announced, it became apparent that Morgan had learned his. The seasoned coach's eyes began to well up with tears. The small boy who had swung at the dangling speed bag and missed was now grown and on target with a clear path to the next level of competition: the State Division.

That consoling notion, along with the roar of the crowd, momentarily numbed the well-concealed pain Morgan had been living with for months now. He forced a smile.

Approaching the coach for his customary victory hug, Evander noticed the old man's strained expression, but in the jubilation of the moment he passed off the wince as nothing. However, what he did not know was that Morgan's subtle grimace was the outward manifestation of the man's hidden inner struggle. The coach was suffering the chronic effects of pulmonary emphysema.

The coach had always been somewhat cranky, so it wasn't difficult to misinterpret his staccato breaths and little irritations as features of his grouchy behavior. At times, Evander figured that Morgan's harshness was somehow personally directed at his own seemingly slow progress. But what he and the majority of his teammates did not know was that Carter Morgan, their longtime coach, was dying.

Blow to the Belly

The disease's gradual effects had been coming on for years. It had probably already begun its destructive work back when Evander first peered through the boxing team's forbidden chain-link portal.

The emphysema slowly invaded Morgan's lungs, robbing him of the oxygen necessary for vitality. No one had noticed that his ruddy complexion had gradually turned an ashen blue, or that his son, assistant coach Ted Morgan, had begun filling in for the old man more frequently. Carter Morgan had kept his long, suffocating struggle to himself.

So when the news eventually broke that the final bell had rung for the old boxing coach, it hit Evander with the force of an unexpected blow to the belly. That sudden knowledge momentarily robbed *him* of the oxygen necessary for vitality, and for an instant, he wondered how he would ever breathe again.

"How can I go on without Mr. Morgan?"

Carter Morgan had been his boxing coach for eight of Evander's sixteen years. He had spent half of his life with the man. Morgan had been his trainer, his mentor, his friend—and a father figure. The coach's grudging approval had become the source of Evander's drive and ongoing incentive. Evander Holyfield and the sport of boxing would never have found each other had it not been for that crusty, old, freckle-faced coach. But now the man was gone.

Standing at the coach's grave, alongside Morgan's family, friends, and members of the team, Evander once more felt the numbness that comes with the admission of helplessness. The reality of Morgan's passing seemed to knock the fight right out of him. He found it difficult even to step inside the Boy's Club gym.

"There's no reason to try anymore. What's the point?" he rationalized. "I can't box without Mr. Morgan! It's over." It seemed as if another mark had been added to his loss column. And all he could think about was the coach's favorite little phrase, "There's no tomorrow."

Wallowing in the realization that he would never again hear Morgan bark out that tired cliché, he let the words replay in his mind repeatedly, like an old scratched phonograph record. There's no tomorrow. . . .

Then, with a jolt of clarity, Evander realized that their last few training sessions together must have been harder on the ailing coach than on himself. With the clear judgment of hindsight, Evander recognized that the old man's relentless goading had not been based on a loss of patience but rather on the loss of time.

There's no tomorrow. . . .

Knowing this gave Evander a glimpse into just how much the coach prized his potential. The old man must have known that his days were limited; still he chose to invest those precious hours in Evander's future. The old man had indeed been like a father to him. And as the reality of Morgan's devotion slowly sunk in, his old adage took on a whole new meaning.

"Come on young'un. Get up! Stop wastin' time. . . . There's no tomorrow!"

And Morgan's legacy gave Evander new hope. "If Mr. Morgan thought my training was worth the effort, maybe I should too. . . . If I stop now, eight years of my life will have been wasted. If I throw in the towel now, all of those bouts I've won, everything I've learned, will have been for nothing. If I don't stick it out, the coach's efforts, and all of his time, will have been spent in vain."

There is no tomorrow . . . only what you decide to do today.

"I've got to try. I've got to go on, but how? How did Coach do it? What had kept Carter Morgan in the gym? What kept him in my face, those last few sessions?"

Evander's mind spun faster, snapping the pieces of this puzzle together. "What drove him? It couldn't have been his body. Physically he was just about gone."

In time the answer that came to mind—the only answer that seemed to fit—was the little phrase he had often heard his mother sigh after a long hard day: "The flesh is weak, but the spirit's still willin'."

"Could the spiritual side of us be that strong?" Evander wondered. And the 90 percent he had used in the ring welled up inside of him and whispered, "Yes!"

"God will never put you in a place where you can't excel," Grandma's words echoed in his memory. "Things may not always go your way, but if you'll trust in Him and keep on—no matter what— He'll give you the strength you need."

With the strength of that realization, Evander got his second wind and was ready for the next round. "Mama and Grandma didn't raise no quitter, and I am not about to start now."

If Mr. Morgan thought that Evander could one day be champ of the world, he had a good shot at it. If he tried and failed, that was one thing. But if he never tried, if he never gave it his 100 percent best, he would be dishonoring more than just Morgan's faith; he would be going against Mama, Grandma, and, most important, God.

To this day, whatever fight Evander finds himself facing, his resolve has remained consistent. "I can't quit. If God doesn't put on me more than I can bear, there is no reason to quit. If I stop now, if I give up, I'll be letting the Lord down."

Evander was not about to let anything, or anyone, deter him from the goals that he and Coach Morgan had set.

It's amazing what that 90 percent edge can accomplish . . . if we let it.

Filling the Void

The two years that followed brought a whirlwind of changes. Evander continued to box, working his way through the State Division under the tutelage of Carter Morgan's son, Ted. During that period, Evander not only added a few extra trophies to his vast collection, he also managed to earn his high school diploma, which Mama proudly displayed among the clutter of his other awards. And if that wasn't enough, he even penciled into his schedule his first full-time job, servicing commuter planes at Atlanta's Epps Airport.

Coach Morgan's death had transformed Evander, matured him in the way that the passing of a father develops the character of a surviving son. To the casual observer it would seem that the scrambled puzzle pieces of Evander's life had all been sorted and were now falling into place with ease. But the puzzle was far from complete, and independence was the largest piece still missing.

Evander was still the only Holyfield sibling living at home. Although his full-time job provided him with the necessary money for self-sufficiency, and his diploma—his sheepskin visa—allowed him to pass Mama's departure requirements, Evander still felt duty-bound to stick around. Why? Because he was "Mama's boy," the last one at home. He felt that his departure would be construed as disloyalty or abandonment. He wasn't sure how Mama would take a "vacancy" sign on our bedroom door.

Evander's apprehension was similar to the "torture" we experienced when Grandma told us not to leave the yard. However, this time Evander was alone, standing just inside the boundary of our home, watching with longing as the rest of world ran and played free. He was nineteen and itching for independence, but he stayed put. Evander was not about to take that departing step without attaining some form of permission.

In the spring of 1982 that signal of consent finally came, but the peculiar way in which it was revealed was most unexpected.

The Great Clothes Caper

One afternoon, upon arriving home from a long day at work, Evander went to his closet for a change of clothes. Sliding the hangers across the horizontal post, he noticed that his best shirt and slacks were missing. Immediately he knew the culprit: our eldest brother, James. Although James lived on his own, he would frequently stop by to check on Mama. During these visits, he would invariably take inventory of Evander's classy wardrobe, and on occasion he would "borrow" an item or two. Taking such liberties, however, did not set well with Evander, and he angrily took his complaint to Mama.

"James is your brother," came her reply. "You boys should share."

"Share!?" Evander's voice bellowed back in frustration. "He goes into my closet and takes whatever he wants without my permission! That's not sharing!" His statement was punctuated by the sudden smack of the kitchen broom against his back.

In his fury at James's misdemeanor, Evander had raised his voice to Mama. And in the Holyfield house, that was just not done!

As Mama followed through with another swing for good measure, Evander's boxing reflexes instinctively blocked the broom's path. That act only inflamed her irritation. And like a pro, Mama swung at him from another angle, and the broom found its mark again.

Evander started to cry, not because Mama had hurt him but because he realized that his angry outburst demonstrated unintentional disrespect—the very thing he had tried to avoid by staying home. His regret was obvious.

Seeing his tears, Mama stopped, and for a long moment the two stared at each other. Assessing the situation as only a mother can, she sensed his dilemma. And in her own wise way, Mama subtly offered him what he needed most: his freedom.

"If you can't obey the rules around here," she slowly whispered with a hint of hesitancy, "then, I-I think it's time you . . . l-left."

Having received Mother's reluctant blessing, Evander solemnly returned to the bedroom and quietly packed his bags. It wasn't the way he wanted to go (Evander would always be "Mama's boy"), but he was not about to let the opportunity pass.

Like old Coach Morgan, when Evander sets his mind to do something, he doesn't waste time. That same afternoon he called up two of his buddies, Ricky and Kenny, and the trio moved into a three-bedroom apartment nearby.

Of course Mama was a little upset. But she recognized that her boy was now a man. In her scarred but understanding heart she knew it was time.

She adjusted. It was one of her many talents.

Relative Ease

Changes and adjustment were not only taking place at home, they were happening in and around the ring, as well. Among the most significant of these transitions was the installation of a new head coach for the Carter Morgan Boxing Team.

Filling the void left by Mr. Morgan's death would have been a difficult task for anyone, but the man chosen to be the new Boy's Club coach definitely made the transition easier. Like his predecessor, the new kid on the block also answered to the surname "Morgan."

At first there was the natural tendency to compare Ted with his revered father. But after a period of adjustment it was obvious that the younger Morgan was his own man. Once you got past the familiar last name and the noticeable family resemblance, it was clear that he was a no-nonsense guy who took the science of boxing seriously. And although he lacked Carter's long years of experience, Ted made up for it with his inbred tenacity and grit. The new head coach filled his father's sneakers well.

The old man had been strict, allowing no discussion, just action. Ted loosened things up considerably. Four inches taller than his 5-foot 4-inch prototype and decidedly younger, the thirty-something Morgan brought a new energy to Evander's game.

The transition and subsequent teamwork between Carter Morgan's biological progeny and his boxing protégé were virtually seamless. With relative ease, young Morgan built on his father's firm foundation and helped Evander to focus and grow. And as he steadily moved up through the State and Regional Divisions, the boxing world began to take notice of the name Holyfield.

Seemingly overnight Evander's reputation began to filter out beyond the ring. At Epps Airport, where he spent his days gassing up private planes, one of his coworkers from the flight crew, David Booker, began calling Evander "Champ." The first time this happened, Evander stopped short.

Champ, Evander thought. *He said, "Champ"?*

It wasn't a medal, just a name, but already Evander saw how his new attitude was paying off. He invited David Booker to watch his next fight.

Amateur bouts are a much more informal affair than the show put on by professionals, so Evander was with David when he first saw the muscle man Evander was up against that particular night.

David's eyes widened. Gesturing incredulously toward the large gladiator, he whispered, "Is that your opponent?"

Evander glanced over at the bodybuilder, then grinned back at his friend. Booker's dismay couldn't hold back an involuntary chuckle. Shaking his head in disbelief he laughed, "Man, that guy's gonna kill ya!"

Evander brushed off the comment. The road to the championship wouldn't be paved by fighting 150-pound straw men; he'd have to take on the biggest and the best—and beat them all.

Confidently Evander stepped into the ring to face the bigger man, who sneered at Evander's smaller frame. His opponent's face was a snarl, his entire visage saying, "What's up with you, small man?"

When he looked into Evander's eyes, however, he saw a ferocity that created just a slight moment of doubt, so he quickly looked away.

The bell rang, and the bodybuilder came out swinging, hoping to overpower Evander before he even had a chance to get going. What the bruiser didn't know was that this was Evander's game. He loves to get down to business. The faster, the fiercer, the better.

David winced when he saw the first blow hit Evander's body. But Evander stayed with his opponent, toe-to-toe, not giving an inch. The bodybuilder's next blow went wide and Evander seized the opportunity. He exploded with an inside shot to the man's ribs, and his opponent's face registered its surprise.

He may be small, the bruiser's face seemed to say, *but that small man can hit!*

The two men traded blows for the rest of the first round—a furious exchange, neither man willing to back off, both relishing the chance to slug it out.

David Booker wasn't sure what he had expected to see, but certainly not this. He had watched a number of prizefights, but Evander had already taken and given more shots than he had seen in many ten rounders.

When the next round started, the bodybuilder seemed more cautious. He was protecting his left side, and Evander jumped on the weakness. Give the opponent credit—he was keeping Evander back—but halfway into the round the muscular fighter dropped his guard for a split second, and Evander punished him with a bruising shot to the side. The pain he felt was palpable on his face and caused him to drop his guard again, just for a second. He was rewarded with an uppercut to the jaw and a hook to the side of his face, which hit him just as his head went back.

The floor was no more merciful than Evander had been. It hit him with a thud, and the man was out. The "giant" had lasted less than six minutes with the "small man."

David Booker was even more excited than Evander. "I've never seen anything like it before," he kept saying.

"I told you," Evander said. "You'd better get my autograph now, while you can."

David carried his enthusiasm into work the next day and began telling everybody every detail of the fight.

The word spread quickly, and soon the spectators' seats around the ring were filled with familiar faces. Everybody wanted to see their friend "Champ" Holyfield in action.

The nickname "Champ" became so popular that it seemed only natural for the company, Epps, to embroider it on Evander's airport uniform. The recognition felt good to Evander. After years of hard work and frequent solitude, the attention was quite therapeutic. It was certainly better than the wisecracks his old classmates used to make about the "crazy man" who "thinks he's Rocky."

The Bottom Line Didn't Add Up

One day while working at Epps Airport, Evander's eyes happened to fall across a discarded piece of paper on the ground. It looked like a check stub. Being the curious type, he picked it up.

Reading the small dot-matrix print, he recognized the name. The check stub belonged to one of the airport employees, a man well over fifty who had worked at Epps for many years. Looking at the numbers, Evander was surprised. The man's pay did not seem to reflect his experience and long years of service. The bottom line just didn't add up.

"Young'un, nothin' in this world is free. If ya want somethin' it's gonna cost ya. You're gonna have to work for it. . . ."

Staring at that fragment of paper, Evander realized that this employee's financial destiny was in the hands of his employer. And despite the man's extensive qualifications and years of experience, it was obvious that he had hit a glass ceiling.

For a split second Evander put himself in the old man's place, and he realized that no one was going to hand him anything. If he wanted something—security, independence, respect, a national title—he was going to have to work very hard.

He flashed on the indelible image of our brother Willie, the artist. He remembered how "Bobo" never fully developed his talents and eventually lost them.

Suddenly Evander realized, to get ahead in the world you have to do more than want and dream; you have to *do* more!

Evander wasn't about to end up a fifty-year-old man, looking back on his half-used life with regrets. He was going to take full advantage of his independence and do more than just the expedient thing.

Crumpling the check stub in his hand, he resolved to employ 100 percent of his abilities to break the glass ceiling that had kept his attitude low.

He also started budgeting his income more judiciously. It didn't take Evander long to notice that his calendar and his checkbook were not balancing. As his number of boxing tournaments mounted, so did his need for extra cash. He discovered that his income was not matching his outgo. And he recognized that if he did not remedy the situation, his insufficient upkeep would quickly become his downfall.

Tabulating the conflicting numbers with care, Evander flashed again on the old airport employee's check stub. And adding that sobering image to his small financial total, the bottom line of the situation became clear: He was going to have to do even more.

To solve this mathematical dilemma Evander decided to add one extra item to his busy schedule. Taking advantage of the certified lifesaving course he once took at the Boy's Club, he signed up to be the weekend lifeguard at Atlanta's local summer refuge, the Thomasville Pool.

Looking back on it now, that practical decision marked a pivotal moment in his life. Ironically Evander managed to step squarely into the path of the "sucker punch" that every fortunate male eventually runs into: The knockout's name was Paulette.

A Welcome Oasis

In the summer, the Thomasville Community Pool was the place to be. It was a refreshing sanctuary from the Georgia heat. Residents throughout the surrounding neighborhoods were drawn to its cool chlorine waters. It was the perfect spot to spend a lazy Saturday.

Filling in as the pool's weekend lifeguard was like a vacation for Evander. Perched in his observation chair, his assignment consisted mainly of surveying the area in and around the pool and maintaining a safe environment for its patrons. The high point of his job was usually reminding some youngster to "walk, don't run on the wet pavement!" Although he was alert and trained for any emergency, Evander's uneventful days at the pool were more like the shift of a "Maytag Repairman" than an action-packed episode of *Baywatch*. Thus, Evander's eyes were not so occupied that he failed to notice the slender frame of Paulette Bowden splashing about with her girlfriends.

From the looks of things, the caramel-skinned beauty was quite popular, and not just with the gals. Each time Evander saw her at the pool she was surrounded by a number of clumsy young men, trying their best to impress her. He too had felt the compulsion to flex his muscles when she passed by his perch, but he could only muster the strength to smile. The sight of her brown eyes left him weak.

Evander has always been somewhat shy and soft-spoken outside the ring. He could go up against a 250-pound bodybuilder without flinching, but put him next to a fragile female, and he would freeze. In his attempt to overcome this shortcoming Evander once took note of how I used to read self-composed "Love Poems" to girls over the phone. Seeing how well it worked, he tried memorizing the lyrics of popular songs and reciting them as his own creations. But, more often than not, his wooing efforts fell flat; the girl usually knew the song.

From his lifeguard station Evander could see that the other boys didn't have his problem. They hovered around Paulette like vultures circling above their prey, waiting for just the right moment to strike. And from where he sat, it looked as if she enjoyed it. So he shrugged his shoulders in resignation, half convincing himself that he already had enough competition in his life.

This went on for a while. But eventually something happened. Maybe it was the hot Georgia sun or Evander's frequent smiles, but somewhere during that summer, he and Paulette began to chat. Those chats soon turned into comfortable conversations. And eventually those conversations evolved into a relationship. Before long the two were inseparable. And to everyone's surprise, including their own, Evander and Paulette became each other's companion.

Love never seems to appear when we're looking for it. And no one can fully describe it once it is found. But its presence, as well as its absence, affects every facet of life. There is nothing like that giddy, barely containable sensation we experience when we lock eyes with our first love. Evander had found someone to fill that void that is common to us all.

I am convinced that finding and filling that void of companionship is the original purpose for which we were created. Back "in the beginning," we were fashioned to keep the Creator company—not as trained pets or unfeeling androids but as thinking individuals with a free will. Had He designed us to involuntarily go through the motions of a relationship with Him, or anyone else, our existence would be meaningless. Companionship is as natural and necessary as the air we breathe; it makes our successes sweeter and our failures easier to bear.

As for Evander, Paulette's companionship was a welcome oasis to his disciplined life of solitude, like a cool, refreshing dip on a summer's day.

No Guarantees, No Excuses

Evander went on to win the Southeastern Tournament in 1982. He beat everyone and afterwards almost seemed disappointed that there was nobody left to fight. Evander's next major tournament was the Amateur Boxing Federation National in Indianapolis. He rolled through his first two bouts, neither fighter being able to give Evander a serious challenge. For a while it looked as if Evander might almost walk into another title.

And then he faced Ronnie Hughes.

Evander's first bout with Hughes was a classic amateur fight. Neither fighter was going to overpower the other. This was a bout of two surgeons, dissecting and cutting through each other's superior defenses; but this was brutal surgery, conducted in the midst of darting and bruising blows, far removed from the quiet of a hospital. This surgery was conducted amidst the roar of the crowd, with the referee darting in and out, a white-and-black striped blur that would appear and then disappear from Evander's view.

But always Evander kept his eyes trained on Ronnie. His concentration was intense, and his exertion was steady. Evander did well in the first round, gaining the edge. He kept Ronnie back and was able to maintain control of the bout. When the second round began, Evander kept up the same furious pace he had displayed in the first round. It looked like he was going for a knockout, but Ronnie was too quick to let a blow hit him that square. Ronnie was more reserved, and though he took his share of punches, he stayed in Evander's face.

Evander was now just three minutes away from dispensing with this menace. When the bell rang to start the third round, however, he felt like he was dragging his entire entourage behind him. His legs were heavy, and his arms lost their quickness. Evander's heart and determination showed through, but Ronnie soon gained a clear advantage. Evander did his best to perk up and regain the pace he maintained during the first two rounds, but his movements started to look more like lunges than darts. Ronnie scored several hits and was clearly in control when the final bell rang.

I thought it was possible that Evander's strong showing in the first two rounds could still carry him past a less-than-stellar performance in the third round, but in this case the judges didn't agree. In a split decision, they went for Ronnie.

Evander is without a doubt the most competitive person I've ever known. He has to win, whether it's sports, board games, or even a family game of cards. In every situation he'll do everything he can to pull out a victory.

But paradoxically he's also one of the best "losers" I've ever known. Once a decision is rendered, Evander accepts it and moves on. He doesn't throw a fit; he just makes plans for the next conquest.

So it wasn't surprising that, after losing, Evander chose to stay at the tournament and learn what he could. As he watched the remaining bouts, he couldn't find a single fighter that was better than him technically. All his loss had come down to was exhaustion in the third round. A third round slump.

Watching the title fight, Evander knew he had what it took to be there, in that ring, fighting for the title. The only thing that stood in his way was more conditioning. He couldn't let himself run out of gas again.

Never again.

Unfortunately many of the same friends who had looked on Evander with a new esteem after his fight with the bodybuilder and his win at the Southeastern Tournament now started to sneer. At work Evander would hear his given name whispered more frequently than the one sewn on his shirt. One coworker openly confronted him, "I don't know why they call you Champ. You're always losin' the big ones."

Evander looked at the man who stood before him. He knew he could drop him with one blow, but it wasn't worth it. Maybe the guy was right. Evander *did* lose the big ones.

This wasn't true, of course; he had won the Southeastern Tournament, after all. But he was learning a hard lesson. To boxing fans, you're never any better than your last bout.

Now the word *Champ* written on Evander's uniform mocked him. What had once felt like an Olympic medal hanging around his neck now felt like a smelly, decaying albatross. Suddenly all the negatives poured in on Evander like a hot, scalding storm: the insults, the doubts, the sneers, the editorials, all of it.

This is the moment of truth for many an amateur. At this point many young boxers decide to quit and return to the streets. Others keep fighting, but they internalize the criticism to such a degree that they destroy their self-confidence and never reach their full potential.

Not so for Evander. He had acquired the necessary training of body and spirit, and he had learned the "fight formula" to make it work. All he had to do now was . . . more!

He redoubled his efforts and began scheduling his time more efficiently. Penciling in a few extra assignments on his "to do" list, Evander went to work on his third round stamina problem. Along with his early-morning run, his daytime job, and his strict regimen of weight lifting, power training, and sparring with the team, he further resolved to add a minimum of 250 to 300 push-ups to his daily roster. And, to supplement his diet, he began downing a daily dose of that clichéd "Rocky Balboa" concoction: raw eggs, milk, and honey.

Momentum

The next few months were a blur of activity. When Evander wasn't on the airport tarmac fueling commuter planes or eating a fast lunch with Paulette, he was in the gym pumping iron, preparing himself for the long list of competitions that lay ahead. He tore through the warm-up tournaments on his way to the national tournament. Pundits started to pick him as the next national champion.

Evander arrived at the 1983 National Golden Gloves Tournament eager to fulfill the pundit's expectations. He finally reached his bout with Sherman Griffin, ranked number one in the world. Griffin's ranking didn't rattle Evander, however. This was a fight that had to happen, and Evander felt ready.

He came out swinging. Griffin was prepared, but Evander's heart leapt when he was able to drop Griffin in the first round with a left hook. The referee let the fight continue, and Evander dropped Griffin again in the second round. This time, the referee gave Griffin a standing eight-count. Evander dropped Sherman yet a third time in the last round. Evander had yet to fall, and watching his opponent pick himself up off the canvas, he could taste victory, taste the title, taste the glory.

But Griffin got up. Evander lifted his weary hands once more and went to work. A hard and bruising battle followed. The final bell sounded, and Evander felt elated. Here he was, an unranked fighter, and he had just dropped the top ranked amateur *three times*. The referee had ruled that one of those knockdowns was a slip, but still Evander believed he had controlled the fight from the beginning. After all the defeats, all the ridicule, all the snide comments, finally, he had vindicated himself.

Evander stood in the middle of the ring while the announcer declared there had been a split decision. That wasn't so surprising. With five judges, in a close fight, a split decision was almost to be expected. Still, Evander felt confident. He had dropped Griffin three times and clearly felt that he had shown his superiority.

When the referee raised Griffin's hand in triumph, Evander felt his heart drop right out of him. The judges went 3–2 for Griffin. Evander couldn't believe it. The postfight elation displayed by the Griffin camp created pandemonium, but through it all, Evander did his best to review the fight in his mind. He replayed it over and over, and still he wondered, *How could they have given it to Griffin?*

Evander felt robbed. He had earned the national title, but another man would wear it. People in the crowd began booing. They knew who had won. Two of the judges knew who had won. The three judges who had scored Griffin the winner were about the only ones in the arena who thought otherwise.

Once again Evander would have to face his coworkers after losing the "big one." The difference this time was that he didn't feel as though he had lost it; he felt that it had been taken from him. Still it wouldn't do any good to make excuses, so when they asked, he just said he lost—end of discussion.

The 90 Percent Edge

Though Evander refused to defend himself, the *Atlanta Constitution* did. The morning paper argued that Evander had been robbed. It was a difficult lesson for such a young fighter, but Evander refused to let it dim his dream of fighting for the Olympic gold. This loss was a setback, certainly, but it wasn't the end of the road. In fact, he could learn from it. No longer would he allow judges any doubt. If a knockdown wasn't enough, then Evander realized he'd just have to learn how to knock them out!

CHAPTER 7

BOXING FOR THE DREAM

The bitterness of the Golden Gloves Tournament was eased somewhat when Evander received a phone call from the Olympic Training Center in Colorado Springs. The frightening thing is that this was a call that almost didn't happen. In spite of a stellar amateur record that eventually reached 160–14 (with seventy-five KOs), Evander had attracted surprisingly little attention, and just one year before the Olympics, he was still an unranked boxer.

There are a number of reasons for this. Before Evander turned professional, boxing and Atlanta were almost never uttered in the same sentence. At the time Atlanta was not the "sports city" it is today. In 1984 the Braves weren't perennial contenders for the World Series, Deion Sanders hadn't donned a Falcons uniform, and most people would have greeted the idea of Atlanta sponsoring the Olympic games with ridicule or disbelief—or both!

Evander himself literally grew up boxing, and that meant he went through weight classes like most people go through dress shoes. He never stayed in one class long enough to become famous. He was like the star athlete whose father was in the military—as soon as everybody found out how good he was, he was off to another neighborhood.

When Evander graduated from high school, he weighed all of 147 pounds and was one of the shortest boys in his class—hardly the picture of a future heavyweight champion of the world. Only gradually did Evander reach his 6-foot 2-inch status and 200-plus pounds.

Fortunately for him, the president of the Amateur Boxing Federation was Lawrence Baker, a Georgian. Baker served as a referee and judge for many amateur fights in Georgia, so he had seen Evander box. Buddy Davis and Bo Davis ran the Georgia Amateur Boxing Federation, and they asked Baker to consider giving Evander a shot. Baker remembered seeing enough to be interested, and Evander got the call.

When the amateur representing Evander's weight division was injured, Evander was invited to train for a dual match with Cuba in April 1983. *Finally,* Evander thought, *a chance to get some national recognition.* The bout was a bruiser, close all the way, but the judges gave the edge to the Cuban. Evander thought he had won, but he was just thankful that he had been given a shot.

His gritty performance was enough to impress the Olympic coach, Roosevelt Sanders. "You're a fighter, kid," Sanders said. "You can go places."

He paused and looked at the young hopeful. "Tell you what. I'm gonna give you another shot, a chance to fight in the Pan-American Games. We'll bring you back to the training camp and see how you do."

Sanders saw the excitement light the young fighter's face. "I want to make it clear to you, though; if you lose, you go home. Understand?"

Evander nodded.

"I think you can win—but if you don't win, you go home," he repeated.

Evander's tryout for the Pan-Am Games occurred at the 1983 Sports Festival in St. Louis. The winner would go on to represent the United States. Because boxing is an individual sport, it's not enough to be good, you have to be the best or you don't make the team. Evander would face all the top-ranked amateurs, and if he wanted to go to the Pan-American Games, he'd have to beat them all.

He couldn't wait to get another shot at Sherman Griffin and Ronnie Hughes, two fighters who had beaten him previously. Evander's family, coworkers, and Paulette attended his bouts against both Griffin and Hughes.

This time Evander won both bouts decisively. He felt elated, until he remembered that the next bout would be with Ricky Womack. In fact he had to fight Womack *twice.*

Womack was being trained by Emanuel Steward (who would one day train Evander for a heavyweight title fight), while Evander was still, at this point, a "homegrown" product from Georgia. It wouldn't be fair, Evander began to think. Womack had all the advantages Evander had never enjoyed.

Womack won the first bout, and afterwards Evander seriously thought about quitting. He called his trainer and said, "Man, I don't know if I can go on and fight tomorrow. I hurt my arm."

"No, Evander, no!" the trainer shouted into the phone. "Don't make any excuses. If you hurt one arm, fight with the other one!"

Evander hung up the phone and laid down on his bed. He still couldn't put the thought of quitting out of his mind. He began to think about all the things that had gone wrong in his life.

It would be so easy to quit. No boxer from the state of Georgia had ever made it to the Pan-American trials, and Evander thought, *If I lose tomorrow, so what? I've already accomplished more than any other boxer from Georgia.*

In that lonely moment Evander lost something he had never lost before: his confidence and his will to win. He didn't know what to do, so he dropped to his knees and prayed.

More than anything else, Evander was just tired. He had fought and won two difficult bouts against two fighters who had beaten him previously, and then lost a tough match against Womack. The adrenaline of facing such competition had created an inevitable letdown once weariness set in, and that was the position Evander found himself in as he prayed, quietly, before his second match with Ricky Womack.

There, on his knees, Evander found his feet. There, facing his God, he realized he couldn't just give up on what God had already given him. God had created him to be a boxer. If he gave up now, he'd be spitting in the face of the Almighty. And everything he had worked for would be brought to an end.

Evander had accomplished a lot for a boxer from Georgia, but he began to set his sights even higher. He remembered his earlier dream—the Olympics. To make the team, it wouldn't be enough to be a good fighter in his weight division. He had to be the best. And to become the best, he had to beat Ricky Womack.

Adrenaline changed his visage. Evander rose, ready to take on the world.

He had learned another important lesson. He was not immune to the usual doubts and weariness that all boxers occasionally encounter, but he had found a potent weapon with which to fight them: prayer. On that day, as he reached the end of his own physical and emotional strength, Evander found a supernatural strength. Prayer entered his arsenal, and in the coming years, prayer would be every bit as essential to his success as was his right hook or left uppercut.

But first he had to face Ricky Womack.

The rush from his prayers allowed Evander to come out and clearly outbox Ricky in the first round. Evander is like a machine when he first gets going, and if an opposing boxer isn't careful, he's going to be chewed up. After the initial rush of excitement, however, Womack began taking charge and won the second round. Evander retired to his stool, weariness clouding his eyes and threatening his courage.

When the bell to start the third round sounded, the last thing Evander felt like doing was fighting. He didn't know why, but he was bone-tired. He was back to that old third-round slump. The doubts sown by exhaustion worked their way into his mind. He had already beaten two strong fighters. What difference would beating a third make?

He wanted to quit, but he knew he couldn't quit on the stool, so he stood when the bell rang. Evander just wanted the fight to be over, even if that meant suffering a quick loss. Shortly after the round began, Ricky worked Evander into a corner. After a few opening exchanges, he landed a clear shot to Evander's head. Evander wasn't hurt, but he was tired.

Here's my chance, Evander thought. *I can let myself fall and the bout will be over.* As he began to go down, Ricky held him up. Womack pushed Evander back, and then intentionally threw his head into Evander's nose.

Nothing affects a fighter's sight like a head-butt to the nose. Even putting aside the pain, the body's reaction to a nose blow is severe. It affects your sight, and a boxer who can't see is a boxer who can't fight. Ironically, if Ricky hadn't thrown the head-butt, he would have won. Evander would have fallen and stayed there. But because Ricky threw in a cheap shot, Evander's tiredness melted before hot anger. He forgot about how much his arm hurt, he forgot about being tired, and he started throwing hard punches back.

Unlike Evander's listless shots earlier in the round, these punches had emotion behind them, and they landed—hard. *It's one thing to get beat by a hard punch,* Evander thought. *It's another thing to get beat by a cheap shot.*

The fight became a grudge match. Womack backed off in the face of Evander's blows, and where seconds before it looked like Evander might go down, now he was literally pushing Womack around the ring. Womack couldn't find a place to make a stand. Evander wouldn't let him. He was all over Womack, and his blows were fierce. The tide had turned, and Evander rode the emotion all the way to victory.

When the bell finally rang, there wasn't a soul in the arena who doubted the outcome. The announcer proclaimed the judges' decision and raised Evander's hand. The young Atlantan was elated. The first thing he did was to thank God for not allowing him to quit boxing. This moment was what boxing was all about—reaching down to the deepest level of your gut, staring fear and weariness in the face, and then discovering just how much you had left. It was postfight eupho- ria, and Evander was flying.

The Pan-American trials marked a watershed in Evander's life and career. Not only did it leave him ranked number one in the United States, but it taught him never to let past records concern him. Never again would he be intimidated by statistics or rankings. Never again would he allow a boxer's association with a special trainer or his training to cause fear. Evander had learned how to take the hardest of punches and still come out swinging. He had found on his knees the strength he needed to tackle anyone who stood in the way. He also saw how God could use anything—even a head-butt to the nose—to encourage him to do his best. Grandma and Mama had been right: All things did work together for good.

Evander finally had the confidence to go with his skill. Back at Epps, he regained his coworker's admiration. No one questioned why he wore *Champ* on his uniform, not anymore.

Birth of a Rivalry

Evander returned to Georgia to fight the Golden Gloves at the Omni. It was here that his rivalry with a young heavyweight named Mike Tyson began. The two young fighters had worked out together in Colorado Springs, and now, as these two boxers tore through their competition in the Golden Gloves, they looked like prime candidates to secure the Most Outstanding Boxer title.

It began as a "battle of the knockouts." To secure the Most Outstanding Boxer award, a fighter needed to win convincingly, and there is no more convincing way to win than a quick knockout. Evander had learned that before—at the distressing end of the Griffin match. Tyson watched as Evander dropped out his first opponent, then climbed into the ring and did the same.

Evander's and Tyson's second and third opponents all met identical fates: three bouts, three knockouts. Evander was determined to get the edge and proceeded to knock out his fourth opponent. Tyson's opponent was disqualified, however, so even though Tyson won the match, he was one knockout behind Evander.

Evander entered his fifth bout eager to wrap things up. True to his earlier form, he knocked his opponent out and became the light heavyweight Golden Gloves champion. Not a single opponent had been able to go the distance.

Tyson also got a knockout in his fifth bout, so Evander had five knockouts in five wins, and Tyson had four knockouts in five wins. When the most outstanding boxer award was announced, however, the judges went for Tyson. The heated competition between the two created an energy that inevitably caused their teammates to wonder how the two fighters would fare against each other in the same ring.

"Oooh, boy, I'd love to see you two guys fight," a teammate said as Evander and Mike sat together.

"I'll fight you," Evander said, turning to Mike. "You want to fight?"

"Naw, man, you're too small," Tyson said. "You're just too small."

"All right, then. Let's spar."

"You want to spar with me?" Tyson asked.

"Yeah, man, I'll spar with you. And you don't even have to pay me." (The Olympic Committee had to pay people to spar with Tyson because too many amateurs were afraid of him. He was known to be a street fighter, a wicked brawler.)

"I like you," Tyson said. "I'll box you with just one hand."

"You better use both, boy," Evander said, "or I'll whip you."

Word about the sparring match between the two knockout kings created an electric atmosphere at the camp. Evander and Tyson climbed into the ring, Evander smiling, Tyson looking serious.

They touched gloves, and once they started, there was no stopping them. Tyson soon discovered that he needed both hands. In fact
both fighters probably would have preferred a third hand at their
disposal. You put two hypercompetitive fighters in the same ring,
and what happens? You end up with a brawl.

Evander made use of his quicker hands, slipping in several
blows. Tyson began to get edgy—he wasn't used to getting tagged—
and he started "loading up," hoping to land a big blow. Most of the
blows that he launched missed; those that landed hit Evander on his
arms and glanced off.

After the first round the Olympic coach walked over and
stopped the action. "You guys aren't sparring," he shouted. "You're
fighting! You're hitting too hard, and somebody's gonna get hurt. I
don't want to see you in the same ring again."

Evander thought he won that round, but his experience with
Tyson left him with nothing but respect. Nobody worked harder than
Mike—including, at times, Evander himself.

"He did everything faster than anybody," Evander recalls. "When
he hit the bag, he hit it faster. When he jumped rope, he jumped
faster. Everything he did, he did faster than anybody."

Evander was now turning heads as an amateur. He had won
both the Sports Festival and the Golden Gloves in convincing fashion.
But there was one tournament that would mean more than all the
others put together: the Olympic Games.

Financing the Dream

Although he was winning major tournaments Evander was still
struggling with financial imbalance; in fact the first big event of
the year 1984 almost tipped the scales—and at eight pounds and
four ounces, that event was certainly heavy enough. You guessed it!
The year 1984 marked the happy arrival of Paulette and Evander's
firstborn: Evander Holyfield, Jr.

The new mom and dad could not have been prouder. But along
with their joy came the weight of added responsibility. That and the
financial burden of going to the Olympics seemed overwhelming. His
only income consisted of the meager wages he earned at Epps Airport, and his time-off to fight in tournaments interrupted this modest
cash flow.

Evander's former math teacher, John Smith, drove Evander around Atlanta to find a sponsor for the Olympics. They visited a man who owned several hair care shops, but he wasn't interested. They visited a man who owned a number of restaurants, and while he seemed to like Evander, he wouldn't commit to any support. They talked to people in construction, in banking, and in other fields, but they still came up with a big zero.

It's difficult to imagine a number one ranked amateur from Atlanta having a difficult time locating a sponsor today, but back then, most Atlanta businesspeople were not boxing fans, and they couldn't fully appreciate the height of Evander's accomplishment as an amateur.

Evander had to sit quietly while businesspeople looked him up and down and thought, *This small kid, a boxer?* It was hard for them to believe that a local boy could be that good.

One businessman actually questioned Evander's drive. "Nice guys don't finish first, kid," he said, "especially in boxing. They always finish last. You're too nice to make it."

Evander found it difficult to keep from becoming disappointed. He had proven himself in the ring and wanted the chance to represent his country in the Olympics. He felt certain he could make it to the Olympics and even bring home the gold. All he'd have to do was repeat what he had already done. To do that he needed his country's support. Unfortunately nobody was willing to help.

When he returned home, rejected and confused, he asked Paulette, "Why, baby, why? Why won't they believe in me? What else do I have to do?"

The last thing Evander wanted to do was borrow money, but as the weeks wore on and the bills piled up, he knew he had no choice. Their 1968 Dodge Stark was in serious need of repair—or junking. When Paulette didn't think the car would make it to the doctor's for one of Evander Jr.'s visits, Evander reluctantly borrowed two thousand dollars and went down to the local Buick dealership in Morrow, Georgia, to see what he could find.

After kicking some tires and wrinkling his nose at a few sticker prices, his eye eventually caught the glint of a 1982 Buick Century. Evander could see himself in this car, the same way he could see himself on an Olympic podium. Spotting a salesman, he called him cover and gestured toward the car with a smile. "I like it," he admitted.

Hearing the sound of a potential customer, the salesman spun around in his practiced manner and involuntarily reached into his shirt pocket for a business card. But after taking a step, he focused on the dark-skinned teenager, and he hesitated.

Evander, however, didn't skip a beat. "Hi, the name's Evander Holyfield." He politely extended his wide hand. "I'm a local amateur boxer. And I'm also a brand new dad. I could use a good car."

"H-Holly-feld?" the salesman stuttered.

"That's 'Holy'—like the Bible. Ho-ly-field." Evander carefully enunciated the two familiar words. "I can put two grand down now," he continued, bending to look through the driver's side window at the dashboard, "and pay off the note in full—in two months."

"Two months, eh?" the man's eyes narrowed in disbelief as he looked at the so-called boxer's compact 170-pound frame. "You got a cosigner, kid?"

"Cosigner?" Evander echoed. "I, uh . . . can we work somethin' out? I've got a good shot at making this year's Olympic team."

"The Olympics!?" The salesman's eyebrows raised. "Well now, that's somethin'."

Evander smiled at the final recognition.

Scratching the back of his head, the salesman turned his gaze upward, in a moment of thought. Then, with a purpose-filled snap of his fingers, he pointed his thumb toward the dealership's office.

"Tell ya what," he motioned for Evander to follow, "let's have a talk with the owner, Mr. Sanders."

Inside the office Evander once more extended his hand and carefully pronounced his name to the man behind the desk. But like the salesman, Ken Sanders had never heard of the young boxer. Nevertheless, he sat back and patiently listened.

Evander mentioned his job at Epps and then talked about his hopes of making the 1984 Olympic team. The determined manner in which Evander explained his situation piqued Sanders's curiosity. And after a few words the businessman was listening very carefully.

Ken then volunteered to be Evander's sponsor for the Olympics, and allowed him to purchase the car without a cosigner.

Evander drove home in a new car—with a new sponsor. He thanked God that even when things seemed to be at their lowest, He always came though. Everything was now in place.

The Olympic dream burned bright.

Pregame Jitters

Although things were now more secure at home, Evander was still a little nervous upon his arrival in Fort Worth, Texas, for the 1984 Olympic tryouts. To qualify for the team Evander had to fight both Sherman Griffin and Ricky Womack once again. In the next couple of days Evander defeated Griffin, but he lost to Womack.

The fact that he *had* defeated Womack was proof enough that he *could* defeat Womack, so Evander was particularly hurt and heart-broken after this fight. The Olympics were still a possibility—the number one and number two fighters would face off in the boxoff two months later, but Evander had hoped to emerge from the trials as the "man to beat." That was not to be, and Evander wore his defeat with an unusual heaviness.

When Mom saw him right after the fight, she was startled by the despondent look on his face.

"Are you all right?" she asked.

"Yeah, Mom, I'll be fine," he said. "Don't worry. I'll get another shot at the boxoff."

Evander was saying it, but none of us were quite sure he actually believed it. Evander had expected to win. He had the skills to win. He was confident that he *would* win.

But he had lost.

An unexpected loss is a tough realization for any athlete, especially just minutes after the contest, when you haven't had the time to figure out what went wrong.

Ironically Evander seemed to feel even worse for others—people he thought he had let down, like Ken Sanders, his new sponsor.

"I lost, Ken," Evander said later over the phone.

"I know," Ken said. "I saw it, but don't let it get you down. You fought a good fight. You should be proud."

Evander was silent. As an amateur, more than his sport was up in the air—his entire future hung in the balance. If he couldn't make it to the Olympics, it'd be all the more difficult to become a professional boxer. And if he couldn't become a professional boxer, how in the world would he feed his growing family?

As if he were reading Evander's mind, Ken assured him. "Hey, keep your head up. If you ever need a job, you've got one right here, so don't worry about that. But you can still fight. You know you can. Maybe you just need a better coach. Either way, it's gonna turn out all right."

Evander was cheered by the call, and he began preparing for the boxoff.

Two months later, in July of 1984, the kid from Atmore was on his way to Caesars Palace in Las Vegas for the Olympic boxoff. Evander was more than just a little nervous as he made his way into the arena where the competition would be held. When one lives with a dream for so long, it becomes a friend, and for years the thought of this Olympic opportunity had pushed Evander out of bed, got him through his hundreds of push-ups and sit-ups, and kept him pummeling the heavy bag long after his aching muscles told him to go home.

But now, the dream's fulfillment—or devastating end—was just a few hours away. Evander recognized Tyson and said "Hi!" Since both of them had lost at the trials, both were entering the boxoff in what is called the "loser's bracket." If you're fighting in the loser's bracket, you have to win both fights to secure a place on the Olympic team.

Evander and Tyson continued to work out together, watching the other bouts as they took place. Evander enjoyed being around Tyson. Though he was aware of Tyson's reputation as a fighter with a vicious edge, Evander was struck by Tyson's warmth and quiet nature.

Boxing can be a lonely sport. You've got your trainers behind you, but when you step in the ring, you're one on one, and all your trainers can do is watch. It takes another boxer to understand the nervousness and the sudden fear that can arise in the midst of a heated battle. Evander knew he could use a friend right now, and Tyson was right there.

Tyson himself had his hands full with Henry Tillman, a young man who would eventually win two very controversial decisions against Tyson and deny the future heavyweight champion a shot at Olympic gold.

Evander's first bout against Womack was scheduled for the evening. If he won, he and Womack would fight for a spot on the team the next morning. If he lost the first bout, his chance to make the Olympics would be lost.

The day of the fight was one of the longest in Evander's life. He tried to pass it by lying on his bed and conserving his energy, but every ten or fifteen minutes he'd jump up and walk through a combination.

"Gotta remember to keep the jab going," he'd say, throwing a couple jabs toward the mirror.

"Gotta keep moving."

He stared into the mirror as if he were facing Womack. "He's going to do this," Evander said aloud, "and I've got to respond with this."

Evander was programming himself to react spontaneously to whatever Womack did. "You can't work and think," he explains. "If you're thinking about throwing a jab out there, it'll already be too late. You have to react."

It was an incredibly tense time for both fighters. After the fists flew, only one lifetime dream would remain standing. Evander was so nervous he wondered if he might slip into an anxiety attack.

Finally the young Olympic hopeful again dropped to his knees and asked for God's help. In such circumstances Evander doesn't pray that he will win ("The Lord doesn't choose sides," he points out), but that God will allow him to do his very best.

"Protect me and Ricky," Evander prayed. "Don't let either of us get seriously hurt. . . . But help me do my best. Just help me to do my very best."

At that moment Evander's heart felt the touch of quiet. A new peace settled on him. He knew God had done His part. Now it was up to Evander to do his.

In one of the most difficult times in such a physical sport—the quiet waiting before the battle begins—Evander had again found solace on his knees. To remain standing in the ring, he began making it a practice to bow down outside it.

Evander entered the bout against a fiercely determined Womack. Womack was ranked number one in the world as an amateur, and the pundits already had the gold medal around his neck. Womack was determined to carve out his place in glory, and the only thing that stood in his way was Evander.

A shot of excitement, fear, and exhilaration went through Evander when he and Ricky finally touched gloves. Womack stayed on Evander with a passion. He stalked and pressured Evander all over the ring, hoping to keep him away from his style. It didn't work. Evander outpointed Womack and earned the right to fight him the next morning for the one Olympic spot.

If Evander thought he was nervous before, this evening was excruciating. If anything, winning the first fight added more pressure. Evander was now just three rounds away from representing the United States in the Olympic Games. Morning couldn't come quickly enough.

His dreams, his desire to be an ambassador for Christ, his need to provide for Paulette and Evander Jr.—all of it would be greatly influenced by less than ten minutes of furious explosions of fists.

Evander knew that more than a match was on the line. His *life* was on the line, and what he'd do for the next twenty or thirty years would be greatly affected by the bout that lay before him.

When the initial bell sounded, Evander was prepared. As before, Womack tried to stalk and outpressure Evander, but Evander was dancing on air. His quickness frustrated Womack's strategy. Evander's defenses proved impenetrable, and Womack slowed noticeably in the second and third rounds.

It was as if Womack could feel the bout slipping away. He kept trying to turn it up a notch, but each move toward Evander was rewarded with a clear shot to the head. Evander had found his zone, and Womack simply couldn't penetrate it. Evander outboxed the number one ranked amateur in the world.

When the final bell rang, Evander lifted his head and his arms and smiled. He had worked as hard as he could; he had fought his heart out. Now everything was in the hands of God and the judges.

Evander's heart beat heavily from the exertion, excitement, and anticipation. Because he had seen the other bouts, he knew that the winner of the bout would be announced as the representing member of the Olympic team.

The referee stood in between the two fighters. After a painful wait, the announcer's voice cut through the air. A lifetime's worth of dreams was in the offing.

"And representing the 1984 United States Olympic Team—"

There was a long pause. Evander couldn't stand it.

"From Atlanta—"

Evander didn't need to hear the rest. Womack was from Detroit. Evander knew he was in. He felt his legs grow weak, while the announcer finished saying, ". . . Georgia, Evander Holyfield!"

Evander lifted his face toward heaven. *I have reached this goal,* he said to himself, with well-deserved satisfaction. *After all these years, I reached the goal. Thank You, God. Thank You, Lord!*

Evander became euphoric. He changed his walk. Strutting outside (*I'm somebody!* he was saying to himself) he raced toward the pool and jumped in, still wearing his boxing gear.

"I reached the goal!" he screamed, splashing around. "I did it!"

Evander thought of all the people who had said he was too small, too nice, too young to box. It had taken him weeks to get Carter Morgan to let him hit the bag. It took him years to become ranked. He had lost sleep, given up fun time, worked his body into exhaustion, but now, every millisecond of it was worthwhile.

Phones started ringing all over Atlanta. People were cheering. Everybody from the Boy's Club to Epps Airport and from the Thomasville Pool to Ken Sanders's Buick were shouting the same incredible news!

"Evander Holyfield just earned a spot on the United States of America's Boxing Team! Our boy's going to compete in the 1984 Olympics!"

CHAPTER 8

OLYMPIC LESSONS

Evander's great athletic gain—a spot on the Olympic team— was followed by a great personal loss.

It was raining that night. I could hear the drops pounding our roof when I got the call. It was dark outside and I had been asleep for several hours, so I'm sure it must have been around 2 or 3 A.M. I picked up the phone and heard the news.

Our grandmother was dead.

She had been fighting various ailments for some time, but the pneumonia finally won and Grandma went home to be with her heavenly Father.

Unless you lived in our house, you couldn't possibly understand what Grandmother meant to Evander and me. All our lives, Grandmother had been the one who disciplined us, who comforted us— and who stopped our mother from whipping us.

I thought of the time this tiny woman, confined to a wheelchair, outmaneuvered and almost outmuscled the future heavyweight champion of the world. I remembered the times she had spent burning a love of God and the Bible into our souls, teaching us never to give up on God because He'd never give up on us. She was clearly the hub of our family's wheel, and we couldn't imagine life without her. And just when Evander was ready to take on the world at the Olympic Games, he lost his most stable foundation at home.

I began to wonder if Evander would ever get a break. The next few days were a blur of mourning. Friends and family gathered; people came from all over the state to express their sympathy and pay their respects.

Evander, Willie, James, and I served as pallbearers. For most of our lives, Grandmother carried us, and it was heartrending to realize that now we were carrying her. Her strength had given Evander the character to keep pursuing his Olympic dream, even when a sponsor couldn't be found and even when his toil in Atlanta kept him from becoming a nationally ranked fighter.

Evander stood erect over the grave. For a moment, he blinked back the tears. He wouldn't look left or right. It was almost impossible for me to maintain composure when the minister began reading the Twenty-third Psalm, one of Grandmother's favorite passages. She had read and explained it to Evander, me, and our siblings many times over. She used it to teach me how to read, and now with its beautiful poetry filling the air, we used it to commend her soul to God.

Evander and I spent some time alone after the funeral. "How are you doing, Chubby?" I asked. He was an Olympian now, but at that moment, he still felt like my little brother, and I was concerned about him.

"I'm all right," he said. Then, more quietly, he added, "You know, Lightning, this isn't a tragedy."

I looked up, surprised, and Evander continued. "Because of Jesus," Evander said, "We should be joyful when there is death. Grandmother had heart problems; you know that. I hated seeing her in pain, and she won't have any of that in heaven. It's all gone, now."

Evander sighed deeply. "God gives the best to His children, and she was one of His. He had a better place for her, that's all."

Training with Terrapins

God's place for our grandmother was heaven, but His next plan for Evander was Gonzales, Texas, where the U.S. Boxing Team gathered to prepare for the Olympic Games. If ever you could devise a place to keep twenty-four young boxers out of trouble, it was Gonzales.

"Ten miles out of nowhere," Evander laughed.

The training grounds were located on a huge, desolate plantation. The boxers didn't have cars, and they would have had to walk over ten miles just to get off the property—not that there was anything to do once you reached the boundary. And the coaches made absolutely sure that every boxer knew that the plantation was swarming with snakes. For the most part, you couldn't see them, at least not at night. Then, it was absolutely black. With no street lamps or store lights to brighten the sky, at night it was so dark you'd look around and wonder if you had lost your eyesight.

There were two houses, each boarding twelve boxers. Each house had one telephone—and that one telephone was the *only* form of recreation outside the ring.

It was in Gonzales where Evander landed the name "Real Deal." Evander liked to listen to music, so he was always trying to come up with rhymes. One day, as he was singing, "Real Deal" slipped out. Evander stopped, and then added the phrase to his name: "Real Deal Holyfield."

A smile broke across his face. Every boxer eventually needed a nickname, and Evander knew he had found his. The rhyme was imperfect—Evander would make a better fighter than a poet—but the name stuck, and soon his Olympic teammates were saying, "What's up, Real Deal?"

Confined to a training camp in Gonzales, the Olympic boxers began to forge lifelong bonds of friendship. Many of them would eventually stand in each other's weddings. They had all worked harder than they had ever worked in their lives to get there. Each one had tasted the sweet euphoria of making the team and returning home a local hero. But after a dozen days of long, hard, and sweaty labor, with nothing to cheer your progress but a bunch of cactus, snakes, and terrapins, they were quickly brought back to reality. The excitement morphed into exhaustion, hard work, and tedium. With no crowds for miles, they cheered each other on. That's exactly what the coaches wanted. The young men came to Gonzales as individuals, bearing individual dreams of glory. They left it as a team, passionately devoted to each member's success.

Walking Toward the Crowd

We're about to get off the plane," the coaches warned the athletes during their descent into Los Angeles. "It's going to get pretty crazy out there. None of you have ever experienced anything like it. I want you to walk *away* from the crowd. Understand me? Walk *away* from the crowd."

The young boxers could hear the cheers before they got off the plane. Flags were waving. Old folks, young children, and middle-aged couples were smiling and jumping up and down. There were dark faces, light faces, Hispanic faces.

To Evander it felt like half the country had shown up to welcome their boxing team to the Olympics.

For the first time in his life, Evander felt like a Beatle. He got off he plane, heard the yells, and walked *directly toward the crowd!*

It was an intoxicating moment for the young boxer from Atmore and then Atlanta, and he was determined to get the most out of it. Evander walked slowly, as close to the crowd as possible. He *wanted* people to touch him. Gonzales had kept the boxers hidden in anonymity. Well, now the secret was out, and Evander was going to savor this moment.

For once he felt that the red, white, and blue of the United States' colors were more noticeable than the blackness of his skin. No racism here. The crowd at the airport greeted him and the other athletes wildly and with a hero's welcome. Because they wore the red, white, and blue, the athletes were instant celebrities.

Evander had overcome much to get here. The racism he had faced in the South was sometimes overt, as in the case with Lassie, and sometimes subtle, as when he sought to secure a loan or solicit a sponsor. But Evander never made excuses. To him, every obstacle was just another challenge that needed to be overcome.

But here, in the rainbow atmosphere of the Olympics, all of that was left behind. It was almost a spiritual experience for Evander as he walked around the Olympic grounds, surrounded by athletes from Africa, China, Korea, and the former Soviet Union. He saw that in this 23rd Olympiad, there was just one human race, joined together in the pursuit of athletic excellence. The athletes respected each other, regardless of skin color, religion, or political philosophy, for each one knew what an accomplishment it was just to make it to the show.

Evander had fun trying to communicate with other athletes who knew just two words of English: "Good!" and "Yes!" The bond each athlete felt with the other athletes overcame any communication problems that erupted. With one African, Evander simply nodded his head and smiled. An Asian came by, and the three athletes carried on a conversation with a makeshift form of improvised sign language.

Once they were safely tucked away in the confines of the Olympic village, the coaches said, "You don't need to leave the village. As soon as you do, you'll be mobbed, so try and stick around."

That was all Evander and his teammates needed to hear. At the first second of free time, they headed for the gates! Evander, Virgil

Hill, and Meldrick Taylor decked themselves out in their Olympic-issued red, white, and blue sweats—nobody within a mile of the young men could miss the fact that they were Olympic team members—and went to one of the most public places they could think of: the Mann Theater in Los Angeles. Everywhere they walked, people shouted out, "Way to go, guys!" "Bring home the gold!" "Go, USA!"

Amidst the lighthearted celebration, however, Evander carried a burden that few other athletes carried, even those from the United States. It is "expected" that a boxer representing the United States will bring home the gold, and already, Evander felt the pressure of those expectations. Since Evander had beaten the number one ranked amateur in the world to earn his spot on the team, anything less than a gold medal would be considered a disappointment. Evander was literally facing the best amateur boxers in his weight class in the entire world—each one of whom had trained with the best his country had to offer.

And Evander was expected to beat them all.

The excitement generated by the opening ceremony was the thrill of his life, but Evander knew he was here to work and get the job done: to bring home the gold medal in the light heavyweight division.

Shortly before the boxing competition began, the entire team turned out for a press conference. Reporters from all over the world had an opportunity to throw their questions at the world's most feared amateur boxing team. After general statements were made, the reporters crowded around Breland, Tillman, and the other well-known boxers.

Evander sat alone at his table, watching even the Georgia reporters go after other fighters. The 1984 boxing team was a highly celebrated bunch; Evander's inclusion over Womack was seen as an anomaly. Few people knew his name, so his comments weren't considered very important. Evander waited, alone and embarrassed, at his table. Not a single reporter came his way, until a young woman looked over and walked up to him.

"I just came up here to talk to you," she said. "I know you must feel kind of embarrassed that none of the reporters are interested. But I think you'll do well."

Evander looked at her and said, "I *will* do well. They'll wish they had come up and talked to me by the time I finish the tournament."

Cosell, the Cuban, and a Kenyan

Evander soon fell into a regular schedule. He would practice every afternoon, shower, and then, in order to relax, he would visit the disco. Virgil Hill, Henry Tillman, and Frank Tate went with him. The dance floor gave Evander a chance to loosen up and also to check out the other athletes' confidence. The "mind games" that precede such high-level competitions are intense, and Evander sought out every edge he could find.

On the morning of his first fight, Evander felt confident and exuberant. His opponent was from Africa, and Evander watched as the other boxer weighed in. He felt the electric thrill of the upcoming competition run down his spine.

Evander wanted to win. The crowd's adulation was intoxicating, and after a lifetime of being ignored or passed over, Evander was finally getting his due. Nothing could have prepared him for this moment. He had traveled a long road of seemingly endless and gritty practice sessions, when nobody was there to see him, much less applaud. But Evander had stuck with it, and now he was about to embark on every amateur athlete's dream: competing in the Olympic Games.

Evander began his chase for the gold by knocking out the African hopeful in the third round. When he also knocked out his second opponent—this one from Iraq—the press finally started taking notice. Evander's opponent in the third round—a young fighter from Kenya—looked to be much tougher, however.

Howard Cosell warned Evander, "The Kenyan will be your toughest opponent. He has fast hands, and he'll use his jab to try and get you out early."

Evander had met Cosell earlier in the year at the Pan-American Games. After Evander's loss there to a Cuban, Cosell had given Evander a hard time about how badly the Cuban had beaten him.

"No, Howard, I beat that man!" Evander had protested.

"I disagree, Evander," Cosell had said.

When they got on camera for an interview, Cosell had started using words that Evander had never heard, so Evander began shaking his head "no." The usually unflappable Cosell was bewildered by this young fighter's reaction, and appeared to be as frustrated by Evander's gestures as Evander was by Cosell's big words.

And all this was being played out in front of the camera!

Evander wasn't trying to be difficult, but he didn't know what Cosell was trying to say and there was no way he was going to just agree with him, especially after the heated discussion about his fight with the Cuban. It was Evander's first major interview, and Cosell intimidated him.

Not surprisingly, ABC programmers opted not to run the interview.

Later, during the Olympic boxoff, Cosell picked Womack to beat Evander. When Evander won both bouts against Womack, Evander was told that Cosell would have to interview him once again.

Evander said, "No way! I'm not talking to that man. He just tries to make me look bad. He uses those big old words so I don't look good."

ABC officials were sent scrambling. Evander had just won the coveted light heavyweight spot on the Olympic team, and he had to be interviewed. Finally, Cosell himself approached Evander and said, "I'm sorry, Evander. I promise I won't make you look bad."

Evander's heart is naturally trusting. He wants to forgive, and he did so here. Out of this experience, he and Cosell became good friends.

Now, at the Olympics, Cosell was acting as an informal advisor. "He may be tough, Howard," Evander said of the Kenyan, "but he's a counterpuncher so he's going out early. He may be waiting for me and I won't give him the opportunity. He's going out early."

"Be careful," Cosell warned. "Don't think about a knockout too much."

"I want to knock them all out so there's no doubt about who won," Evander said.

This conversation eerily presaged the future controversy. Because boxing is "scored," judges can allow political affiliations to influence the outcome of a match. It can be heartbreaking for an athlete to realize that a lifetime of pain, training, and sacrifice can be wiped out through a prejudicial political judgment, but several sports in the Olympics are subject to that danger.

Boxing is one of them.

Adding to the danger of a "political decision" was the growing frustration many of the nations were feeling as the United States began to dominate the Eastern-bloc-boycotted games. Without the Eastern bloc, few countries could match the United States' overall effort—and some people were getting tired of hearing "The Star-Spangled Banner" every time an awards ceremony was held.

That's why Evander was so intent on knocking everyone out. If only one fighter was left standing, nobody could doubt who the winner was—or so he thought.

Cosell nodded. He was well aware of the intrusion of politics into sports. "You can do it, Evander," he said.

It was a delight to watch my brother tear through his competition. Evander wasn't well-known internationally, so prior to his first two fights I heard many fans sit down, read their program, and say, "Who is this kid, Evander Holly-field? I never heard of him."

With each knockout, however, Evander began to erase that anonymity for the rest of his life. Suddenly, the young man looked like a favored candidate to win the coveted title of "Most Outstanding Boxer of the Games." Now, reporters would come up to him and say, "Man, you've been very impressive! Where have you been? Why have we never heard of you?"

Evander Holyfield, the Real Deal from Atlanta, had arrived, and the entire world was watching. Almost unwillingly, the fans and media were forced to learn how to pronounce his name correctly. Evander no longer had to say, "*Holy*-field, like the Bible." Soon, everybody knew.

One of the reasons that people started gravitating toward Evander was that he embodied the American Dream. Evander was proof that the victory doesn't always go to the fighter who is the quickest or the strongest or the biggest. Sometimes, it goes to the one who endures, the one who hangs in there until finally, no one else is standing.

Evander had lived that dream. He began his life as a poor black youth, without a father, and he grew up in a tiny community called Summerhill. Through it all, Evander developed a spiritual strength that would teach the entire world a lesson in Los Angeles. It was impossible for a reporter to talk to Evander without him bringing up the source of his strength. "First of all, I want to give thanks to my Lord and Savior, Jesus Christ," he'd say, and the reporter would move impatiently on. But Evander hung in there. When asked what kept him going, he replied, "When we start out with Jesus Christ, we start out winners, and no matter what the final score is on the judges' card, when we stay with Christ, we end up winners."

As Evander's success in the ring grew, his boldness in mentioning Christ also grew. He no longer worried about praying silently before a fight. Now, he didn't care if the whole world heard. He believed in praying in secret, but he wouldn't hide his faith.

As he had promised Howard Cosell, Evander easily dispensed with the Kenyan, knocking him out in the first round. Howard was very impressed, and as soon as he got on the air, he literally raved about the young fighter from Atlanta.

"E-*van*-der Holyfield," Cosell began the interview. "He really knows what he's talking about! He said he would get a knockout, and he *did!*"

The Gold Hush

Evander's next opponent was Kevin Barry from New Zealand. According to Cosell, Evander had won his toughest fight. Neither Barry nor the boxer from Yugoslavia (who was slated to face the winner of Evander's next bout) could compare to the Kenyan Evander had already knocked out. It looked like the gold medal was all but his.

Even so, Evander stayed focused on his upcoming fight with Barry. If he beat Barry, he was assured of at least a silver medal and a chance to fight a Yugoslav boxer named Anton Josipovic for the gold. Evander didn't think twice when he was told his referee for the fight with Barry was from Yugoslavia. At the time, nobody did.

Evander exploded as soon as the fight started, and Barry never really had a chance. The New Zealander almost went down in the first round. He found his legs to begin the second round, but again, Evander had the young man reeling. The fight looked like a classic mismatch, and everyone watching thought it was just a matter of time.

As the round wore on, it became clear that Barry was just trying to hang on. He didn't want to be knocked out, but from the style of his fighting, it was clear that he had given up any hope of victory. He just wanted to save face and go the distance.

Evander remembered the danger of relying on decisions, though, so he kept jabbing and bobbing, working to get Barry onto the canvas. Now, it was time to go to work, and he wouldn't rest until the New Zealander was off his feet, in the same way Evander had left his earlier opponents. Finally, in desperation, Barry grabbed

Evander in a clinch. The crowd was yelling, and the noise was filling all corners. You couldn't hear yourself screaming, it was so loud. The many languages of the crowd rose in a crescendo of unintelligible shouting as Evander sought to end the bout.

He couldn't do it with Barry clinging to him, however, so he tried to push away, but Barry held him by the head. The noise was still deafening. The crowd sensed a knockout, and the smell of such a feat can whip a crowd into a frenzy. Evander's ears were filled with a cacophonous roar, but his eyes revealed the cool detachment of an iron-will focus.

Finally, Evander managed to twist away and break free. Barry knew what was coming and braced himself. Both fighters swung at each other, and Evander felt his glove connect. Barry's swing just missed Evander, and Evander's blow sent Barry sprawling to the canvas.

The tingling thrill of competition raced through Evander's spine, and he almost regretted the fact that Barry had fallen. *I'm not finished with him yet,* he thought. *I want him to get up so I can get him real good.*

Barry was out, though, and Evander knew he had earned at least a silver medal. His next bout would be for the gold! In the rush of the moment, the referee sent Evander to a neutral corner. The New Zealander was clearly dazed and defeated. Then, in the midst of what seemed almost like a demonic confusion, Evander saw the referee point at him and tell him he was disqualified.

Evander's first thought was *For what?* He couldn't ask because the referee didn't speak English.

Later, the referee would claim that he had asked the fighters to stop—even though *both* kept swinging. Evander *had* knocked Barry out, but the referee had still managed to take the fight away.

Evander couldn't believe it. Barry had covered his head in the clinch, so there was no way Evander could hear the referee say, "Break!" In his mind, Evander replayed the last few seconds of the bout. When fighters are clinched, the referee is supposed to step in and put his hand between the fighters to signal that they're supposed to stop. That didn't happen. The referee had relied on a voice command in the midst of a noisy crowd while Evander's opponent covered his ear in a clinch.

The political fallout soon became obvious to even the most unenlightened of observers. According to amateur rules, because Barry had been knocked out, he was ineligible to fight for ninety days. That meant that Evander's disqualification (by the Yugoslav referee) guaranteed the Yugoslav fighter the gold medal *without having to fight for it.*

The crowd of many languages found one voice in condemning such an unjust decision. When the announcer got on the intercom and announced that Evander Holyfield had been disqualified and raised the arm of Kevin Barry, I thought a riot was going to erupt. Cups full of ice and soda were hurled into the air. "Boo" is "boo" in any language, and the sneer from the crowd was so frightening that security guards quickly came to the ring to escort the referee from the arena.

As the referee was led out, the crowd reached out to tear his clothes and get a piece of the man who had stolen another man's dream. The anger was so intense, I thought the crowd would never settle down. The crowd was like a bomb, just waiting for one spark to set it off and make it explode.

There was one calm man in the arena, however, and that was my brother, Evander Holyfield. He stoically walked out of the arena with the same confident detachment with which he had entered it.

"I thought they would reverse the decision," he later told me. "We're from the United States!" I thought. "They can't do this. They have to reverse it."

Howard Cosell didn't seem so positive. "I've never seen a decision reversed, Evander," Cosell warned him. "I wouldn't get my hopes up."

After the fight, Evander's friendship with Cosell paid off. Cosell led the disappointed and shocked boxer through a national interview.

"Now Evander," Cosell began, "you didn't hear that referee say 'Break,' did you?"

"No Howard," Evander said, "I absolutely did not."

"This is so bizarre," Cosell added. "Never in my career have I seen a decision this bad. I can't believe this."

Cosell guided the dazed Evander through the rest of the analysis. His caring dissection of the bout was in marked contrast to the belligerent interview after the Pan-American Games. To this day, Evander remains very fond of Cosell's memory.

Finding Good in Bad, Bad, Bad!

Evander still held out hope that justice would be done. It all seemed like such a bad dream that it was only natural for him to expect that he would wake up and everything would be "fixed." Loring Baker, the president of the Amateur Boxing Federation, filed a formal complaint on Evander's behalf. But as the hours and then the next two days passed, Evander began to have doubts.

When he heard the news, he was on the beach. Evander walked by a television and saw Howard Cosell's face on the screen. He stopped to hear what his friend had to say: "There's good news and bad news for Evander Holyfield. The good news is, his bronze medal won't be taken away. The bad news is, he won't be allowed to fight for the gold."

Evander's jaw dropped as he thought, *That's not good news/ bad news; that's bad, bad, bad!*

At the time, the bronze medal didn't seem important. Evander wanted the gold or nothing. The bizarre decision was an attempt to uphold justice and save face at the same time. Because he had been disqualified, Evander shouldn't have been eligible for *any* medal. The fact that he was given one showed that the Olympic committee believed he hadn't been treated entirely fairly. They didn't have the courage to overturn the decision, but they decided they couldn't completely deny a young fighter something he had earned.

Suddenly, the boxer whom everybody had ignored at the start of the games became the hottest interview property in the Olympic Village. Now, everybody wanted to talk to Evander. Unfortunately, Evander was still reeling from being told he wouldn't get his shot at the gold medal. But the media wouldn't wait. They wanted a reaction *right now.*

But the twenty-one-year-old felt too stunned by the news to go toe to toe with broadcasters. He was hurt and disappointed beyond belief. It's one thing to fall short. It's another thing altogether to have something taken from you. For the first time in his career, Evander began to feel the pinch of celebrity. Duty called him to face the camera, even though the only thing he really wanted to do was be alone.

People came up and patted Evander on the back, telling him it was okay. One of his teammates said, "Real Deal, it looks like you got a raw deal." Evander appreciated these comments, but they didn't remove the sting.

"None of those pats put the gold medal around my neck," he said.

What hurt Evander as much as anything was realizing that statistics don't contain asterisks. Fifty years from now, people would read the results and assume that both Barry and the Yugoslav fighter were superior boxers. The controversy would be forgotten, while the medals and printed results would be remembered.

Looking back now, however, Evander finally agrees with Cosell's "good news/bad news" analysis.

"At first, I didn't care about the medal," Evander explains, "but now I'm glad I've got it, even if it's bronze." He laughs. "Though sometimes, I want to get it dipped in gold. Still, not too many people can look at an Olympic medal they've earned."

It could have been a bitter moment, but Evander chose not to become angry.

"It won't do any good to blame the ref or Barry," Evander told me at the time. "They couldn't change the decision even if they wanted to. I'm just thankful God answered my prayers and let me make the Olympic team. This is still going to be the greatest experience of my life."

I was amazed that Evander could say such a thing after such a bitter ending, but even today, after twice winning the heavyweight championship of the world and earning more than $120 million in the ring, Evander still points back to the Olympics as his greatest accomplishment.

Boxing is an individual sport, but at the Olympics, Evander finally felt he was part of a team. He wasn't just fighting for himself; he was fighting for all the other United States Olympians as well. He was fighting for every United States citizen and all his friends and family in Atlanta, Georgia.

As a young man who had faced his share of racism, it was impossible for Evander not to be moved when he saw that for two weeks people didn't care about their outward differences. Instead they respected each other on the basis of their skill. During the Olympics, no one cared whether you were a black pole vaulter from Ghana or a white boxer from Poland; whether you were a Muslim wrestler from Saudi Arabia or a Roman Catholic swimmer from Italy; whether you came from the working class of France or the upper class of England. You were an athlete and a part of one human race.

In many ways, the Olympics brought a taste of the unity, harmony, peace, and universality that Evander looked forward to as a Christian on his way to heaven. Evander knew firsthand how brutal the world could be, both inside and outside the ring. But for about a dozen days, he was able to enjoy a new world, and no amount of later glory, fame, or financial success would ever compare with the Olympic flame that was lit in his heart that year.

As a boy, Evander had fought largely for Morgan's approval. When Morgan died, Evander's motivation died with him. Watching the 1976 Olympics rekindled a desire in Evander, and for once the fighter from Atlanta began to fight for himself.

So in that sense it was still a dream come true for the young Atlantan to stand on an Olympic awards platform, even though it was the sound of the Yugoslav national anthem that filled the arena. Evander stood still and gracefully as he watched the three flags ascend to the rafters. The New Zealand flag came up behind the Yugoslav flag, followed by the Stars and Stripes. Evander took his place on the bronze medal platform, standing slightly below the silver medal winner, Kevin Barry, the man he had clearly beaten. As the music died down, however, Barry reached out and lifted Evander's arm, showing his support for the bronze medal winner.

The crowd erupted into a standing ovation. Tears flowed freely, and people saw the young boxers embody the Olympic spirit. Evander and Kevin Barry remain friends to this day.

It Takes a While to See the Good

I had mixed emotions when Evander and I hugged after the ceremony. I was as proud of him as I've ever been, but I also hurt for his loss. Evander told me not to.

"I learned a valuable lesson about accepting the things I have no control over," he said. "After something bad happens like this, something special always happens later."

What good could come out of this? I thought. Well, the publicity that Evander received from the bad decision catapulted the previously unknown fighter to the heights of celebrity—not a bad place to be when negotiating for gate receipts as a professional.

Following the Olympics, Evander joined the Olympians on a visit to the White House to meet with President Ronald Reagan. Evander was also invited to join the gold medal winners on a parade-tour in five different U.S. cities. Even though Evander had won a bronze, not a gold, the U.S. Olympic Committee decided that he had earned the right to join the other gold medal winners.

The parades did much to soothe Evander's disappointment. For the first time in his life, he saw people who had made homemade signs in his honor. "We Love You Evander Holyfield!" "We're Proud of You, Evander!" "You're a Gold Medal Winner Too, Evander!"

As I returned home with Mom, we realized instantly that Evander's world had changed forever. Our mailbox was stuffed with mail. People from all over the world sent telegrams, postcards, and letters to the man who had accepted disappointment with so much grace and class.

The mail continued to pour in for several weeks after the Olympics, and each day, the new delivery made Grandma's words ring true. "All things—even controversial decisions—work together for good, for those that love God and are called according to His purposes."

Grandma had been so proud of Evander, often calling him her "little prize fighter." We knew she was cheering him on in heaven.

When Evander finally returned home, there was a period of adjustment for him. He had been so high on the crowd's adulation and attention, it was a shock to come home to the same house and have everything return to normal. Half of him wished the Olympics could last forever.

In fact, his real challenge—and his real fame—was still ahead of him. Evander would no longer fight as an amateur. The professional boxing world was waiting.

CHAPTER 9

TWO FIGHTS IN ONE

The day that Evander was disqualified in the Olympics, his phone started ringing. Suddenly, every promoter in the country wanted to represent him. He was "hot property" now, his name recognition was high, and offers started coming in from all over. A couple months ago, Evander needed a sponsor to purchase a used car. Now, he was being offered enough money to buy a comfortable house.

From our family's perspective, much more than money was at stake, of course. Turning professional would mean longer bouts, tougher competition, and fighting without headgear. It also meant more danger. This is one element that the ordinary fan takes far too much for granted.

Boxing can be a dangerous sport. Any one of the several hundred blows suffered by a professional boxer would be enough to do serious damage to an untrained and ill-prepared participant. Boxing produces the same nervousness that precedes any significant challenge or competition, but it has the added flavor of potential danger. An unexpected blow—the one "lucky shot"—can wrench victory out of a seemingly certain defeat. That's why watching my baby brother box can be scary at times, and why our mother refused to watch her son fight. You never know, for sure, just what kind of shape a fighter will be in once the final bell sounds.

Thus it's not a small step to take the leap from amateur to professional. The potential financial rewards are great, certainly, but even that doesn't come easily—and only the most successful fighters make significant money. To win at the elite level, you have to fight the biggest and the best and beat them all. A baseball or basketball team can suffer one or two losses a *week* and still make the playoffs. A premier boxer can barely afford one or two losses in an entire *career*. Also, the fifth best baseball player in the world will be a superstar. The fifth best boxer will barely rate a footnote as a potential contender.

To succeed in boxing, you have to be the very best.

Thus, competent management is essential for every potential champion. Evander could fight his heart out in the ring, but he'd need somebody who'd do their work outside the ring, lining up the appropriate fights and grooming him to go all the way.

The 1984 Olympic boxing team was broad enough to attract a lot of attention from various professional management and promotion organizations. Mark Breland was the most heavily recruited Olympian, but other boxers from the team—including Meldrick Taylor, Pernell Whitaker, Paul Gonzales, and Tyrell Biggs—also received considerable attention and "courting."

Ironically, Ricky Womack, who Evander defeated in his quest to make the Olympic team, received even more aggressive offers than did Evander. A number of businesspeople in the boxing community still doubted that the "quiet fighter from Atlanta" had what it took to be a world champion. Even with his increased recognition, Evander continued to struggle against the "nice guys finish last" school of thought.

In hindsight, however, I think it's safe to say that of all the Olympic boxers from Evander's era, none have shared his level of success. Certainly, there isn't a single boxer in history who has earned what Evander has earned inside the ring, and Evander was the first Olympian from his team actually to win a world title. *He* knew he had what it took, even if others doubted.

That's why Evander chose to sign with Main Events Promotions. They offered a better package and seemed more career-oriented than the others. Evander didn't bother following up on offers that were lukewarm and half-hearted. He never boxed that way, and he didn't want to join a management team that recruited that way.

Main Events offered Evander $250,000 to sign, and promised him another $2 million within four years. When Evander signed the contract and looked at the check, a big smile broke out across his face. He had never seen this much money before in his life. In fact, the check he was holding was worth more than all the paychecks he had ever received combined—and he got it just for signing a contract!

He drove home with a lighter heart. *Two hundred and fifty thousand dollars,* he laughed to himself.

It didn't take long, however, for the downside of reaching affluence to show its ugly face. Suddenly, friends, relatives, and even casual acquaintances came calling. All had pressing needs and were seeking a "loan."

"I'm so thankful for my mom," Evander says. She sat our family down and set everybody straight. "Y'all had the same opportunities as Evander," she said. "I raised you all the same. I raised you all Christians. If you chose not to use the talents God gave you, that's your fault, not Evander's. I won't have you all trying to pressure Evander for his money. It's his. He earned it." Of course, Mother could talk to us, but there was no way she could reach all his friends and acquaintances.

It's not like Evander's financial worries were over. Two hundred and fifty thousand dollars is a lot of money, but Evander was realistic. A couple hundred thousand is hardly enough to retire on when you're only in your early twenties. Though there was a promise of an additional $2 million within four years, Evander was mature enough to know that spending *if*come instead of *in*come was dangerous. As far as Evander was concerned, if the money wasn't in his pocket, it wasn't really his.

Just as important, Evander was only a few years removed from living a lower-middle-class life. He realized it would be more difficult to taste "the good life" and then have to go back because of financial mismanagement than to never have tasted it at all. He decided he'd rather leave the expensive toys for another day and instead save all he could.

Evander's first investment was in Mama. He took out two mortgages—one for himself (a condo in Atlanta) and one for our mother. The latter action was the fulfillment of a boyhood dream and promise. I don't know how many times Evander had said, "Mama, someday I'm gonna buy you a house." Nothing gave him more satisfaction than handing the keys to our teary-eyed, hardworking mother, and saying, "Mama, I told you I'd do it. Here it is, your new house."

"Your mom will always love you," he explained. "You can always go home if you take care of your mom. Anything else is kind of questionable, but you can always go home to Mom, so I wanted to make sure she had a place I could go home to."

With two mortgages to pay, Evander's money concerns didn't go away. If anything, they intensified. After making the down payments, Evander saved the rest of his money. He had tasted the struggle of searching for bottles all day long and caddying in the hot sun to raise a few dollars, and he knew he had just a high school education. He was determined to make this money last as long as possible.

Then he discovered taxes. When he got off the phone after talking with his accountant, he threw up his hands and said, "I knew it." He replayed the figure the accountant had given him.

"Fifty thousand dollars. For *taxes!*"

"Man, this is just a trick," Evander told me. "They let you hold it for a while, but then they come back for it."

Evander became a passionate saver. He wanted to have money in the bank, where he could touch it. "I need to save as much as possible, because eventually, somebody else is going to want their share, and when they come back, I'd better have something to give them."

So while Evander's immediate financial concerns were over, he knew he'd have to keep earning more to fulfill his new obligations. He hadn't yet reached his twenty-fifth birthday, and he had two mortgages to pay.

The stage was set for Evander to move forward. He had won a medal at the Olympics, announced his intention to turn pro, and signed on with a management team. Little did he know that a conversation with our mother was about to send him back to his roots on a visit to Atmore, Alabama.

Evander was about to meet his father.

A New Family

During the Olympics, the citizens of the tiny town of Atmore all scratched their heads when Evander's biography was mentioned in the telecasts.

"That boy's from Atmore!" they said. "You know him?"

"Nope. Do you?"

"No, never heard of him."

"Anybody here named Holyfield?" another asked.

"Can't remember that name," a longtime farmer added.

Evander bore his mother's name. Our mother and Evander's father severed all contact, so Evander's dad had no idea where Evander was or what he was doing. Since Evander had left Atmore at a very early age, nobody could remember what he looked like.

After the Olympics, Mother took Evander aside and said she had something to tell him. It was time he learned about his father. "I think it's time you meet him, if you want to," she said.

Evander eagerly agreed. The Olympics gave him more than a medal. They gave him a relationship with his father, Ison Coley.

Imagine the shock Evander's father felt when he received a phone call, telling him that the courageous and classy Olympian from Atmore was actually his son. As the two men finally faced each other, there was an awkward moment. Evander immediately felt a son's love, but he didn't know how to share it with a virtual stranger. Besides, what if he said the wrong thing? What would make his dad happy? What would make him angry? He knew he couldn't treat him like a casual acquaintance—"Oh, hi, how ya doing? Where do you work?"

Not very much was said at that first meeting, though Evander made it clear that he would welcome and even cherish a future relationship. Soon, his newly discovered dad was being invited to all of Evander's bouts.

The lack of emotion exhibited by the newly reunited father and son was more than made up for by the enthusiasm of Evander's newly discovered brothers and sisters. When they found out Evander was their brother, they went crazy.

"We was trying to figure out who this kid from Atmore, Alabama, was," they gushed. "And now we find out, you're *our brother!*"

One of the brothers, Ricky, was the first to introduce Evander to the others. He delighted in showing Evander's now familiar face to them, and then saying, "Hey, this is your *brother.*"

"No kidding?!" one yelled. "Man, everybody was saying how much we looked alike!" (Evander bears more physical resemblance to his father than he does to any of us on his mother's side.)

His new family paraded him all over Atmore. "Hey, remember him?" they yelled out. "The guy from the Olympics? He's our brother!"

Goin' Pro

Evander was eager to turn pro, but when he was alone with his trainers, one of the first things he told them was that he was worried about his endurance. Evander was used to knocking most of the amateurs out, and he now wondered if he had the stamina to go three full professional rounds, let alone the six or eight rounds of most pro light heavyweight bouts.

Everything about Evander's life—from the hours he slept to the food he ate to the way he spent his free time—now came under review.

At the time, Evander would walk to a local store and stock up on the "fun food"—potato chips, corn chips, and his favorite, apple pies. Since it was cold out, he'd buy a large quantity and then store the bags in his room.

One afternoon, another boxer ran short and tried to get Evander to start handing out his junk food stash. But Evander had paid for it—he was still concerned about finances and very conservative with his money—and he had walked through the cold weather to get it, and he wasn't about to just hand it out because somebody else lacked his foresight.

Well, the other boxer played the trump card. He went to trainer Lou Duva and told him about the stash.

Evander was in his room when he heard the knock on his door. "Come in!" he called out.

Duva sauntered in and Evander offered him a seat. Evander began to wonder why Duva would pay him an unannounced visit and not say anything. Duva was just making small talk, until he leaned back in his chair, lifted up the corner of Evander's bedspread, and eyed a bag of potato chips.

"What's this?" he said, pulling out the bag and holding it up.

Evander shrugged. Duva got up and walked around the room. He went to Evander's desk and lifted up a bag of corn chips.

"What's this?" he asked. He walked to the other side of the room and found three or four apple pies. "And this?"

"That's my food," Evander said.

"Wrong!" Duva said. "It *was* your food, but it's not anymore!"

Ironically enough, Evander had started to eat like this to make weight. As his body continued to grow well into his early twenties, it became increasingly difficult for him to keep below the 175 threshold of a light heavyweight. Sugar stopped Evander's appetite cold, so he became accustomed to eating one apple pie a day.

Every habit like that would have to be reviewed, however. Evander realized he had to put every part of his life under a microscope. It was one thing to eat like he did when most of his opponents didn't last more than two rounds. It would be another thing altogether to eat like that as he trained to face professionals.

And Evander was soon to find out just how grueling a sport professional boxing can be.

First Blood

Evander faced his first professional fight in November 1984. It's the management team's job to use great care when choosing the first opponent. If the opponent is too tough, the young fighter might become punch-shy and take on a defensive fighting style. Also, a first-fight defeat can be disastrous to a new professional's career and end it in one night. On the other hand, you don't want to choose someone who provides no real challenge. Otherwise, the fighter won't develop properly. He'll also get a reputation for dodging the real fighters and will be taken less seriously.

The way to get through all of this is for a management team to evaluate their boxer's strengths and weaknesses, and then find a credible fighter who will present a challenge and at the same time help the new fighter to improve on his weaknesses. That way, they can stage a good, tough fight, without giving their man too big of a scare.

That's the way it's *supposed* to work, anyway, but, as with so many things, nothing easy was going to come to Evander. In fact, his first professional fight proved to be one of his most difficult *ever*.

The fight was held in New York City's Madison Square Garden. Everyone on the card—except for Evander—had won an Olympic gold medal, so the evening was billed as "A Night of Gold." Mark Breland, Meldrick Taylor, Pernell Whitaker, and Tyrell Biggs joined Evander in their professional "opening night." Evander was eager and ready to go. He watched as the other fighters scored knockouts or technical knockouts. Everything was going as planned. The Olympians were getting their chins tested, but they were prevailing. It was a good initiation into the professional ranks.

And then Evander stepped into the ring. Just seconds after the bell sounded to inaugurate round one, I knew somebody in management had made a mistake. If you've been around boxing for a while, you can ascertain a boxer's technical skills within a few minutes. I felt a prickly sensation creep up the back of my neck as I watched Evander's opponent. Evander's first professional bout proved to be an all-out brawl.

Lionel Byarm was tough, tenacious, and dangerous. He looked strangely similar to Joe Louis, with his slightly slanted eyes, his low-cropped haircut, and Louis's famous icy stare. Byarm was the Philadelphia State Champion in the light heavyweight division, so his reputation was on the line. He wasn't about to just fall down as the first stepping-stone for Evander's future career. He came ready to do more than fight. He came prepared to win.

Byarm used Joe Louis's nickname, the "Brown Bomber," and he came out determined to prove that it was no misnomer. He left an arena full of convinced spectators. Byarm's arms were swinging before the first bell had stopped vibrating. He didn't want to just beat Evander. He wanted to knock him out.

Byarm is a persistent and relentless fighter. Evander managed to slip punches and counter with his own bombs, but the Philadelphia champion would not let up. He caught Evander with a crushing right, which temporarily stunned him. My heart stopped beating for just a second, until I saw Evander counter with his own combination. Evander backed up and circled, in a desperate attempt to break Byarm's rhythm, but Byarm was relentless and stayed in Evander's chest until the bell signaling the end of the first round pulled him away.

By now the crowd was on its feet, clapping. Nobody expected this kind of fight. This was an entirely new world for Evander. He hit Byarm with everything he had, but Byarm was still standing! In the amateurs, that just didn't happen. Evander knocked out every opponent in both the Golden Gloves Tournament and the Olympic Games. But Byarm wouldn't fall down. Evander kept swinging, and Byarm kept standing.

"This ain't no initiation," Evander told his corner at the end of round one. "This is war."

Lou Duva slapped Evander's shoulders. "He's tough all right, but you can get him. Stay in there."

The second round started, and Evander came out ready to give this professional thing another try. He was shocked as Byarm willingly ate combinations and uppercuts just to land one punishing blow. Byarm's strategy was to disarm Evander and make him afraid of the "big shot" so that he'd stop boxing and become defensive. Since it was Evander's first fight as a professional, Byarm was hoping to shake the rookie's confidence.

Fortunately, Evander had faced similarly tough battles, most notably against Ricky Womack. But that was as an amateur, with both men wearing headgear, and the fight limited to three rounds. This bout was scheduled for six, and Byarm was prepared to bide his time until Evander entered new territory—the fourth and fifth rounds.

Punishing hooks, vicious right hands, and pummeling body shots flew between both fighters. Their styles were distinct, but brutal in both cases. Evander's quickness allowed him to generate head shot after head shot, while Byarm slipped in some devastating body shots.

This was an extremely difficult fight for me to watch. Evander boxed a superb five rounds, but he faced a stellar opponent. As the two fighters rose from their corner for the sixth and final round, everyone knew the outcome was still undecided. Whoever won the sixth round would win the match. But unlike Byarm, Evander had never fought a sixth round before.

The concluding round contained everything the first five rounds did, except that everything was intensified. If I hadn't seen it, I don't know if I could have believed it. The fighters met at the center of the ring and proceeded to pummel each other without mercy. The crowd once again jumped to its feet. This was boxing at its most furious pace, and they were loving it.

I was scared and angry. I couldn't believe that Evander's team had matched him against such an experienced, tough, tenacious, and wily fighter for his first professional bout. Byarm's experience gave him an advantage, but Evander hung in there. This was new territory, but he found his way through it.

After what seemed like an unbelievable display of exertion, the bell signaling the end of the match finally rang. The crowd roared its approval. Evander had survived his first bout, but had he won?

I thought he had, but I held my breath as I remembered the Olympics. My palms sweated until I heard the announcer call out Evander's name.

Even to this day, I get chills watching the tape of that fight. It was a brutal initiation, but Evander got through it. As he went back to his corner after the sixth round, Ace Marotta, his cornerman, encouraged him, "You fought two fights tonight, Evander." As an amateur, Evander had fought three-rounders, so going six rounds really was the equivalent of two bouts.

"You proved to yourself you could do it. You fought two fights, and you won them both. Way to go."

Evander was a professional now, and he was prepared to create one of the most successful and brilliant careers in the history of boxing.

CHAPTER 10

HOMETOWN HERO

L ord, help me last."
    The despairing man's prayer didn't seem as though it could be coming from the lips of Evander Holyfield, but it was. Evander was in the middle of what many boxing journalists would call "the fight of the year." He had rolled through ten victorious professional bouts in the last eighteen months, winning eight of them by knockout. In one, Evander had hit a fighter so hard that the boxer lost both a tooth and a root when his mouth became overly familiar with Evander's fist.

    As I watched Evander march through these victories and into this fight with Dwight Qawi Braxton, I saw my baby brother turn into a man. He was married now, and his wife, Paulette, was pregnant with Evander's second child, Ashley. Evander had taken on several business concerns, and he was proving his character outside the ring as well as in it. The car dealership that now bore Evander's name had become the number one volume dealership in the Southeast.

    Evander's name and popularity as a boxer had risen as ABC televised most of his early professional bouts. Soon, he began to be recognized at airports. He was a star on the rise, and boxing fans began clamoring for a bout with a ferocious fighter named Dwight Qawi Braxton. Most commentators said Evander was still too young to face as tough and experienced a fighter as Qawi. They doubted that Evander had the experience to go up against the cagey and hardened ex-convict who had become known as a brutal and punishing ring warrior. Evander agreed with them, but his success virtually insured that such a bout would soon take place.

    In his earlier bouts, Evander routinely earned about $65,000. When promoters floated a figure more than three times that— $200,000—to fight Qawi, Evander could hardly say no. Even better, he was being offered a chance to gain Qawi's title of World Boxing Association (WBA) Junior Heavyweight Champion of the World.

That's how Evander found himself sitting on a stool, hurting as much as he had ever hurt, feeling as tired as he had ever felt, and wondering how he was going to finish this bout.

As I watched my brother bleed and pant for air between the fourth and fifth rounds, I wondered if the experts weren't right. The fight was scheduled for fifteen rounds. Evander had never fought more than eight—a fact that the Qawi people hoped to exploit when they demanded the longer fifteen-round bout. They reasoned that Evander's lack of experience in the later rounds would eventually show and make it easy for Qawi to capitalize on Evander's exhaustion.

To make matters even more intense, Evander was fighting in his hometown, Atlanta. It was the first time his friends and former coworkers would get to see him fight as a professional. Evander had insisted—at great financial cost to him—that the gate be free. He wanted anyone to be able to come and watch him fight. Evander's high school teachers were there; his Little League football coach was there; his former Sunday school teachers and coworkers at Epps Airport were there, as were his friends from the neighborhood in Summerhill.

Qawi wasn't just fighting Evander Holyfield. He was fighting Summerhill, Fulton High School, the Warren Memorial Boy's Club, and the entire city of Atlanta. All this added to the burden that Evander felt between rounds. He hadn't lost a bout as a professional, and now he prayed, "Please Lord, don't let it happen here, not in Atlanta."

Before the fight, I had the privilege of leading Evander into the arena. The place literally erupted with shouts as we entered. I thought the noise would shake the very foundations of the building. The deafening roar would occasionally be pierced with a high "Chubbee!" I'd look around to see who had spoken, but the movement and sound was so chaotic that you could never tell.

Evander fed off the crowd's energy. The cheers and shouts fired his soul and made him eager to do his best. He couldn't wait to get going.

As I sat down ringside, a man next to me said something that shocked me. "You Holyfield's brother?" he asked.

I nodded yes.

Ten-year-old Evander (far right) with his boxing coach, Carter Morgan, his wife, and other young boxers.

Sixteen-year-old Evander instructs John Williams at the Warren Memorial Boy's Club.

A 1979 fight in Fort Payne, Alabama, between teenagers Holyfield and David. Holyfield won.

Photo on the 1980 boxing contract of competitor Evander Holyfield, Carter Boxing Team, Open Division—17 years old, 147 pounds, record of fights: 48 wins, 11 losses.

A close-up of the seventeen-year-old fighter.

Graduation picture from Fulton High School, Atlanta, in 1980.

Evander servicing commuter planes at Atlanta's Epps Airport.

1984 Olympic bronze medal winner.

(Below) Evander participating in the
1984 Olympics in Los Angeles.

Evander, Eloise McCoy, sister, Bernard, and mother, Annie, in front.

Holyfield vs. Pinklon Thomas, December 9, 1988, Atlantic City, New Jersey. TKO in the seventh round.

Bernard in front of the Evander Holyfield Buick/Subaru dealership.

In the corner with Lou Duva and cut man Ace Morotta.

Team Holyfield: Mike Weaver, trainer and nephew; Willie Holyfield, trainer and brother; and Evander.

Evander weighing in for the Holyfield vs. James "Buster" Douglas fight, October 25, 1990, Las Vegas, Nevada. TKO in third round. Won undisputed World Heavyweight title.

PHOTO BY MARC MORRISON/KAREN WULFFRAAT

(Top) Sparring before the
Holyfield/Cooper fight.

Holyfield vs. Burt Cooper,
November 23, 1991, Atlanta.
TKO in the seventh round.
Retained WBA/IBF World
Heavyweight titles.

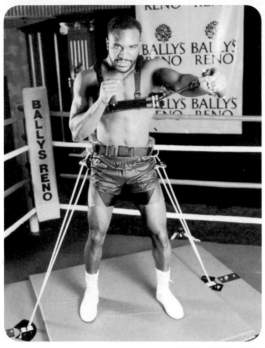

Evander is strapped into the "Reaction Piece," an invention designed and built especially to hone the fighter's instincts. While Evander's legs are strapped to the platform, he must duck, block, and counter five thin, padded poles that are coming at him from all sides.

PHOTO BY WILL HART

Victory over Riddick Bowe, November 6, 1993, Las Vegas, Nevada. Won WBA/IBF Heavyweight titles.

"Evander is going to get knocked out. I remember him in the amateur divisions; he always lost the ones that really counted."

I wanted to belt him right there, especially when he added, "Even in the Olympics, he lost to a fighter from New Zealand."

The sneer in his tone made me sick. I looked at him and knew he couldn't last ten seconds in a ring with Kevin Barry, much less Evander Holyfield. But for some reason he counted himself an expert when it came to boxing.

Evander's chiseled 6-foot 2-inch frame looked lean and taut, and almost out of place with his boyish face and eyes. Qawi was considerably shorter—5 foot 7 inches—but he was thick and solid, reminding me of a pit bull. His arms and thighs were massive, and his dark eyes were menacing. The only similarity between the two opponents was the boxing gloves tied to their wrists.

Lou Duva warned Evander before the fight, "He's going to come right at you. If he bangs you, bang him right back. *Don't give him any respect.*" Duva was practically shouting now. "Stay with him for six rounds, then we'll turn it on."

Evander nodded. He glanced over at Qawi, knowing that for the next forty-five minutes, that face would be his obsession. He'd watch it through sweat-stinging eyes, he'd see it darting left and right, and he'd do his best to mark it with his gloves.

Evander's punching speed was piston-like compared with Qawi's slower swings, and he rattled his shorter opponent's chin with a flurry of four to six punches in combination. It felt good to connect, but he stayed cautious. Qawi was clearly stronger, and he seemed willing to endure Evander's jabs while he waited to unleash some horrendous blows in return. When one of those bombs landed, I heard someone behind me scream, "Evander! Stay away from him!"

Evander didn't need the advice. He kept his eyes open, knowing that any lapse in concentration could provide Qawi with the one—and only—opening he needed.

Qawi's strategy was clear. He wanted to wear Evander down and take him out in the later rounds. Evander believed he could outbox Qawi. If he could avoid Qawi's bombs, the title would be his.

Unfortunately, boxing is a sport in which your mind and body are both under attack. During the sixth round, Evander's back started screaming. The pain climbed up his spine and mercilessly seized him during some of the bout's most intense moments. Qawi kept pressuring him, never letting up, and as Evander's back felt like it was on fire, he began to wonder, *What am I doing in here?* Between rounds, however, he worked hard to talk himself back into the fight. *You can't quit,* he told himself. *You have to go on.*

He did, but the pain in his back kept up its malicious assault, and Qawi kept coming as well. The younger fighter had to win the first bout—the mental one—before he could win the physical one. It wasn't easy.

You're young, his weary mind teased him. *It won't matter if you quit. It won't hurt you to lose one.*

But then he'd reject that thought. *No, you're not a quitter, and you're not a loser. Finish the fight.*

Evander's corner was pleased that he had stayed even with Qawi in the early rounds. But now they wanted him to step it up. "Keep jabbing!" Duva shouted above the roar. "Keep turning! Work his body some more! Let's go to work!"

Evander bounced off his stool and did exactly as Duva told him. He started pounding Qawi's arms and lower body. Qawi didn't change his approach, and he paid dearly because of it. Evander could sense that his blows were making an impact.

By the tenth round, however, the momentum began to shift away from Evander. Qawi began to connect more frequently, and the pounding began to cloud Evander's mind. His hand speed started to slow, allowing Qawi to duck more punches. Even worse, Evander's mobility had slowed, making him vulnerable to Qawi's bombs. Qawi sensed Evander's fatigue and dove at him like a shark that smells fresh blood. Evander did his best to mask his weariness, but he knew Qawi sensed it, and the defending champ's recognition energized the more experienced fighter. Qawi began to unleash a barrage of punches rather than holding back with one-two combinations.

The pace was unbelievable, and it marked completely new territory for Evander. He had never gone beyond eight rounds, and now he was in the tenth. His body was used to quitting at that point, but he used his strength of spirit to force himself to continue.

Qawi's heightened intensity began to feed Evander's adrenaline, waking him up. The two fighters exchanged some furious blows, and the need for quick and decisive action forced Evander to concentrate. When the bell signaled the end of the round, the crowd jumped to their feet with thunderous applause.

Evander stepped back, took in a deep breath, and headed to his corner. I saw Qawi smile at Evander. He saw him slowing down, and his sneer betrayed his belief that Evander would soon be lying down.

I heard somebody behind me say, "He's always talking about God. Let's see if God can help him now."

Evander's corner people hurriedly placed the stool in the corner with a bucket of ice and water. Evander plopped down. Sweat cascaded off him like waterfalls. His boxing trunks clung to him. His arms were tired and sore. One of the trainers frantically fanned him with a towel while another trainer gave him water. Ace Marotta applied ice in a desperate and only slightly successful attempt to stop the swelling around Evander's eyes and cheekbones.

"Keep circling!" George Benton, Evander's strategist, now took over. "Keep the jab in front of him."

I watched Evander and my heart went sick. His chest heaved up and down as he took in large gulps of oxygen. I knew him well enough to know that he was questioning his own ability and stamina to continue the pace that Qawi was intent on keeping.

Evander had never fought anyone like Qawi, who kept the pressure on him from round one. There was absolutely no letup. In fact, round after round, Qawi seemed to be getting stronger and stronger rather than weaker. Evander was exhausted and began to question whether he could go on. He sat on the stool, the trainers fanning him and shouting at him, and he prayed, "Lord, give me the strength to finish this fight. I can't make it on my own, but with You I can do all things." The last word scarcely escaped his lips when the bell rang to begin the fifth round.

Qawi came out eager for the kill. The home crowd was strangely silent, expecting the worst. Like me, they had seen the exhaustion on Evander's face. The man sitting next to me said smugly, "Looks like this is the last round for your boy. He barely made it through the last one."

Evander and Qawi literally clashed in the center of the ring. Qawi was hungry and attacked Evander with a vengeance, as if this were the fifteenth and final round. Evander braced himself, planted his feet, and landed a flurry of combinations on Qawi's chin. Qawi stumbled backwards, dazed by the barrage of powerful punches, his eyes blinking quickly, momentarily stunned and surprised by the sudden burst of strength from the young challenger.

The Atlanta crowd leapt back to its feet and poured their desire into the ring.

"Hit him again, Evander!"

"There must be a God somewhere, 'cause he sho' heard my prayers tonight!"

"Knock him down, Chubby!"

Evander was up on his toes now, his heart racing, his feet dancing, and his head bobbing left to right, deftly eluding Qawi's counterpunches. This is when boxing becomes *fun*. Suddenly, Evander became the aggressor and Qawi's chin paid the price. Qawi wobbled, retreated, and ducked his head, but Evander stayed in his face and hammered him. Qawi was in serious danger when the bell sounded.

Cheers cascaded throughout the arena. Atlanta had come alive with their challenger. Evander had bought their seats; now, with his fists, he had bought their hearts, and they were all his. The crowd's excitement further fed Evander's recovery. At this moment, he knew the fight could be his.

What caused the change? Evander felt God empowering him. In an average lightweight fight, a boxer throws sixty, maybe seventy punches a round. Qawi was about average here, but Evander unleashed an astounding average of eighty-five blows per round. In a fifteen-round bout, that's more than a thousand swings. In doing this, Evander literally felt the strength of God pour into him as he finished the bout. Between the time the first bell rang and the last bell sounded, Evander had shed fifteen pounds!

Once the final bell stopped the action, a cautious optimism hushed the crowd. Finally, the announcer's voice rang out, "And the New!"—the crowd erupted—"Jun-ior Heavee-weight Champ-ion of the Worrrrllld, Evander 'The Real Deal' Hooollyfield!"

The crowd began to chant, "Ho-ly! Ho-ly! Ho-ly!"

Evander lifted his arms, a smile breaking across his beaten face. He whispered an elated prayer of thanks. The hardest fought battles are the most satisfying, and this was doubly so, as it was a bruising battle for the title. Evander had become the first member from the 1984 United States Olympic team to win a world title. He was now the Junior Heavyweight Champion of the World. Suddenly, Evander felt he could go another ten rounds!

His opponent didn't share Evander's newfound energy, though. Qawi felt as though he had faced a buzz saw. "Maybe I'm getting too old for this," he told a reporter. "Maybe I'd better start looking for something else to do."

Except for Qawi and the referee, Evander had been all alone in the ring. Now everybody wanted to be around him. His trainers, the crowd, the reporters—suddenly nobody could get close enough to him. Evander felt as though he were in the midst of a swirling sea.

The hometown crowd was euphoric. His teachers cried. His coworkers from Epps cheered. A hometown boy had done it.

In the midst of all these strange faces, Evander took particular comfort in being hugged by Willie, our older brother and one of Evander's trainers. Even the enthusiastic adulation of the entire world can't compete with your older brother saying, "Chubby, I'm proud of you. You did good, man. Way to go, Champ!"

Evander wanted to cry, he felt so happy. It was almost impossible for him to get alone long enough to take a shower. Everybody wanted to be with him.

I looked next to me, trying to find the guy who told me Evander would lose, but he was gone. I smiled. Always loses the big ones, huh? This had been the biggest fight of Evander's career, and he had won.

Counting the Cost

As Evander got ready to shower, he felt his aching back tighten up, the sinews contorting themselves in mad and ruthless knots. Wave after wave of nausea attacked him, and his head was seized by a brutal ache.

Evander called his doctor and described the symptoms.

"We got to get you to the hospital," he said.

"Everybody's waiting for me downstairs," Evander complained.

"Listen, Champ, your body's burning muscle. Your kidneys could fail. You need help now."

They rushed the new champion to the hospital, where they immediately put him on an IV. They pumped nine containers of fluid—nine!—into his radically dehydrated body.

When Evander woke up, he weighed 201 pounds, more than he had ever weighed in his life, and he could feel much of that weight sloshing around inside him.

He was stiff, sore, and bruised. His lungs were burnt from the exertion, and his hands were swollen to grotesque proportions. It would take his hands an entire month to return to their prefight size.

Evander had to ask himself, *Was it worth it? If I have to fight this hard to be champ, do I really want to fight anymore?*

For the first time since Carter Morgan died, Evander felt his dreams diminish. He had never been hit so many times in his entire career, and he never imagined that being a professional would be this tough.

The question kept repeating itself: *I have the belt, but do I ever really want to fight again?*

Yet at the same time, Evander was worshiping God. Nobody else knew the full story: how tired he had been, how he wondered if he could even go the distance, and how God not only answered his prayer but gave him more energy than he could have dreamed of.

When you're at the end of your strength, and God proves Himself faithful, it creates a tremendous bond, and Evander felt it now more intimately than he had ever felt it before.

While the belt belonged to Evander Holyfield, the glory belonged to God. But did Evander want to fight again? Was he willing to pay the price?

CHAPTER 11

MILESTONES

When Evander woke up the next morning, the magnitude of his accomplishment finally dawned on him. It had all happened so fast—the Olympics, turning pro, and now the junior heavyweight title. His body took weeks to recover, but during that time, people came up to him and said, "You're the man, Holyfield!"

"I can't believe how good you looked!"

"Man, you were tough!"

Evander thought to himself, *This isn't so bad. I kind of like this*. As the swelling left his hands, he thought, *Well, maybe I can do this one more time.*

Evander fought Qawi in July of 1986. He faced Michael Brothers five months later. The bout was held in France and constituted Evander's first junior heavyweight title defense.

By now, Evander's exposure on ABC made it inevitable that he would be stopped and recognized at airports in the United States, but he didn't expect anybody to know him in France. Thus he was shocked when he walked down the streets of Paris and noticed that people were suddenly stopping their cars, even in the middle of the street, and jumping out.

Evander began to get nervous. What was going on? He looked around to see what was causing the commotion, and it took him several minutes to realize that *he* was causing the traffic jams.

Evander laughed. This was too much. After signing some autographs, he turned and walked into a pizza restaurant, and the Parisians followed him in! Here he was, in a foreign country, and the people knew his name!

Evander was elated, and he rewarded the Parisians for their loyalty by knocking out Brothers in the third round. As Evander watched Brothers fall, he couldn't help but compare this bout with his fifteen-round brawl with Qawi.

Maybe this isn't so bad, being champ, Evander thought. If he could earn the pay and recognition by going three rounds instead of fifteen, maybe he really did have a future in boxing.

Just two months later, Evander was slated to meet a close friend from the 1984 Olympic Team, Henry Tillman. Evander wasn't eager to fight his friend, but he was offered $200,000.

Still, Evander asked himself, *Why does Henry want to fight me? We're friends, and there's three belts out there. Why does he want to take my belt?*

Nevertheless, the two boxers squared off in Reno, Nevada. Evander scored a technical knockout in the seventh round.

Just a few weeks later, Evander flew into Chicago to be in Tillman's wedding. Some people who don't understand boxing might find this strange—why would two friends beat up on each other? In fact, somebody asked Evander about this after the Tillman fight.

"I thought Henry was your friend," the man said.

"Not in the ring, he isn't," Evander replied. "When I'm in the ring, it's either him or me. If somebody's coming after my belt, I'm not going to just give it to him."

To the fighters, boxing is a *sport,* not a personal vendetta. The same linebacker who tries to tear off a quarterback's head during a game can be seen shaking that same quarterback's hand afterwards. A similar phenomenon occurs in boxing. Professional fighters don't take hits personally.

"If you don't want to get hit," Evander explains, "what are you doing boxing?"

When Evander got into Chicago, he and Henry realized that their promoters had pulled one over on them.

"Why did you want to fight me?" Evander asked Henry as soon as he got off the plane.

"They said you wanted to fight *me,*" Henry protested.

"No, I didn't want to fight you," Evander laughed.

Henry laughed, and the two young fighters prepared for their new roles in life—Henry as a husband and Evander as Showtime's new main event. Showtime signed Evander after the Tillman fight, guaranteeing him $200,000 for the next bout but promising him more for later bouts—if he kept winning.

Evander kept winning, and Showtime made good on their promise. In time, Evander was making $1.4 million for one fight.

In 1987, Evander reached several milestones. He had a million dollars cash in the bank ("I could go in there and touch it," he said), and he moved up to cruiserweight. Major sports magazines, like *Sports Illustrated,* were soon running articles entitled, "Tuning Up for Tyson." They recognized that the junior heavyweight championship and even the cruiserweight championship was just a stepping-stone for Evander. Evander recognized it too.

Some have questioned why a former light heavyweight who had to move up to become a cruiserweight, would then venture into the bulky world of mammoth heavyweights. The truth is, Evander never felt comfortable as a junior heavyweight. The upper limit for that class is 175 pounds, and Evander often had to limit himself to one meal a day to maintain that weight. Combined with his grueling training, he could practically feel his body begin eating muscle as it craved something to burn.

Crusierweight allowed him a few extra pounds (fighting at 190), and Evander could have stayed there rather comfortably, but the competition couldn't handle him. Evander had unified all the cruiserweight titles by the spring of 1988, and then gradually, with the help of trainer Tim Hallmark, built his body into a heavyweight.

It was a glorious construction. Evander's slow weight addition allowed him to put muscle on top of muscle until he achieved the most chiseled body in the sport. Not too many men weighing more than 200 pounds can boast a thirty-one-inch waist.

Trying to Bag the Champ

Even though Evander won his first two fights as a heavyweight, critics dismissed the bouts as tussles with "aging journeymen." This irritated, but didn't discourage, Evander. He had become used to people doubting him. After Evander stopped Michael Dokes, however, even the critics had to admit that Evander Holyfield did indeed look like "the real deal." A Showtime analyst called Evander's bout with Dokes "the greatest heavyweight fight in ten years," but that phrase would virtually become a cliché by the time Evander reached the twilight of his career.

In July of 1989, Evander followed up his victory over Dokes with a convincing knockout of Adilson Rodrigues, who was ranked second and third, respectively, by the World Boxing Council (WBC) and the World Boxing Association (WBA). Following that fight, *Sports Illustrated* proclaimed that "Holyfield is the only genuine challenger to heavyweight champion Mike Tyson." Evander told the media, "I hope Tyson was watching. Now he has to know that Evander Holyfield is coming."

By this time, Evander and his management became increasingly exasperated by their inability to get Tyson into the ring. Two major obstacles held everything up. First, it's a matter of getting not just two fighters but two *teams* together. Evander and Tyson would have agreed to fight in about sixty seconds, but when you add promoters, trainers, and managers, it's like putting a dozen cooks in a very small kitchen; nobody can agree on how to break the first egg.

Don King, Tyson's promoter, and Dan Duva, Evander's promoter, are rivals. It was inevitable that serious problems would erupt. The politics of boxing are such that whoever controls the heavyweight contenders controls the heavyweight division. When a promoter refuses to allow his fighter to fight, he affects his rival's income: people won't pay top dollar to see a "straw man" fight the champ.

Unfortunately, promoters sometimes work with divided interests. If they did what was best for their fighters, the next step would be relatively clear. But promoters too often think about what kind of power they'll wield ten years from now, when their current fighter will be retired on a rural farm. By giving in too quickly, they may empower their rival and cut their own future. It's exasperating but true: promoters promote themselves better than they promote anyone else.

I think there was a second element in King's hesitation to let Evander fight Tyson, however. Buster Douglas's defeat of Tyson wasn't a fluke. Don't get me wrong—flukes happen. Sometimes a superior boxer really can get beat by a lucky, undefended blow. A good, strong heavyweight can knock out *anybody* with the right shot.

But Douglas didn't beat Tyson with a lucky blow. He beat him throughout ten rounds. Douglas outboxed Tyson and then finished him off. Tyson is a brawler, not a boxer. Most of the fighters he faced were scared before they put their shorts on. Consequently, they let the fight become a brawl, which played right into Tyson's hands.

King knew that a boxer could give Tyson trouble, and there are no better boxers fighting today than Evander Holyfield. If I were King, from a strictly business standpoint, I would have put off a

Tyson/Holyfield fight as long as possible, riding Tyson's money machine until Holyfield broke it up.

But back in the summer of 1989, everyone knew that King's ride on the Tyson money machine was rushing toward an end. If Tyson didn't sign to fight the WBA's number one contender (Evander) by November 1, 1989, he'd forfeit his title. Tyson was also required to sign with the WBC's top contender (also Evander) by February 25, 1990, or he would lose that belt as well. The entire boxing world understood that even King couldn't stop the "Brawl for It All."

Ironically, it was reported that Dan Duva warned King about putting the Tyson/Holyfield fight off for too long. Duva had once lost millions of dollars when a fighter he was promoting, Tony Ayala, was convicted of rape just months before he was scheduled to fight for the junior middleweight championship of the world. Therefore, Duva warned King not to take too long because you never know how long fighters like Ayala and Tyson are going to be around.

King laughed as if to say, "Don't worry about Mike."

Well, there wouldn't be any need to worry, because Evander wouldn't get his shot at Mike. Tyson's loss to Douglas and subsequent conviction on a rape charge precluded any such meeting.

Will Evander and Tyson ever fight? I think so. In fact, it looks more likely now than ever. Evander has a good shot at winning one of the titles in the fall of 1996. That would set up the ultimate "Brawl for It All," with Evander facing Tyson in the spring of 1997—a full eight years after the first fight should have occurred.

With Tyson out of the way in 1990, however, Evander was finally given his chance to fight for the heavyweight title. To prepare Evander, his trainers took him through an even more grueling training regimen. Virtually everything he ate had to be approved. On one occasion, Holyfield's conditioning specialist, Tim Hallmark, vetoed Evander's choice of home fries and butter on his pancakes. Evander turned to Hallmark and said, "You'd better take out some stock in Burger King, because when I get back to Atlanta, I'm going to spend a whole week on burgers."

Hallmark was more than a trainer to Evander—he became a close friend. The two shared a solid faith in God. Their motto was, "If a man has done everything in his power to get ready, then he can get on his hands and knees and ask God to be with him." Consequently, the two would work to the point of exhaustion in training—

Hallmark increased Evander's strength by 33 percent, and he decreased Evander's recovery time dramatically—and then pray like a couple of monks before a fight, an open Bible inevitably lying on the floor between them.

Just before going out to the ring, Hallmark would repeat, over and over, "You have wisdom, you have security, you have paid your dues."

Evander would nod. God had seen him through many fights. He'd get him through this one, as well.

Although it sounds laughable in hindsight, many of the early critics and commentators thought Buster Douglas would stop Evander cold; some even suggesting that Evander wouldn't last three rounds. The same trumped-up "blown-up heavyweight" charges flew off the newspapers and into the airwaves.

Evander didn't listen. He had heard it all before—even the particularly absurd charge that he was "too nice to be champion." Evander had been training for this title fight for more than twenty years. He began using every negative comment for "fuel and motivation." "I'm starving my doubts and feeding my faith, Lightning," he told me.

I saw a fire in his eyes that told me, Buster Douglas better watch out.

King of the Ring

Things started going badly for Douglas before the ring was set up for the fight. As I said before, a management team often tries to get an edge on the other fighter weeks before the bout by slanting the publicity. Evander's trainer, Lou Duva, put a spiritual twist on his preparation.

On the Sunday before the fight, Duva went into a Roman Catholic church, put in a small offering, and lit a votive candle. As he was leaving, however, he thought he spied someone from the Douglas camp doing the same thing. Duva waited until the man left, then went over and blew out the other candle.

The fighters themselves have an opportunity to psych each other out during the traditional weigh-in, and Evander won this battle hands down. When Buster Douglas weighed in at 246 pounds—heavier than expected—the crowd actually booed. Evander watched a cloud cover Douglas's face, and he knew he had a golden opportunity.

Evander stepped up onto the scale, flexed his muscles as tightly as he could, and assumed a confident pose. Sportswriters said, "Holyfield's physique looks like bronze or chiseled steel" and "Holyfield must be the most conditioned athlete in the world."

Evander gained confidence from the room's reaction and looked over at Douglas, who turned his head away. Right then, Evander knew he was just hours away from becoming the new heavyweight champion of the world.

Nobody else felt that way, however. The day before the fight, thirty major newspapers were asked to give their prediction. Without exception, every one of them—including our hometown newspaper—picked Douglas. They all felt that however well Evander boxed, Douglas's most feared weapon—the uppercut that downed Tyson in Tokyo—would eventually drop Evander as well.

The arena at the Mirage Hotel in Las Vegas was filled to capacity on October 25, 1990. The promoters had billed this fight as "The Moment of Truth." They couldn't have picked a better title for Evander. Evander was fighting for something that went beyond a fancy belt and a prestigious title. All his life Evander had faced the doubters—the ones who said he was too small, too poor, too black ever to succeed. And now Evander wanted to show the world that spiritual strength—an inner reality that comes from a relationship with Jesus Christ—could lift anybody out of his limitations and help him achieve his potential. It could lift a 208-pounder against a 246-pound giant; it could lift a single parent out of poverty, and an earnest young man into the job of his dreams.

"When I win, Lightning," Evander told me, "everybody's gonna know they can do whatever they need to do—get that college degree, get a promotion, break the addiction—and I'm gonna tell them it's all because of Christ."

Evander marched into the arena to the music of his friend, rap artist M. C. Hammer: "That's why we pray / We have to pray just to make it today."

The words, "That's why we pray . . . That's why we pray . . . That's why we pray, just to make it today," kept floating through his mind, stirring up a euphoric feeling. This night was already fulfilling a dream. This night was why Evander had prayed. From the time he was eight years old, Evander had worked, fought, and prayed for this "moment of truth."

As millions of people watched Evander walk out to fight Buster Douglas for the heavyweight championship of the world, Evander silently prayed to his God. *Thank You, Lord,* he prayed. *Thank You for letting me meet another dream.*

An enormous confidence overcame Evander. *I'm already champ,* he thought. *I just gotta go up there and get it.* Many people had questioned Evander's ability to handle this fight: was he really just a beefed-up light heavyweight with an unrealistic dream? Well, those people were about to find out just how powerful a dream can be.

The fact that a heavyweight championship was on the line gave an intensity to this night that outshone any other fight Evander had ever been a part of. Winston Marsalis played the national anthem beautifully, and Sugar Ray Leonard served as the ring announcer. Leonard's smooth voice broke through the night air, "Ladies and Gentlemen, in the blue corner, weighing a chiseled 208 pounds, bronze medalist of the 1984 Olympics, undisputed cruiserweight champion, undefeated in six professional bouts as a heavyweight, the challenger from Atlanta, Georgia, E-van-der 'The Real Deal' Hoooolyfield!"

The crowd roared.

"And his opponent, the current WBA, WBC, and IBF Champion, the un-dis-pu-ted heavyweight champion of the world, James 'Bus-ter' Douglas!"

Again thunderous applause followed.

The fighters and the coaches went to the center of the ring where the referee gave them their final instructions: "Okay, fellows, I want a good clean fight here tonight. I want you to break when I say break. And if a fighter gets hurt, I'll send the opposing fighter to the neutral corner. Touch gloves, and let's get it on."

During these prefight instructions, Evander looked straight at Buster Douglas, who wore a sneer of disrespect on his face. Douglas looked everywhere—everywhere, that is, except at Evander. The two men came to the fight with radically different mindsets. In everything that seemed to matter—size, strength, you name it—Douglas came out on top of Evander. But nobody keeps statistics on spiritual strength, and I don't think there's a fighter yet who can match Evander in that regard.

Evander responded to the opening bell by dancing in the center of the ring, keeping on his toes, jabbing Douglas with great frequency but with little serious damage. He was just warming up, following the game plan that had been developed ahead of time. Buster was much slower, and he boxed with very little bounce in his step. He was content to wait and dodge the quick flicking jabs, countering with his own jabs as best he could.

The second round began the same as the first. Evander was all over Douglas, landing a series of combinations that Douglas was able only occasionally to answer with shots of his own. In the first two rounds, Evander connected on three blows for every one that Douglas landed.

Near the end of the second round, however, Evander opened himself up for a counterpunch from Buster. When Douglas connected with Evander's head, the crowd jumped up, lusting and hungry for another bruising war that would spill other men's blood. Douglas managed to follow up by throwing several of his fierce uppercuts, punishing Evander for getting too close.

Evander survived, however, and Buster opened the third round by doing what is called "crowding a boxer." You "crowd" a boxer to take away his jab and quickness, cutting off the ring and forcing your opponent to get into a slugfest. Evander realized what Douglas was trying to do. The larger fighter wanted to stop Evander's jabs and tie him up long enough to drop him with an uppercut.

This is what everybody expected would happen, but Evander was too quick and cagey for this trap. Every time Buster moved in to pressure and corner him, Evander countered with a quick combination. His quick foot movement allowed him to dance out of the reach of Buster's bombs.

Keep moving, Evander told himself. *Keep moving.*

Douglas grew increasingly impatient. There are few things more frustrating and irritating to a boxer than being pummeled by an opponent without being able to land a retaliating blow. If the boxer isn't careful, he can take the blows personally, forget all about boxing, and make a fatal error. That's exactly what Buster did.

When Evander was pressed into Buster's chest, Buster put everything he had into a vicious uppercut, but Evander saw it coming. He had watched the tape of Buster's fight with Tyson more times than he could remember. He never let the threat of that uppercut leave his mind. When Buster planted his feet, reared back on his right thigh, and coiled his right hand back, Evander knew what was about to happen. In a split second, he hopped to his right, and the wind from

Buster's potential knockout blow fanned Evander's chin from at least a foot away.

The follow-through of Douglas's blow left him completely defenseless. Evander almost smiled. He had planned for this to happen, and now Buster's jaw carried an address that even a blind mailman couldn't miss. As Buster's body followed his errant swing, Evander met the side of Buster's jaw with a right cross that had his entire 208 pounds behind it.

Douglas's knees collapsed, but he tried to stay up by hanging onto Evander's neck. This resulted in a second blow as the two fighter's foreheads collided. Douglas dropped with a thud, and his massive body slammed against the canvas. Propped up on one elbow, he wiped his face with his glove no fewer than three times, obviously his brain rattled beyond reason.

The critics said, "Buster lacked heart," but who can really judge the heart, or the lack thereof, of another man except God? It appeared to me that Douglas lacked a sense of consciousness and was unable to get up. During this dazed stupor, the referee stopped counting at eight, and the fight ended.

Pandemonium followed. The little guy had won. Evander became the first cruiserweight champion to win the heavyweight title. Dan and Lou Duva were so excited they both took nitroglycerin tablets for their hearts. Everybody surrounded the new champion. Evander was so focused on the fight, so intent on the task in front of him, that it took a while for the truth to come upon him. In less than eight minutes of fighting, he had become the undisputed heavyweight champion of the world.

"I did it," he thought, "I achieved my dream—and I didn't even have to work twelve rounds to get it!"

He was elated, he was surprised, he was basking in a well-deserved self-satisfaction. But he also didn't forget who got him there. A sportscaster stuck a microphone in front of Evander's still-sweating face and the first words Evander spoke were, "First, I want to thank my Lord and Savior, Jesus Christ, for the victory. I dedicate this victory to all the kids out there who were told they couldn't make it. People told me I couldn't be the champ, but here I am, the champ. Don't let anybody tell you that you can't do what you want."

Evander looks back on those magical moments after his victory over Buster Douglas as a time of personal revelation. "It dawned on me that all the things other people had told me all my life weren't true. 'You won't make it, you can't do it, you're too small.'" He pauses. "I was set *free*."

After the initial postfight celebration, Evander went back to his room to change. The first thing the new heavyweight champion of the world did was to drop to his knees. "Lord, I thank You for letting me reach my goal. I couldn't have done it without You." Evander shifted his weight forward and clenched his hands even tighter. He couldn't believe what he was about to say, it was so delicious, so unbelievable, yet now, so true. *I'm the heavyweight champion of the world, Lord! Please don't let fame and all the fortune that follows take me away from You.*

Evander had seen people discard their God after riches and renown came calling. He didn't want to use God like an adolescent uses a bicycle, only to discard it once he gets his driver's license. God was the center of his life. He wasn't just the heavyweight champion of the world; he was *God's* heavyweight champion of the world.

Protect me from myself, Evander kept praying.

Evander couldn't remember a time he had been this happy. He got dressed as quickly as he could, eager to see Mother. She didn't attend the fight, but Evander knew she'd be there for the party.

When he walked into the room, everybody broke out into a large cheer. My brother looked larger than life that night. Evander walked up to a microphone and thanked his supporters, but then quickly ended his talk.

"Now that I'm heavyweight champion of the world," he said, "the one thing I really want to do is . . ."

There was a pause, and everybody waited.

". . . The thing I really want to do is dance with my mom."

Mother's eyes brightened and then moistened as her son, the new champ, walked down from the stage and took her in his arms. Evander wanted her to share in this moment, and she did. This was the woman who had worked two jobs to keep Evander's stomach full. This was the woman who managed to squeeze out a few extra dollars so that Evander could join the Boy's Club. This was the woman who loved him, disciplined him, and cared for him enough to ask him to leave home when it was time. This was the woman who prayed during every one of his fights.

She would never know poverty again.

Later, Evander was besieged by autograph hounds, and after every autograph he wrote the inscription "Phil. 4:13" ("I can do all things through Christ who strengthens me."). That verse was the theme of his career and his message to the entire world. When Evander got tired of signing autographs, he often limited his inscription to "Holyfield, Phil. 4:13." People who hadn't picked up a Bible in years dusted off the old King James to see what the champ had to say.

After the fight, promotion for the follow-up with George Foreman began almost immediately. ESPN rigged a special hookup that allowed the then forty-two-year-old Foreman to talk to Evander.

"Nobody can stop me," Foreman said. "The world says, 'We're behind you, George.' I'm the poor man; you're a rich man now. I'm going to whup you, rich man."

Evander responded in a good-natured tone. "George," he said, "you've had your day. Don't you think your day is done?"

Foreman reacted with his melodramatic-serious style: "I'm going to Baskin-Robbins and eat every flavor. When you start pushing and shoving me, you're going to be pushing a whole franchise. My foot weighs more than you."

Evander responded with the truth of his life. "It's not the size of the man," he said. "It's the size of the heart."

After the interviews, parties, and autographs were over and everybody was tucked into bed, the new champ couldn't sleep. He slipped out of his room and walked the deserted streets of Las Vegas. It was 4 A.M. and not a single person shared the sidewalk.

Man, you did all that, Evander said to himself, *and you excite people, then you stay up and they sleep.* He laughed. Evander loved entertaining others. He's always been happiest making other people happy. Once he was asked if he got tired of signing autographs.

"It makes the kids so happy," Evander said. "I'll never get tired of making people happy."

The desert night air was crisp and clear. *You're the heavyweight champion of the world,* Evander said to himself, still laughing. *Don't feel no different, though,* and he laughed again, a deep joy cascading over him.

Evander returned to the hotel in time to get ready for an interview with religious broadcaster Pat Robertson, who had asked him to appear on *The 700 Club.* To Evander, appearing on this show was the crowning point of his victory.

"What made it worthwhile," he said, "was that now people could say, 'He did all that, and he's a *Christian*.' God's people are supposed to be number one."

Evander's success fueled his already spiritually hungry heart. On his flight to Birmingham (to watch our brother Michael play in an Alabama A & M game), Evander asked a flight attendant for a Bible. He was traveling with a young protégé, Anthony Williams, whom he had coached on a football team.

On that flight, Evander the fighter became Evander the evangelist. "Tony," he said, "you got to do more than just read the Bible. You got to read it so much that you *know* it. The purpose of the Bible is not to read it and then put it down; it's to read it in such a way that it becomes a part of your life."

A man who sat across the aisle from Evander heard what was going on, leaned over, and said, "With the Lord on your side, it's no wonder you're the champ."

This was classic Evander. Less than twelve hours after being crowned heavyweight champion of the world, he was making sure that his younger friend was taking his Bible seriously.

When Evander got to our brother's football game, the Alabama A & M coach invited him to share a few words. Evander spoke very briefly, but long enough to tell his story: "I won my fight even though I was the smaller man. It's not the size of the man; it's the size of the heart. I'm a little guy, but I have a big heart and a big determination. I work hard. I pray hard. I believe in Christ."

Nothing could have prepared Evander for this moment. Not that long ago, he was an Olympic hopeful, without a sponsor, seeking a used car loan. Now he was the heavyweight champion of the world. The limousine driver asked Evander what car he drove and acted surprised when Evander replied, "A Buick."

"What kind?" the driver asked.

"Any kind I want," Evander smiled. He didn't need a loan anymore. He *owned* the dealership now.

In just six years, Evander had climbed from poverty to wealth, from anonymity to fame. Now, everybody wanted to be around him. The mayor of Atlanta gave him the key to the city. His financial future was secure.

Evander Holyfield wasn't just the toast of the town. He was King of the Ring, Heavyweight Champion of the World.

CHAPTER 12

BIG GEORGE

The explosion of Evander's success inside the ring began to threaten his world outside the ring. It is almost impossible for somebody who hasn't experienced worldwide fame to understand the responsibilities that come with being a celebrity. Evander refused to let people call him a star: "Ain't no stars but what's up in the sky," he'd say. "I ain't no star." But regardless of how Evander saw himself, the way other people saw him began to change.

That fame began to take a toll on his personal life. There should be a class for the spouses of famous people. Evander's fame, wealth, and physique (*Sports Illustrated* once called him "the body beautiful") made him alluring to countless women, and the boldness with which these women approached him was astonishing. On several occasions, as Evander stood next to Paulette, another woman (or women) would ask for an autograph and picture. Evander knew this was part of being champ, so usually he'd agree. After the autograph, the women would gather around Evander, and just as the flash went off, they'd reach up and kiss him—right in front of Paulette.

Other times, Paulette would be pushed away in the throng. When she'd complain, "Hey, I'm his wife!" she'd usually get an apology, but still, it wasn't easy.

Evander's training regimen didn't make it any easier. Not only did an upcoming fight require months of training in Houston, but Evander had to balance personal appearances, promotion schedules, and the routine demands of the general public as well.

Evander was determined to give his best to his family, but his marriage became strained. The next blow proved to be too much.

In the heart of Atlanta, Evander had lent his name to the dealership that sponsored him for the Olympics. Evander had formed a partnership with Ken Sanders, giving his name to the dealership, but leaving all day-to-day operations under Ken's jurisdiction.

The dealership was more than just a business to Evander—it was a symbol of hope to a generation of future entrepreneurs. The dealership employed young people from nearby colleges and from the Summerhill community in which we grew up. Initial plans called for Evander to eventually buy the dealership outright, and I would manage the day-to-day operation as the general manager after I graduated from the General Motors Dealership Management Program. We would be partners: Evander would provide the finance, and I would provide the management. But in the meantime, the management of the dealership was still solidly in the hands of Ken Sanders, Evander's manager.

Unfortunately for us, before the ink could dry on my diploma from General Motors, the management at the dealer hit rock bottom. Though Evander's name was on the dealership, his participation was limited to personal appearances and autograph signing. His success ensured that the dealership was busier than ever, but the store became rife with mismanagement. As Evander toiled away at a Houston camp training for the Buster Douglas fight, the car dealership was placed in chapter 11 bankruptcy.

It was then that I realized we had made a profound error by being totally dependent on others to manage our business. After the dust cleared, the only thing left for us to manage was a mountain of debt, a sea of irate customers, and a constant assault on our family's good name and reputation as Christians and honest businessmen.

Looking back over that experience, we understand more clearly now what Mama meant when she said, "Sons, never let anyone rob you of your independence by making you totally dependent upon them for your livelihood. To be totally dependent on others is to be in a position to be totally controlled and manipulated by others. Always maintain your independence by being self-sufficient." Some of life's lessons we learn the hard way.

"What do you mean the dealership's in chapter 11?" Evander asked after the fight. Although he had plenty of personal cash to reinvest, Evander's accountant convinced him that putting more money into a sinking ship wouldn't help it float.

As the dealership began to unravel, however, Evander finally sought the services of his own attorney. At the time Evander entered the dealership agreement with Sanders, Evander, with Sanders's encouragement, used Sanders's attorney. It was suggested that they could save money this way. Since Sanders was also serving as Evander's manager, the conflict of interest was bold, by any measure. Ostensibly, Sanders's attorney was supposed to look after the interests of both men, but those experienced in business realize it rarely happens that way.

Evander's success in the ring fed his confidence outside the ring, however, and he took charge. All parties tied to the plundering of the car dealership were legally made accountable, and a settlement was reached out of court. Evander had no personal grievance against Ken—in fact, he still had a strong love for the man—but he also realized that he couldn't afford to ignore the advice of his own attorney and accountants, and that meant he had to fire Ken Sanders. It was an extremely difficult thing for Evander to do. Ken had given Evander his break and had been willing to sponsor him when nobody else would. On the other hand, most of Evander's friends—including Ken—had been paid very generously for their services, and several of them had become wealthy off their association with Team Holyfield.

Firing Ken was just the first step in an arduous process that eventually led to the closing of the dealership. It couldn't have come at a worse time, especially for Evander's marriage. The public demands, the professional demands, and the court battle surrounding the closing of the dealership all converged like a giant arrow striking at the heart of his marriage.

What the public didn't know was just how heroic it was for Evander to even show up for the Buster Douglas fight, let alone win it. He was actually served with divorce papers from Paulette the week before he faced Buster Douglas, and just days after his car dealership was placed in chapter 11.

True to form, Evander refused to let the bad timing prove detrimental. "I used it as motivation," he said.

But now that the dealership, divorce, and Douglas battles were behind him, Evander developed a new strategy to hold onto his family. Prior to the divorce, Evander prepared for his bouts by working out in Houston, flying his kids in on the weekends. Now, he built a gymnasium on his estate so that he could train at home at least sixty of the ninety days prior to the next bout.

Schoolchildren who visit the gymnasium are often surprised to see a name inscribed in the cement just outside Evander's gym: "Mike Tyson." Mike Tyson is the name of one of the laborers who helped build the gym. He's about as unlike the boxer as he can be, but he and the former heavyweight champion share the same name, and that's how Evander's rival earned a presence on Evander's home turf.

Now that Evander had a gym at home, he was able to stay away from Houston longer and begin taking his children to school. He attended special programs at school and was there for the baseball games, track meets, and football games.

Evander was elated to have become heavyweight champion of the world, but it would be an empty achievement if he couldn't also become heavyweight champion of his children's hearts. "It's great being recognized as a boxing champion," he told me, "but it's more important to me that my children recognize me as a good father."

What Evander showed in these quiet, unseen actions is that life doesn't stop for anybody, including the heavyweight champion of the world. Every dream worth achieving is a dream that must be sought in the midst of outside distractions and even crises.

Big George

"Nobody can stop me," Evander remembered "Big" George Foreman saying. "The world says, 'We're behind you, George.' I'm the poor man, you're a rich man now. I'm going to whup you, rich man."

Foreman was one of just a few men in their forties who fought for the heavyweight title, but he was certainly the only "poor man" ever who was worth tens of millions of dollars. And it was this colorful figure who would constitute Evander's first title defense.

There was a lot to like about Foreman (literally). His huge girth, his playful banter, and his concern for youth all made him the world's favorite contender.

But Evander knew there was also a lot to respect about the man. Sure, Foreman had fought some journeymen as he warmed up to face serious competition, but in the previous months he had still earned twenty-three knockouts in twenty-four wins, and two of those knockouts were against respected fighters like Dwight Qawi Braxton, who was now known as Dwight Muhammad Qawi, and Adilson Rodrigues.

Evander expected that his first title defense would be a tough one. Unfortunately for Evander, George had everything to gain by fighting and Evander had everything to lose. Foreman could make history by becoming the oldest heavyweight champion in boxing history. Evander, on the other hand, would be expected to win. The *most* he could do would be to fulfill expectations.

There was a second factor that made this fight a little more difficult. Foreman was a born-again Christian minister who went back into boxing to raise money for his youth ministry. One of Evander's edges had always been his spiritual strength—a strength that, for the first time, his opponent knew as well as he.

Evander believed that "through Christ, all things are possible," and he knew that the same verse held as much truth for Foreman as it did for him. With Christ in his life, it *was* possible for Foreman to win.

Foreman was not Evander's first choice. Since some people in the boxing world still thought of Tyson as the champ, Evander was eager to fight Mike. After he watched the Tyson/Ruddock bout, he knew that Tyson was a reckless fighter who often got imbalanced, and Evander was confident that, in such a circumstance, he could defeat Tyson, like he had Douglas. Even Foreman publicly said that "Tyson would be an easy fight for me, easier than Evander." But King had Tyson wrapped up in a rematch with "Razor" Ruddock and said that he was going to make Holyfield "wait," so there was nothing Evander could do. He had to fight George to get to Mike.

Evander wasn't about to take Foreman for granted, however. "You can't forget what got you there," he said. "And that's hard work."

And few boxers worked harder than Evander. Lou Duva lined up some huge sparring partners, but Evander sent many of them packing. One left with a bruised rib. Another tried to excuse himself by showing Duva a purple arm, the result of a Holyfield blow to his left bicep that burst a blood vessel.

Hallmark put Evander on the "Reaction Piece," a new invention that was designed and built specifically for Evander. Evander's legs were strapped to a platform, creating constant resistance, while Hallmark quickly moved five thin, padded poles around, forcing Evander to duck, block, and counter the poles that came at him from all sides.

Evander would need it. When you removed the age factor, Foreman looked especially formidable. He came in outweighing Evander by almost fifty pounds. He had an almost two-inch advantage in both height and reach. Foreman also had sixty-five knockouts in his sixty-nine victories. Ten of those knockouts had come in the last two years.

On the night of the fight, Evander invited three members of the 1984 Olympic team to join him: lightweight champion Pernell Whitaker, WBA welterweight champion Meldrick Taylor, and former WBA welterweight champion Mark Breland. Evander surprised everyone—especially me—when he asked Willie and me to carry his belts into the ring. Such an honor is usually reserved for the fighter's trainers, but Evander was never one to forget his family.

It was a rush to step outside into the arena and lead Evander out of the locker room. Evander wore a short, white satin robe and a fierce look of determination. He and George weren't getting together for Sunday school.

When round one began, Evander surprised everyone by staying close to Foreman. Commentators had predicted that Evander would want to stay away from Foreman's heavy blows, but George Benton—Evander's strategist—reasoned that the more Evander kept Foreman on the defensive, the less time he'd have to unleash a killer shot.

Evander quickly began to build up points with quick jabs and landed combinations. George couldn't dodge most of them—his lateral movement was atrocious—but he countered with some bruising body blows that made us wince. Our sister Annette screamed, "Chubby, don't let him hit you in the body!"

As the fight took shape, it became clear that George would focus on pummeling body shots, bruising Evander's rib cage, liver, hips, or anything he could connect with. Evander, in turn, was determined to keep a barrage of combinations and jabs flying at George's head. A punch-drunk Foreman, Evander's corner reasoned, would lose some of his power.

The second round proved that Foreman was much more than a "great pretender." George managed to slip in a jab that snapped back Evander's head. He followed his initial stunning blow with two quick but hard head clubs. As Evander moved in to retaliate, Foreman unleashed a low blow to Evander's throat.

I grimaced. Foreman was warned, but that warning didn't take away the hurt. The thought of Foreman's strength pummeling into my brother's neck forced me to the edge of my seat. Annette began twisting her hands.

Evander was in another war.

In the third round, Evander had Foreman in serious trouble. He stunned George with a powerful hook, then followed it up with a furious assault of more than a dozen blows. George tried to grab

Evander to lock him up, but Evander was too quick. Foreman knew he was in trouble, but he bought himself some time with another low blow—this one landing perilously close to Evander's cup.

Foreman the preacher must have left his ethics in the pulpit, because very few of them made their way into the ring.

The sixth round was especially painful for me to watch. Foreman's body shots had begun to take their toll on Evander, and I could see my brother grimace when yet another blow pounded into his side. The bruising blows reduced Evander's mobility, and George capitalized on it by unleashing a gut-wrenching body shot to the rib cage that practically lifted Evander off the ground. Evander felt his breath leave him and the painful residue of the blow work its way through his nervous system.

He vaguely heard Benton screaming, "Evander! Turn him! Stay in the circle! Don't stand directly in front of him!"

Time can stand still for a boxer during such moments. You become almost an observer, willing your body to wake up and prepare for the coming assault.

George followed with a solid combination to the chin that rocked Evander back. The crowd gasped, sensing Evander's vulnerability. Benton kept shouting his instructions: "Evander, circle him! Don't stand directly in front of him!"

Evander survived the round—the bell was an incredibly welcome sound—and dropped onto his stool. Lou Duva encouraged him to keep the jabs and combinations going. Sweat ran off Evander's body like melting snow. A small mouse began to grow high on his cheekbone. One of the trainers massaged Evander's increasingly sore rib cage. Evander's body was being punished in the worst way.

Fans often moan about how boxers can make millions of dollars in six minutes of fighting, but when a bout goes the distance, the pain and punishment is unlike anything any nonathlete has ever felt. Imagine being in twelve car accidents within the space of about an hour and a half, and you'll begin to get the idea of what Evander often forces himself to endure in a title fight.

Evander reached down. At this point in the fight, he knew it was about spirit more than flesh. His body was bruised and hurting. To win it now, he'd have to dig deep and find the strength in his heart.

Meanwhile, Foreman actually stood in the opposing corner. He stared at Evander, never taking his beady eyes off him. Angelo Dundee, the famous boxing coach who trained Muhammad Ali, whispered strategy in George's ear. George would nod, but he wouldn't take his eyes off Evander.

The seventh round proved to be one of the most spectacular rounds in all of modern boxing. Foreman came out hungrily, sensing that Evander was tired. He began pounding Evander's body and then landed a solid right to Evander's head. Evander staggered back, but Foreman was on him, pressuring him and using his size to push him around the ring.

This is where Evander comes alive. It shouldn't surprise boxers by now, but still, it usually does. Evander views the moment of his greatest weakness as his greatest opportunity. Because the opposing fighter smells a knockout, he's liable to get careless. Evander forces himself to stay clear and look for the opening.

He found it. His hook to Foreman's head caught George completely by surprise, and now the tide turned in a ferocious way. Evander hit Foreman with blow after unanswered blow—twenty-one of them in all. He hit George on the left and right side of his face, under his rib cage, on top of the forehead, on the left and right side of his ear, on his shoulders, arms, and chest. Evander was like a surgeon, searching for that vulnerable point, the one area that would bring Big George down.

The crowd became hushed while the announcer exclaimed, "George is hurt! He's still standing, but he's certainly hurt!"

George wobbled, teetered, and tottered all over the ring, but he wouldn't fall. He carried the same spiritual strength that Evander knew. Evander felt like he was just hitting the bag: pow, pow, pow, pow!

"Ain't nothing but God," Evander said to himself, as George kept standing. "Ain't nothing but the Lord. Just ain't His plan for George to go down."

At this point, Evander kept the ultimate objective in mind: He wanted to win. If that meant a knockout, great. If not, that was okay, too, as long as he kept the title. What he didn't want to do was exert himself so much for a knockout that he became exhausted and opened the door for George to salvage a late victory.

The bell finally stopped the assault. George, still visibly shaken from the beating he had just endured, half-walked, half-stumbled into his corner.

The crowd was on its feet and going crazy. Such a display of inner strength and spirit is rare in the entire world of sports, much less boxing. The rules of boxing insist that there can only be one winner, but in the crowd's hearts, both fighters were proving themselves to be champions.

Here again I'd like to take you inside the mind of a fighter. Imagine that you're as tired as you've ever been in your entire life. Imagine that your body has been pummeled by an opposing fighter who weighs more than 250 pounds and has arms as wide as many people's thighs. Now imagine rallying yourself for one intense barrage of twenty-one blows, each one of them packed with as much strength as you can muster, hoping that one of them will be the punch that finally brings the fight to an end. Throwing those blows is almost as exhausting as receiving them.

And still your opponent is standing!

And still you have five more rounds to fight!

That's where Evander was at the end of the seventh round. It is in times such as these that Evander dives inward to find his strength. Physical prowess can get a fighter through the early rounds, but Evander's courage is best displayed when his body is spent and only his spirit can fight on.

The rest of the fight contained more of the same. Evander nearly dropped Foreman two rounds later, but it was near the end of the round and, again, George was saved by the bell. Both fighters kept coming at each other—neither one was sitting back—until the final few seconds of the twelfth and final round. Evander and George fell into each other. Clinches are common in long matches, but this one looked more like a hug. The bell rang and ended the bout.

Evander had great respect for George, and he appreciated the aging fighter even more when George reached out and hugged Evander once again, just before the announcer gave the decision. Some Christians have a problem with boxing, but that's mostly because they don't understand the sport and the goodwill that often exists between the two combatants even after a fight. George thanked Evander for giving him the chance to fight for the title, then admitted, "You won."

Duva, who was standing nearby, said, "Absolutely."

All the judges agreed.

Foreman took more punishment in twelve rounds than most people could take in twelve years. He put on an astonishing display of perseverance, and I doubt there is another human being who could have stood up to the assault that George endured. Unfortunately, Evander's beating left a lasting mark on Foreman. If you watch his later fights, you see an appreciable decline in his quickness and reflexes. It's impossible for a man George's age to take the abuse he did and walk away unscathed.

At the same time, both Evander and I believe that God worked everything out in such a way that both fighters won. Evander retained his title, but George's popularity skyrocketed after the bout. He received more endorsements, more money, and more adulation from the fans.

Evander had faced quicker boxers, younger boxers, and more offensive boxers, but he had never faced one with the spiritual strength displayed by Foreman. It was good training ground, for now Evander knew he could enter the ring with anybody and find what he needed to pull out the victory.

Even before the postfight celebration ended, the next step was obvious. The commentators knew it. The fans knew it. Evander knew it.

The time to fight Tyson had come.

CHAPTER 13

THE MIKE MYTH

With Foreman out of the way, Evander was especially eager for a shot at Tyson. He knew he'd never get the respect he deserved until he disposed, once and for all, of the "Mike Myth"—the idea that Douglas's victory was a fluke and that no other boxer could really face Tyson in the ring and win. Evander already had the title; now he wanted the chance to fight for respect.

Evander had a different perspective than many of the boxers who had fought Tyson earlier. He had climbed through the amateur ranks with Tyson, and he had seen Tyson get beat. The aura of invincibility that surrounded Tyson as a heavyweight just didn't penetrate Evander's mind. Of course Tyson could lose. He had lost as an amateur. He had lost to a man—Buster Douglas—that Evander had dropped in the third round. He could fall again.

Evander was confident that his experience with Tyson would be considerably different from that of the other heavyweights Tyson had knocked out. "I'm the fighter that fears no man," Evander explains, "because the Bible says, 'Don't fear the man who can hurt your body, fear the God who can hurt your soul.'"

If Tyson didn't knock somebody out, he often lost. Evander thought, *If I'm at my best, and he's at his best, I can win.*

On the other hand, Evander respected Mike's skills. No question, Tyson was one of the most talented challengers around, and Evander's goal was not just to lay claim to the title but to beat the top contenders of his era. To do that, he needed to fight Mike. After Evander's victory over Foreman, some people said, "So what? You fought an old man. What does that prove?"

Evander felt he could fight Tyson, win the respect that comes from beating a feared former champion, and then retire.

It would be a classic confrontation. *Inside Boxing* wrote, "The fight will boil down to the inner strength of Holyfield versus the bad boy in Mike Tyson." Evander's heavyweight belts have the Bible verse Philippians 4:13 inscribed on them.

Evander knew he needed a great opponent to reach the level of a great champion. Tyson knew the same. One of Tyson's trainers, Jay Bright, said, "Mike is viewing Evander as the best fighter he is ever going to fight." Already, writers were comparing Holyfield/Tyson to Ali/Frazier. Evander knew he could beat Tyson, but he also knew he'd have to dig deep to pull it out and that in the process, history could be made.

The road to such a bout looked bleak, at best. King was making unbelievable demands. He wanted 45 percent of the purse to go to Tyson—even though Evander was the champion. Duva was offering Tyson $15 million—an unprecedented figure for a challenger to receive, but still not enough for King. Where King got really ridiculous was in seeking an option to promote Holyfield's future fights.

King was down to just a few marquee fighters. If he lost Tyson, he didn't have much left. In many ways, the first boxing match was between Duva and King. Only after they locked it up were Holyfield and Tyson released to do their business.

Duva was able to one-up King by scheduling a rematch with Foreman. King had actually approached Foreman about a bout with Tyson—hoping to run around Holyfield one more time—but Foreman rebuffed him, saying instead he wanted to fight Holyfield again.

Duva jumped on the opportunity and actually reached a verbal agreement—though making it clear that Team Holyfield would get back to Foreman before finalizing the details.

With Foreman as the trump card, Duva and company met with King and laid their package on the table. King made a counteroffer, and Duva and company retreated once again to consider their options.

At this point, the fighters themselves got the fight scheduled. Tyson apparently told King to "forget the money." He wanted to fight Evander, period.

When Duva reached Evander in Hawaii, Evander had mixed feelings. He wanted to fight Tyson, but he respected Foreman and didn't want to leave him "out in the cold" now that negotiations had gone so far. Evander was willing to fight Foreman one more time, then face Tyson in the spring. King countered by saying that Foreman was simply using Holyfield to get a richer fight with Tyson.

It was Evander's call. He told Duva to go ahead and sign Tyson (for the $15 million), but insisted that the contract include a clause requiring the winner of the bout to make a "best effort" to fight Foreman in the spring.

Team Holyfield was elated when the fight was finally scheduled for November 8, 1991, in Caesars Palace, Las Vegas. The winner of this fight would be recognized as the undisputed heavyweight champion of the decade. The announcement of the bout electrified the boxing world. This was the fight everybody wanted to see. It would be the richest fight in history, with Tyson guaranteed $15 million and Evander guaranteed $30 million. The two fighters would split the purse, 40–60 respectively, after the first $45 million.

Evander began training immediately and with a new excitement. People started flocking to the gym, wanting to know how the champ was training. This interest fed Evander's own motivation, and though tough training had never been something that Evander avoided, now he seemed to relish it. The many deposits of pain that he was making would reap rich dividends.

Evander was willing to pay the price.

His prefight motto was, "No mistakes allowed." He had only so much time to prepare for Tyson, and he was passionate about using every second of it to get ready. He knew Tyson was tough, and that toughness called for him to enter the ring more prepared than he had ever been in his life. Evander was determined to be faster and stronger and have more endurance.

George Benton and Evander implemented a sound strategy. Evander would attempt to outbox Tyson, duplicating his performance against Buster Douglas thereby defeating Tyson.

Evander was as focused as he had ever been as he worked out in his Houston gym. He was in his prime, Tyson was in his prime, and Evander couldn't wait to explode into the match of the decade.

Canceled!

Five years later, Evander can still remember the date and the call. It was October 18. Evander had just completed a grueling workout. When he got back to his room, he listened in silence as Shelly Finkel, his manager, told him, "The fight is canceled. Tyson messed up his ribs."

Evander sank back into a chair, holding his head in his hands. He turned on ESPN and listened to the details.

I trained all this time for this fight, Evander thought, *and now it ain't gonna happen.* The pace of preparation for a world championship title fight is intense. Evander was in the best shape of his life. Conditioning involves mental as well as physical training, and Evander was gunning for the early November bout. Now, all that energy was left hanging.

"Well," he finally said, "I might as well go to the Braves game tomorrow." It was Atlanta's first time in the World Series, and Evander was catching the fever. The next day, Evander watched baseball as the nation was informed that the fight everybody wanted to see wasn't going to happen, at least not any time soon.

Duva and company met Saturday morning to reschedule the bout. At first they began talking about a mid-January date in the same venue, but Evander is from Atlanta, and he didn't relish the thought of fighting outdoors in weather that frequently dives into the thirties and forties at night. Evander hates the cold. When he vacations, he goes to Hawaii or other warm, tropical islands.

Even worse, Evander realized that now the fight might never happen. Tyson's arrest on rape charges was headed for a trial. It would be impossible to fight Tyson during a trial, and if Tyson was found guilty, he could face a number of years in jail. The financial figures for the fight were now well-known, and Evander knew there was little chance that anyone would have sympathy for an accused rapist who wanted to make a quick $15 to $20 million before going to jail.

Evander faced this setback like he has faced every other. At first he was extremely disappointed, and then he grew to accept it. As negotiations dragged on, and speculation arose about how Tyson's judge would rule, Evander finally told the press, "It's up to the court. I can't fight Tyson if he's in jail. But it won't bother me if I don't fight him. I want to fight the best man available, and if he's not available, then we will find the next best guy and fight him."

Evander's perspective was that *he* was the champion. Whether or not he fought Tyson, he was still the champion. If Tyson blew his chance, it was Tyson's loss, not his. Evander's responsibility as champ was to climb into the ring with every credible challenger. Tyson was just one of several hopefuls. In other words, Tyson needed the fight more than he did.

"When all this business came up," Evander said, "my attitude was, *he missed his opportunity. I'm the champ. He has to get it from me.*"

When others tried to insist Evander had missed something, he disagreed. "I didn't miss nothing. I'm still the champ. My goal has always been to be the heavyweight champion of the world. My goal was not to fight Mike Tyson. I'm *still* the heavyweight champion of the world, so how can I be disappointed?"

Since Evander had been training for months, his management suggested that they find a replacement so that Evander's sacrifice wouldn't be wasted. Initially, they identified an Italian fighter named Franceso Damiani. Evander didn't know anything about him. His trainers told him that all they knew was that he was flat-footed and a hard puncher. Evander dutifully switched his game plan and prepared to fight a plodding, flat-footed, hard-punching heavyweight instead of the quick, hard-punching Tyson.

After several weeks, Damiani's people called and said he had fallen out of the ring and wouldn't be able to fight. Evander's management team went digging and found another boxer named "Smoking" Bert Cooper. Again, Evander's team knew little about Cooper, but they heard he was a solid puncher. In all honesty, they were desperate. Evander was "primed" and ready to fight, but they had to find somebody willing to face him on short notice.

Again, put yourself in Evander's shoes. You're preparing for the fight of your career against the premier challenger of your day. Just weeks before the fight, that challenger drops out. Next, you change your regimen to face another fighter, and several weeks later, that boxer bows out. Finally, you manage to land a 32-to-1 underdog. How do you prepare yourself mentally?

One thing you can do is to hold the bout in your hometown. Team Holyfield negotiated the venue change, and it was announced that for the first time, Evander would defend his heavyweight title in Atlanta.

Givin' a Show to the Homeboys

The Omni was packed. Local and national dignitaries came out in support of Evander. It had been five years since Evander had fought in his hometown, and the excitement surrounding this bout knit the city together.

The first two rounds unfolded as everybody expected. Evander dropped Cooper in the first round with a body shot. He looked like a champ, and Cooper looked like a 32-to-1 underdog. But in heavyweight boxing, any fighter is just one swing away from victory.

During the middle of the third round, Cooper nailed Evander with a right cross that sent him reeling into the ropes. Cooper followed it up with another right, and Evander began to sink. The hometown crowd became hushed. They were holding their breath, hoping Evander would survive long enough to complete the third round and be revived by his corner. The announcer's voice rang out, "Smoking Bert Cooper has knocked the champion down. The champ is still on his feet, but can he hold on?"

Evander didn't fall, but the referee moved in and gave him a standing eight count. It had been over a decade since Evander had been counted down.

While the crowd worried about their champ, Evander was actually quite calm. His mind was clear; his body just wasn't functioning right. He was busy trying to figure out how to get his body to respond.

One of Evander's great strengths is being able to "think" his way out of these desperate situations. Rather than panic, Evander said to himself, *This is good. He'll think I'm hurt, and he'll get desperate and punch himself out.*

"The punch wobbled me," Evander explained later, "but I knew Cooper was a hard puncher. I wasn't worried. Your body is made to relieve pressure by having the lights go out. When you get hurt real bad is when you get hit going down. That's when you don't have your senses and the guy can do some real damage, but that's not what happened here."

In other words, the real damage is done when a fighter falls slowly, giving his opponent a chance to step in and finish the job. It's usually the unexpected or undefended blows that knock a trained fighter out. Once Evander had a chance to recover, his training insured that the blow's damage was past him and wouldn't affect the rest of the fight.

Cooper was back on Evander as soon as the referee stepped away. Evander tried to cover, but the force of Bert's punches kept him off balance. Then, Evander saw his moment and countered with his own combination, hitting Bert squarely on the chin and causing him to stumble.

Cooper was tasting victory. He thought he had it wrapped up. In fact, after the fight he claimed he had been just "one punch away from the world championship." What Cooper didn't realize was that Evander was simply letting Cooper burn himself out. Then, when Cooper least expected it, Evander unleashed an equally furious barrage. Cooper's face registered his surprise, and he was able to do little but cover up against Evander's new arsenal.

The bell rang and the crowd was on its feet. Evander had looked like he was out of it, but he came back so strongly that he might even have taken the round.

His trainers were irate. They had seen how close Evander had come to falling, and they were less than impressed by his retaliation, which they viewed as reckless. "What are you doing?" Duva screamed at him. "You're not fighting your fight, you're fighting *his* fight. Move, jab, turn him, and look for your spots. If you slug it out, you're going to let this guy get lucky."

Evander didn't say anything, but inside, he wasn't listening. At this point in his career, Evander knew that he was in charge. His trainers and strategists and business partners could offer advice, but they couldn't tell him what to do. Evander had matured. He had watched a marriage go down. He had broken with and then fired his manager. He was the heavyweight champion of the world, and if he wanted to stay in someone's face and fight, then he was going to do it.

Evander believed that pulling back would result in a long fight, and he was determined to get Cooper out. "I'm the captain when I'm in the ring," he's said since then.

Captain Evander came out swinging and backed Cooper up. In the fifth round Evander hit Cooper so hard that one of Evander's gloves burst open. The fight was stopped and the glove changed.

Finally, in the seventh round, Evander decided to end it. He unleashed two dozen unanswered blows. Cooper was still standing, but the referee recognized that Cooper was finished and stopped the fight.

Evander was pleased just to have the fight over with. The entire training period had been a fiasco—planning on a rematch with Foreman, then preparing for Tyson, then for Damiani, then, in just a few days, for Cooper. His concentration had been broken and twisted several times over. He never wanted to fight Cooper in the first place, so his mind was never really in it. But the final conclusion was a win, and not just a win, but a knockout.

We had a little celebration after the bout. Team Holyfield was really coming together, finding its pace and proving its worth. As we danced, laughed, and talked long into the night—we were home in Atlanta, after all—none of us could imagine that one of the most crucial members of Team Hoyfield, not to mention a cherished member of the Holyfield family, was participating in his last postfight celebration.

Oh, there'd be more victories, but this brother wouldn't live to see them.

CHAPTER 14

BOBO, BAD BOYS, AND NICE GUYS

Evander was now 9–0 as a heavyweight. Only one heavyweight—George Foreman—had been able to go the distance. Evander was proving himself to be a major champion.

The tragedies of life don't take detours around champions, however, and as Evander recovered from the blows he suffered while fighting Cooper, he was forced to endure an enormous blow outside the ring. This one threatened to become a knockout punch.

One night, at about 2 A.M., our brother Willie was sleeping peacefully in his bed. Willie's fiancée, Renee, was also sleeping quietly when her brother, Michael, began pounding on the front door. One of Renee's children got up and let him in. Michael charged over to one of the bedroom doors and began pounding on it, accusing one of Renee's sons of stealing something that belonged to him.

The young man's cries woke Willie, who instantly recognized that Michael was drunk. Willie stumbled out of bed and opened his door. Michael waved a shotgun in the air, shouting that he was going to shoot Renee's son.

Willie could easily take on two guys in a fight, but because of his outgoing, fun-loving, and good-natured personality, he never got into any frays. Willie was the type of guy that everyone wanted to be around. He made you feel good about yourself, and if you were doing wrong, he made you want to do better.

But even Willie's patience was being tried as Michael's drunken display played itself out.

At first, Willie tried to talk Michael into relaxing. He and Michael were very good friends, but the words bounced off Michael like rubber. Finally, Willie tried a different approach. "Michael," he said, "take that gun off him! What's your problem? Are you crazy?"

Michael waved the shotgun toward Willie, finally pressing it against his chest. "Oh, you want some of this, too?" he asked.

Willie had a strong relationship with Michael, so he wasn't worried about Michael shooting him. He knew that Michael respected him, and he just wanted to find a way to bring as swift and quiet a resolution as was possible.

Alcohol, however, changes everything. Before Willie could answer him, Michael's drunken fingers had touched the trigger and the shotgun exploded right into Willie's chest.

I received a phone call about 3 o'clock in the morning. There's something about phone calls after midnight that sends chills down your spine even before you answer them. Nobody calls at 3 A.M. unless there's trouble.

Renee was crying, and at first it was difficult to make out what she was saying. Finally, I heard the words that shocked me. "Lightning," she wept, "Bobo is dead."

"What happened?"

"He was shot."

"Where?"

"Here, at home."

I dropped the phone. "Baby, what's wrong?" my wife asked. It was difficult to talk. I threw on my clothes and managed to say, "Bobo's been shot."

She reached out and held me. I needed her touch and quietness to collect my thoughts.

"We better call the rest of the family," she said.

Her call woke Evander. She was crying, but she managed to get out the two words Evander needed to hear.

"Bo's dead," she said.

"What do you mean Bo's dead?" Evander asked.

"He just got shot."

Evander hung up the phone and began the short drive to Willie's house.

My tears further blurred the already rain-drenched highway. As I drove, I remembered the time that Evander and I were about nine and ten years old. We had spent all day working as caddies for local golfers. At the end of the hot afternoon, we collected our tips and began walking home when we were stopped by two teenagers who made a living out of robbing younger caddies. They waited like vultures just a few blocks from the golf course.

"Where you two been?" the teenagers asked.

Evander looked at me. I was the older brother. I had to do something. "Nowhere," I said.

"Give us the money," the bigger one said, stepping toward me. "Now."

I instinctively covered my pocket, and the smaller of the two boys walked up to Evander. They began pushing us around, and I prepared myself for the worst when all of the sudden I heard the most welcome sound in the world: the voice of our brother Willie.

"What's this?" he asked.

"They want to take our money," Evander said.

Willie instantly sized up the situation. There were two of them, but his little brothers were involved.

"You two go along," he said. "I'll be along in a bit."

"But Bobo—" I protested.

Willie was firm with us. "I said, you two go along. I'll be fine."

Bobo was fine, but those boys weren't. And they never bothered us again.

That night, as I pulled up, I saw the swirling blue lights outside of Willie's house. Not long after I arrived, Evander pulled up. Renee walked us through what happened. We could see Willie's bloodstains on the floor and walls.

It was an awful sight, and it wrenched unchartered emotions from my soul. Sensing my distress, Renee cried, "It was an accident, I swear to God it was an accident. Michael wouldn't have shot Willie on purpose."

Evander didn't say a word. He turned and walked away.

I joined him on the porch, both of us staring out into the distance, the sound of raindrops pelting the roof.

Finally, we walked down the steps to the ambulance. Bobo's body was in a bag.

"Let me see if that's him," Evander said to one of the attendants. Neither of us could quite believe this had really happened.

The man nodded and slowly unzipped the bag. Evander and I looked down on the face of our protector, our older brother, the strength of our family. He died with his eyes open. I almost wanted to speak to him, his death seemed so impossible. Everybody loved Willie. Nobody would want to shoot him.

Evander and I stood next to Willie, the rain running down our heads and drenching our clothes. We didn't want our last time together to end. Neither of us said a word, but both Evander and I were remembering. Rain fell the day Lassie was shot. Rain fell when Grandma died, and now rain fell for Willie. Willie came as close to being a father to us as anyone ever could.

But now, our Bobo was gone.

It couldn't have come at a worse time for Evander. He had lost more than a brother; he had lost an essential member of Team Holyfield. Evander doesn't travel with a large entourage, like some fighters. He's always preferred to keep his circle small. If you're around Evander before a fight, you're either a family member or a very close friend.

Willie, in his own unique way, was both. He was Evander's older brother, and he was a close friend. As an older brother, Willie commanded Evander's respect. Because of this, Willie was able to get Evander to do what others couldn't: "Come on, Champ, you can give me two more reps. Let's do it!" Willie helped organize and orchestrate Evander's training regimen. Everybody knew Tyson was in Evander's future, and Evander always knew—at least he always *thought*—that Willie would be right beside him, all the way.

And since Evander had become a world champion, Willie had been more than just a trainer—he provided a place of solace. With Willie around, Evander could be "Chubby" again instead of the knockout artist. Willie had provided the connecting bridge between Evander's past and his promising future. He could not possibly be replaced.

To make matters worse, Evander had just begun to suffer the media's assault. All the writers and television commentators delighted in pitting Holyfield against Tyson, while at the same time saying that Evander was too small to be a true heavyweight champion. They called him the "blown-up cruiserweight."

Willie had been able to protect Evander from many of these assaults. There's no one like an older brother to give a man perspective, to keep him focused, to keep him believing.

Most fans don't realize that a fight starts long before the two combatants enter a ring. Promoters "wage war" through the press. They do everything they can to psyche the other fighter out. The next thing the boxer knows, everybody he's talking to is saying, "So, you're going to fight Tyson?" Or in this case, "You're going to fight Bowe? Man, at 240 pounds, he's going to kill you."

Now, just when Evander needed his older brother's perspective the most, Bobo was gone.

Fighting Outside the Ring

Willie's death came at a particularly difficult time in Evander's career. Evander was still stinging from the effects of his divorce. "I have all this money," he told me, "more than anybody imagined a boxer could make, but what does this money matter if I can't wake up and see my kids?"

Outside the home, Evander began to grow weary of the demands that others were placing on him. Hardly a day went by when somebody didn't want a significant chunk of his time. Some of the groups, perhaps not fully aware of the staggering number of requests that Evander received, seemed to take it personally when Evander couldn't accommodate them.

This hurt Evander, because his desire really was to help as many people as possible. Even so, he realized he was just one man. "Being the heavyweight champion of the world, everybody wants your time," he said, "but God doesn't give me any more hours in the day than he gives anybody else."

These demands made it difficult for Evander to grieve privately over Willie's death and the divorce. Evander was forced to overcome his pain and loss in the midst of very public appearances and demands. He understood this. He didn't expect a five-year-old boy to realize what it felt like to love your kids more than you love life itself but to wake up to an empty house. He knew most seven-year-old girls couldn't comprehend the pain of losing an older brother. So when they asked him for an autograph, he did his best to smile and encourage them. He gave of himself as willingly as he could, trying to fulfill his public obligations while working through his personal griefs.

Unfortunately, people can marginalize the difficulties of a celebrity. *How can Evander Holyfield hurt?* they think. *He's got all that money, he's famous the world over, what could go wrong in his life?*

What these people don't realize is that fame and fortune have never been able to satisfy a person's soul. These things may act as tranquilizers for a while, but eventually the soul wakes up to the pain and real life has to be dealt with.

Evander turned to the Bible to renew his strength. He read Psalm 23, "The LORD is my shepherd; I shall not want. He makes me to lie down in green pastures; He leads me beside the still waters. *He restores my soul.*"

That's what I need, Lord, Evander prayed. *I need You to restore my soul.* That familiar passage became more than words to Evander: it was his spiritual food, helping him keep himself together.

Many times, as Evander drove around town or came home to his now quiet house, thoughts of retirement taunted him. *Should I be in the ring or out of the ring? I've already made enough money to live, I've reached my goals . . . I love what I'm doing, but my kids need me . . .*

Many a day passed as Evander worked through these questions. As soon as he was alone, they rose up before him and demanded his attention.

To make matters worse, some people in the boxing community almost seemed to resent Evander's success. With Tyson firmly en-sconced in jail, Tyson's "bad-boy" image ballooned and presented a stark contrast to Evander's "nice-guy" image. Evander had decided long ago to follow Jesus Christ inside and outside the ring, but some elements of the public—particularly the sportswriters, commenta-tors, and pundits—seemed to resent the fact that Evander lacked the "obligatory vice" expected of a heavyweight boxer. Don King proclaimed that Evander "couldn't draw flies to a picnic," and even Kathy Duva, Evander's own publicist, said that marketing Evander's "nice-guy, clean image" in a "mean sport" has been "almost im-possible."

When somebody like Dennis Rodman wears a dress and head-butts an official, his name is everywhere and his popularity rises. When Kathy Duva tried to get *People* magazine to do a profile on Evander as a positive role model, however, the magazine balked.

A New York newspaper called Evander "dull material," yet the same paper ran a front-page story of three baseball players who were accused of rape. When an elite athlete resists such temptations, the news people act as though they resent it. What is there to write about when a heavyweight champion defeats his opponents, doesn't use drugs, and refuses to talk trash?

The Senior Circuit

Also adding to his travails, Evander was caught by a historical moment in boxing. It wasn't his fault that aging, formerly retired boxers like George Foreman and Larry Holmes decided to fight again. The same papers that profiled the two men's returns and generated public interest, virtually forcing a fight onto Evander's handlers, then turned around and faulted Evander for fighting the forty-year-olds.

Evander knew that agreeing to fight these men would prove to be a lose-lose situation. They were old but still strong, and any fight can turn on one, unexpected blow. Evander knew this, and he realized he had everything to lose and virtually nothing to gain. If he defeated them, he did only what was expected. If he didn't knock them out in the first two or three rounds, well, that just proves "he's a blown-up crusierweight."

Evander was disappointed that though he convincingly won eight of the twelve rounds against Big George, people still criticized him because he did not knock George out. These fans just didn't understand the complexities of boxing, or how difficult it can be to drop a 250-pound man who doesn't want to go down. Finally, Evander got to the point where he just didn't care. "I found out that critics are going to say what they want, regardless of what you do."

Boxing faced a vacuum when Tyson lost to Douglas and then went to jail, and writers were looking for a scapegoat. As the heavyweight champion, Evander was an easy target. The same writers that used to complain that Tyson was ruining the sport by knocking out people early on (making fans think twice about paying the big bucks to watch ninety-second bouts) now faulted Evander for engaging in long and often grueling fights that stretched into the later rounds.

But even in the midst of all this, the thoughts of retirement were never strong enough to take Evander away. He was a boxer, that's what he did, that's how God made him, and that's what gave him the platform to talk to others about Jesus.

Even so, he was less than excited about facing Larry Holmes. He had wanted to fight a young challenger named Riddick Bowe, but Bowe's promoters wouldn't accept the $6 million payoff they had been offered. Evander then agreed to fight the winner of the Holmes-Mercer bout, fully expecting that Mercer would win. When Holmes beat Mercer, Evander was stuck.

Evander gave in to his handlers and agreed to fight Holmes, but Holmes, he said, was the last aging boxer he would fight. "I'm through with the senior circuit," he insisted.

It can be perilous, navigating the ratings, rankings, and contractual wars in professional boxing. Whenever you're talking about millions of dollars changing hands, a seemingly simple task—getting two fighters together on the same day, in the same place, for about an hour and a half—suddenly becomes extremely complicated. Also, each of the three major boxing federations require title defenses. If the International Boxing Federation (IBF) tells Evander he has to fight Foreman or lose his title, what is Evander supposed to do?

In the spring of 1992, Evander believed that the two most credible contenders were Razor Ruddock and Lennox Lewis, and he was eager to fight both of them. Those two weren't scheduled to meet until the fall, however, with the winner emerging as the number one contender of the WBC.

That meant Evander had to fight somebody else sooner, and with Bowe refusing to accept $6 million, that somebody else was going to have to be Larry Holmes. Evander was attacked as soon as the fight was announced.

"He's dodging all the good fighters," one writer said.

"He only fights the has-beens," another writer charged.

Dodging the good fighters? Evander thought. He had signed *twice* to fight Tyson, and in both cases, it was Tyson who backed out.

"I'm not dodging all the good fighters," Evander said. "I'm just trying to follow the rules and regulations and fight everybody in the top ten. They have to be patient, like me. I was the number one contender for two years before fighting for the title."

Fortunately, others came to Evander's defense. Bernie Dillion, the TVKO vice president of programming, said, "Evander pursued Tyson for three years. He was the one fighter going after a man everyone called 'The Baddest Man on the Planet.'"

Evander refused to let the criticism get him down, even laughing it off. "I'm sure there's a guy on the street who thinks he can kick my butt," Evander said. "But I don't worry about what people say."

Bowe would get his chance. In the meantime, Evander had to face Larry Holmes.

Blown-Up Charges

The Holmes-Holyfield fight was getting little publicity until one of Holmes's promoters figured out a way to generate controversy. It wasn't one of the prettiest moments in the history of boxing, but it became lucrative. First, Bob Arum faxed a letter to national boxing writers, suggesting that Evander had used steroids to grow into the heavyweight division.

Evander was furious. He wanted to be a positive role model. He wanted people to know that they could become whatever they wanted to be. Through hard work and faith in Jesus Christ, all things were possible, and you didn't need drugs to get there.

There was absolutely no evidence to support Arum's completely false accusation. Evander built himself up through hard and pro-longed work, and he resented the fact that Arum was now attacking his main message. "I don't like the idea of using lies about me to promote the fight," Evander said. "I'm a grown man. I can take it. But it hurts the kids who look up to the heavyweight champion."

Evander told the kids, "Don't believe the hype. I'm not a cheater and never have been."

Arum showed his character when he actually tried to blame the sportswriters for the controversy. During the final prefight news conference, he said, "I only issue these releases. It's up to the news editors to use their judgment on whether they're true or not."

Larry Holmes eventually apologized, but the entire incident became one of the decade's lowest points in boxing. Finally, the boxing world had a champion that young men could look up to, but in order to generate more revenue, a contending promoter was willing to manufacture a scandal.

Arum's next move came just three days before the fight. He unveiled a poster announcing a "title fight" between the "new heavy-weight champion" Larry Holmes, and George Foreman, scheduled for November 13.

Evander responded by turning Arum's antics into motivation. He came to the ring ready to do battle, and Holmes suffered for it. Holmes was simply outboxed, and Evander won a unanimous decision. It wasn't a pretty fight, but Evander did what he had to do to win.

Now, the stage was set, and one of the most colorful and dra-matic rivalries in all of boxing history was about to begin in Holyfield-Bowe I.

CHAPTER 15

HOLYFIELD AND BOWE: ROUND ONE

Evander and Bowe are two radically different fighters. Bowe came into the first bout at twenty-five years of age, five years Evander's junior. He is known as a boxer with questionable stamina, an "underachiever," while *People* called Evander "a major overachiever." Bowe has been known to weigh as much as 275 pounds. Evander had to work hard to build himself up to 210 pounds. Bowe is a Muslim; Evander is an outspoken Christian. People questioned Bowe's conditioning. Evander may be the most well-conditioned athlete of the decade.

A potentially fight-delaying incident revealed Evander's advanced conditioning. Once, when Evander crossed the floor of his training gym, he slipped on some water and did a side split. The people watching grimaced, certain that something must be pulled or injured. Evander's flexibility coach was in the room at the time and simply told Evander to get up.

He did—smiling. Everything was fine.

If the same thing happened to Bowe, Douglas, or Foreman, it would take some heavy equipment or at least half a dozen firemen to lift them off the floor.

Holyfield-Bowe I occurred on Friday the 13th (November) in 1992. Promoters billed the fight as "Friday the 13th: Anything Can Happen," and nobody left disappointed. For boxing, it was a magical night, the biggest bout in years.

Celebrities came out in droves. Andre Agassi, with his then long and tri-colored hair; Magic Johnson, with people swarming around him; Jack Nicholson and Mr. T.; Kareem Abdul-Jabbar with (I'm not kidding) a 5-foot 2-inch date; Sylvester Stallone; Mel Gibson; Kevin Costner; Bruce Willis; and others.

Sports Illustrated called the twelve-round bout a "portrait of courage that will hang forever in the memories of those who watched." The *Houston Chronicle* said it was "one of the most exciting heavyweight title fights ever." In truth, it was an all-out war, with both fighters refusing to back down, giving everything they had for the most coveted title in sports.

Evander entered the fight confident he would win—maybe even a little overconfident. He believed that the best-conditioned fighter would win, and the way he trained, it was hard for him to believe that another fighter could be in as good shape. He had sparred with Bowe several years prior to this fight, and Bowe always had a stamina problem. Evander figured he'd just have to hang in there until Bowe ran out of gas.

For this bout, Evander focused on training for speed and mobility. He wanted to stick Bowe with a jab or combination, then move. And that's just what he did—for the first two rounds. Evander remained very much in control, dictating the pace, scoring with his jabs, slipping and countering the punches of his larger and somewhat slower opponent. It looked like Evander would win this fight easily.

But late in the second round, something changed. Nobody in the arena saw it, for it was an internal change. For months, Evander had listened to the media, and for once, he let its criticism get under his skin. A number of writers kept saying that Evander's fights were boring. It wasn't enough for Evander to win, he had to knock his opponents out. They talked about how Bowe was younger, bigger, and stronger, and about how he was going to prove that Evander was just a "blown-up" cruiserweight.

As Evander outboxed Bowe through the first five minutes, these taunts came back to his mind with unusual strength. Early on, Evander set them aside and focused on what he knew would win—moving, dancing, and outboxing the larger Bowe. It was working, and Evander's confidence grew. Bowe was clearly puzzled. Evander was hitting him almost at will, and Bowe couldn't figure out how to stop him.

Then, as the two fighters clinched near the end of the second round, the referee said, "Break!" Bowe slipped in a shot on the break, and Evander got angry. It was just a stupid cheap shot—it didn't even hurt that much—but something inside Evander snapped, and he got angry. That anger and the critics' accusations mixed a potent cocktail.

So, the critics wanted a knockout, he thought. He was going to provide it. "I lost my cool," Evander said. "I started going toe-to-toe with him, and I started rumbling real hard with him. I stopped thinking about boxing him and started thinking about knocking him out."

Evander decided to "bowl him over." Of course, one of the factors working against him was that Evander weighed 206 pounds and Bowe weighed 235.

The fight became personal—against Bowe's cheap shot and against the critics' cheap words. Winning was no longer Evander's obsession. Now, only a knockout would suffice. He went at him with everything he had.

From that moment on—the end of the second round until the tenth round, my family and I witnessed one of the most horrifying fights that we have ever had to endure. For the first time, I could appreciate why our mother refused to watch Evander fight. This was beyond scary. It was a nightmare.

The same action that makes a fight exciting to the casual on-looker makes a family grimace and sweat. We know that there is always the possibility that a fighter can get seriously—even permanently—hurt. A tennis player might turn an ankle, and a hockey player might lose a few teeth, but boxers have actually *died*. When it's your brother's head that's getting hit, you don't look at a fight in the same way.

Mother was at home, praying. "I don't pray that my son win," she told me, "I pray that God protects him and the other young man in there with him. I realize that just like me, there's another mother who is worried about her child."

Mother went on her knees just before the fight, and stayed there until after the fight was over. Since she doesn't know exactly when a fight ends, she usually keeps praying long after the bout, so Evander calls her as soon as possible to say, "Mother, I'm fine."

Both men would need her prayers tonight.

In round three, Evander began scoring early with big shots, but Bowe was countering, and many of Bowe's shots carried a mercilessly powerful momentum. Evander's chin snapped back, and his body was racked by the blows. Evander has almost no body fat so you can't see the blows shake him, but sitting up close, you can feel them.

At this point, Evander slipped into his zone. In fights such as these, Evander can become so determined, and the adrenaline can begin pumping so furiously, that he becomes virtually impervious to the pain. His concentration was intense, and he simply planted himself in front of Bowe and unleashed a thunderous combination to the head and body. Bowe would be momentarily stunned, but then respond with a powerful combination of his own. Evander would grimace, but he wouldn't back up. He stayed in there and fought.

This went on for several more rounds, and the damage became ugly. After the ninth round, Ace Marotta, Evander's cut man, worked frantically to keep Evander's right eye from swelling shut and his left eye from bleeding. Lou Duva shouted at Evander to fight his match, not Bowe's; Benton urged him to use his boxing skills. But at this point, Evander knew he had to dig down and find something within himself to keep going. The critics wanted a knockout, and he was determined to provide it.

The tenth round would be one that would go down in the annals of boxing history. Evander welcomed Bowe into it with two solid combinations that exploded off Bowe's chin, but Bowe countered with four bruising combinations that staggered the champion's legs. Evander quit jabbing; instead, he was determined to unleash the knockout blow that would drop Bowe to the floor.

Bowe found an opening, however, and that's when time seemed to stop and then proceed in slow motion. I saw Evander leaning on Bowe's chest, trying to regroup after throwing a hard combination. Bowe, by now having tagged the pattern of the champion, took one quick step back on his right leg, and drew on the force of his massive thighs and hips to throw a gut-wrenching uppercut that connected squarely with Evander's face. Evander's legs wobbled. The blow had so much power that it catapulted Evander's head from a bowed position to vertically erect.

Evander rocked back, instantly recognized his precarious position, and prayed, *Help me, Lord!*

Help is there. All you gotta do is not quit. The voice Evander heard calmed him. His mind became clear.

Realizing that Evander was dazed, Bowe jumped all over him, pushing him into the ropes. I couldn't believe Evander was still standing, but in times like these, Evander rules his body almost like a detached observer. He never loses his mind, and with that mind he tries to figure out how to make his legs steady. Falling down is simply not an option.

Still, Evander was slowing down. His chest was heaving as his deprived body sucked the air for more oxygen while a 235-pound man drove his fists into his body and face. Evander realized that his attempts at knocking Bowe out had left him seriously drained. Bowe sensed this as well, and Evander watched as the challenger flew into him with the hungry rage of a would-be champion.

Bowe unleashed more than forty blows in the first minute of round ten. Evander endured more punishment in that one minute than most people will suffer in a lifetime. After the forty-punch barrage, there was an eerie lull on that Friday the 13th. Both boxers clinched and sucked for air. People were shocked that Evander was still standing, and Bowe was arm-weary from throwing everything he had at Evander's head.

In that clinch, Evander, though groggy, saw his opportunity. *Now he thinks I'm hurt,* Evander thought. *Now's my chance.* Remembering Bowe's tendency to become tired, Evander expected that Bowe was exhausted after throwing so many punches. As spectators all over the world expected to see Evander fall, Evander dug down and prepared himself to launch a horrendous assault.

Evander's resurrection stunned the crowd. Before the eyes of millions of spectators, he transformed himself from a tired, clinching fighter into a boxer determined to bring his man down. His eyes were swollen and his vision was cut—it's a surreal view to look out through two swollen eyes, catching glimpses of a bloody face bobbing in front of you—but Evander saw enough to connect, and he landed a hook, two stunning combinations, and then three uppercuts.

Bowe couldn't figure it out. Evander should have dropped by now, but suddenly, he had discovered an arsenal of his own. Bowe tried to keep the champion off with three lazy jabs, but Evander went right through them and slammed his fists into Bowe's bruised and battered face.

Evander had withstood forty shots in sixty seconds, and now Bowe endured fourteen shots in fifteen seconds.

But both fighters stood their ground. The crowd couldn't believe it. They had never seen such a pace. The intensity slowed somewhat for the rest of the round—it had to—but both men continued to pound the other. Neither stepped back, both kept moving forward in a wild display of courage and elan.

When the bell rang to end one of the most brutal rounds ever fought, the crowd jumped to their feet to give the two fighters a standing ovation. A writer from *Sports Illustrated* said, "No heavyweight champion and challenger have ever fought a more heroic round. Other boxers have been linked in three-minute essays in raw courage—Muhammad Ali and Joe Frazier, Larry Holmes and Ken Norton, Tommy Hearns and Marvin Hagler—but none can claim to have been in a round fought more ferociously."

Evander dug down deep after the tenth round. He didn't just want to survive this fight, he wanted to win it. He had worked his entire life to become heavyweight champion of the world, and he'd just as soon die before he willingly gave the title up.

Evander surprised Bowe by charging into the eleventh round. Evander's conditioning was paying off. He could get tired, but his recovery was nothing short of amazing, and Evander still thought he could win it. He knew he needed a knockout, however, and in his efforts to land the big blow, he suffered another uppercut, then a combination that sent him sprawling toward the ropes. Evander was suddenly down on both knees. It was a rare moment for him, but all he could think about was getting up.

"How you feeling? You all right?" the referee asked.

In spite of the pain, Evander wanted to say, "What are you talking about? Let me at him!" He just wanted to get on with the fight, viewing the knockdown as a momentary distraction that temporarily kept him from finding a way past Bowe's defenses. Bowe would have to make Evander lose consciousness if he wanted to stop the champ.

Then, after enduring another Bowe assault, Evander stunned the crowd by once again going on the offensive.

As the eleventh round ended, just one word cascaded through Evander's mind: *knockout.* If a boxer is putting everything he has into a close match, he won't know who's ahead. Rather than keeping a tab on who's winning each round, he is concentrating on the fight. When Evander sat down, however, his trainers made it clear to him, "You need a knockout."

Evander realized he had just three minutes to defend his crown, only 180 seconds to drop the man who was laying claim to a prize that had driven him for more than a decade.

Evander threw everything he had into the twelfth and final round. Bowe knew he was up on points, however, and was content to box and move, keeping out of harm's way. As each second ticked off, Evander could feel the title slipping away, and he redoubled his efforts to break past Bowe's wall, but Bowe held firm.

Evander rose up against his weariness, his stinging cuts, his swollen eyes, his oxygen-deprived and burning lungs, in a desperate attempt to land the blow that would bring the fight his way. He was searching everywhere to find an opening for a knockout. As his tired legs and arms screamed their defiance, Evander pushed himself by saying, "The fight ain't over yet 'cause the bell hasn't rung." He never stopped searching for the knockout. It was inspiring, but it wasn't enough. Fittingly, each man threw a last shot at the final bell.

As soon as Evander heard the bell, he felt the disappointment wash over him. "I didn't knock him out!" he lamented.

As the announcer proclaimed the winner, Evander good-naturedly pointed in Bowe's direction. Bowe's people erupted into pandemonium. Evander watched dispassionately, until he heard Bowe say, "I guess I knocked Christ off his crown."

Evander felt his heart drop right out of him. "It's going to take a strong man to learn how to lose," he prayed. "Lord, help me be that kind of man."

Evander didn't feel that God had let him down; on the contrary, he felt that he had let God down. "I didn't fight my best fight. God isn't a respector of persons when it comes to boxing. I didn't use all that God has given me, and that's why Bowe won."

Outside the ring, I didn't hear Bowe's comment, but I saw Bowe's camp celebrate. I knew what it felt like. Team Holyfield had experienced it many times before. Now, we were facing an entirely new phenomenon: defeat.

The Stranger Named Defeat

I followed my brother into the locker room. None of us were quite sure how to act. Evander hadn't lost since the Olympics—eight years before—and even then, he had really won. This was the first time in almost a decade that someone had actually earned a victory against Evander inside the ring.

Evander sat alone in the dressing room. His eyes were partially closed, his cheekbones had swelled, and the fatigue that covered him kept his head down.

After all of Evander's previous professional fights, the locker room was a place of wild exuberance, dancing, and celebration. Celebrities usually lined up at the door to congratulate Evander, while autograph hounds did their best to smuggle in a piece of paper, a shirt, or a hat, to be signed. Unauthorized photographers sought to make a few easy bucks by stealing a photo here or there.

On this night, not a single celebrity came by to say "good fight." All the autograph hounds were crowded around Bowe's room. For the first time, Evander recovered from a fight without the *pop pop popping* of flashbulbs going off. There was just one single and glaring light from the lone cameraman whose job it was to capture the loser's comment. Then a sportscaster stuck a microphone in Evander's face and asked, "Evander, you lost tonight. How do you feel after your first professional loss?"

Evander had always remembered Christ in victory. He wasn't about to forget Him in defeat. "First," he said, "I want to give praise and thanks to my Lord and Savior, Jesus Christ."

"Yeah, that's fine, Evander, but how do you feel about losing your title to Bowe?"

"I feel fine. I gave it the best I had and Bowe won. He was a better man tonight. He fought a better fight tonight."

The sportscaster pointed to a small television set. "Evander," he said, "I have a monitor here with me, and I want to show you the tenth round when Bowe had you in trouble."

The screen lit up with the two boxers facing off. Evander had fought in that round less than half an hour before, yet now he was watching himself on the screen.

"Okay, there it is," the announcer said. "Bowe has you hurt badly with the uppercut."

Evander watched the slow-motion action. He saw himself covering up and stumbling over the ring as Bowe pursued him.

"Evander, what were you thinking about when Bowe was trying to knock you out here?"

Evander looked up at him. The sweat had stopped dripping off his face by now, but his eyes were still puffy. "At that moment, I was thinking to myself that this is my greatest opportunity to knock him out. Bowe caught me with a good uppercut that wobbled me, but the next shot missed, which gave me time to recover. But Bowe became very confident, and he stumbled all over his feet trying to knock me out, throwing big, hard shots.

"I could see that Bowe was overconfident, so I expected him to make himself vulnerable. But more importantly—"

Evander knew the announcer wasn't going to like this, but the empty locker room had already shown him that there are only a few friends who stay with you, win or lose, and Evander wasn't about to slight the most important one.

"But more importantly," he went on, "I believe that, with Christ, when you are at your weakest, you are at your strongest because you learn to believe in God and not yourself. When we are at our weakest is when we rely on God the most."

Evander looked back at the monitor. "At that time, I just believed that God was going to give me the energy to come back. And it was happening. I really believe that if the bell had not rung when it did, I would have taken Bowe out."

Ever in search of a new, sensational story, the announcer asked, "Are you going to retire now, Evander?"

Evander paused and dropped his shoulders. He had just been pummeled by one of the strongest fighters on the planet. His body was sore, his eyes stung, his head was somewhat foggy from the blows.

"Right now, I don't care to fight anymore. I am going to go home and really think about it."

After such a brutal bout, it was impossible to think with any real clarity. "When Bowe hit me," Evander recalled later, "he hit me *hard*." For now, Evander just wanted to take some time off and be with the family who had suffered his absence during the previous months of training. Evander knew his kids would always be there, and right then, he just wanted to be there for them.

At the postfight press conference, reporters kept pushing Evander for an excuse. "There ain't no excuse," he insisted. "I went out there to give my best, and the other guy's best was better than mine, so here I am, a former champion."

Evander had already learned how to win; now he was learning how to lose. He called Bowe the next day to congratulate him and to offer some advice.

"Look, Bowe," Evander said. "This game is a money business. You're the new champion now, and you can make a lot of money.

All your kinfolks are gonna show up. The rules have changed now. You better get ready."

Bowe was listening attentively.

"Don't ever fight for under $10 million," Evander went on. "If you do it once, they'll try to hold you there."

The two men who had fought so viciously less than twenty-four hours earlier were now swapping stories.

"It's more difficult as a champion than as a challenger," Evander warned. "Everybody feels you owe them something. If you can't handle that, you'll be in trouble."

Evander was talking almost as a big brother would to a younger brother. In spite of their roles as adversaries within the ring, Evander doesn't deny his affection for Bowe outside the ring. "I couldn't call him a sweet kid," Evander admits, "but Bowe's a very nice person when you really get to know him. It might surprise you, but he's a very courteous person."

Bowe responded to Evander's call with outright enthusiasm. He told Evander that he hoped the two of them could become "buddies."

When Evander flew back to Atlanta, no cheering fans, high school bands, or local dignitaries greeted him. It was a startling contrast to the pandemonium that followed his other bouts. Even though Bowe himself has said Evander fought "with the heart of a lion," second place just wasn't good enough for boxing fans.

We walked through the corridor of the airport uncontested and unmolested. Nobody stopped five feet in front of us and pleaded for a photograph.

Instead, we were like pariahs. Whenever we looked in the direction of services personnel, they quickly averted their eyes to stare at a blank computer screen, or started polishing the receiver in a telephone booth. Where were the people who could say, "We'll get him next time, Champ"? It was difficult and even irritating for me to watch.

Evander's response, however, was somewhat different. He decided right then he wasn't going to let the fans' reaction get him down. For him, the loss was a temporary setback, not a national catastrophe. "The true fans, Lightning," he said, "the true fans told me, 'That was a great fight. I'm sorry you lost, but that was a great fight,' and that's okay.

"Don't think anything about the others. They just don't know how to approach me. 'Better luck next time,' is just a hard thing to say. They don't want to remind me that I lost. I understand that. It doesn't bother me."

As I watched him walk on, I wondered if boxing recognized the character of the man who had just been knocked off its throne.

CHAPTER 16

RETIRED, RESTED, AND RESTLESS

B owe whipped your behind."
The skinny man who said this looked like he would have lacked the courage to approach Evander for an autograph two weeks ago, but now Evander's loss seemed to make some people bolder.

Another guy came up and complained, "Man, I was winning money on you all the time, but this time you lost, and it cost me."

"Okay," Evander smiled, "but you won more on me than you lost, didn't you, in the long run?"

"Yeah," the young man admitted.

"All right, then, what you complaining about?"

Still, everybody became an expert, eager to offer advice.

"You gotta get him back, Champ!"

"You should quit. He's too young. You're past your prime."

Evander weathered all these comments with heroic patience. He brought the speculation to an early end by announcing his retirement the next Monday. Evander realized he simply lacked the hunger to prepare for and endure another bruising battle. He had made more money than he could possibly spend. He had won an Olympic medal and had fought his way into the heavyweight championship of the world. What more could he prove?

Also, Evander was still sore from what boxing had cost him. The training had shaped his eating, sleeping, and vacationing habits for his entire teenage and adult life. Boxing, he felt, had taken away his wife, and it had kept him away from his kids.

To make matters worse, Evander's bruises weren't even healed by the time the Duvas, who had made millions of dollars promoting Evander's fights, were negotiating to make millions more promoting the Riddock Bowe and Lennox Lewis fight. Duva had used his leverage with Evander to ensure a slice of Bowe's future if Evander lost—the same thing King had demanded of Evander to face Tyson, which Duva had vehemently rejected. Initially, Evander saw Duva's divided loyalties as a clear conflict of interest.

"Dan's my promoter," Evander said. "We've been together since the Olympics. When I saw on television Lennox Lewis beat Razor Ruddock, I saw Dan climb into the ring to congratulate Lennox. My man congratulating a man I might fight. Don't tell me there's no conflict."

Critics were all over Don King in the early 1980s when he controlled the top ten heavyweights. During that time, the championship changed hands more frequently than ever in the history of boxing. Evander—and everyone else—knew this was no accident. A promoter and a fighter have to work together as a team to build a career that goes down in the history books. If the promoter operates with divided loyalties, the payoff, not what's best for the fighter, becomes paramount.

Evander felt betrayed. One of the things that bothered him most about the bout with Bowe was the Nevada Athletic Commission's choice of referees, Joe Cortez. Cortez refused to penalize Bowe for the low blows, one of which infuriated Evander and led him to stop boxing and to start slugging it out. The Duvas didn't protest the choice, even though Evander had made it clear to them that he wanted Mills Lane, who had worked some of Evander's earlier fights. In fact, the Duvas told Evander that Lane *would* be the referee.

So, view the situation from Evander's perspective: He shows up for the fight and finds out the referee is Cortez. Cortez doesn't call a clean fight, Bowe wins, and all of a sudden, the Duvas stand to make millions off of Bowe—just weeks after they ended their ties with Evander.

"Promoters shouldn't have such a conflict of interest," Evander protested. "Promoters should be fighting for their man. Say what you want about Don King, but when Mike Tyson lost to Buster Douglas, you didn't see King running over to Douglas to be his promoter. He stuck by his man."

Evander felt betrayed. The Duvas had made their millions, yet still it hadn't been enough to guarantee their loyalty. This was more than a professional slight—it became a personal wound. Evander realized that to a few of his close associates, he wasn't the "friend" he thought he was, but a "money machine" that they were going to ride and discard as soon as he began to slow down.

Evander was concerned for the younger fighters—men like Riddick Bowe, Lennox Lewis, and Michael Moorer. They were in the stage of their careers where they would soon be negotiating for tens of millions of dollars. Evander wanted to warn them that the same people who express such an undying friendship are often more interested in promoting themselves than they are in promoting the best interests of the fighters.

Later, Evander's take on the situation would change, and the Duvas would once again promote one of his comeback fights. What happened in between? New York sportswriter Mike Katz explained to Evander that a promoter's role was different from a manager's role. A promoter sells an *event* more than he sells a fighter. After Evander was defeated, the Duvas said it was only right that they spend time congratulating Bowe. Now, they said, they were promoters of the entire *fight,* not just Evander. Besides, if Evander was talking retirement, were they obligated to retire as well?

"They're just doing their job, Evander," Katz said. "That's what a promoter does."

When Evander also learned that the Duvas had negotiated a mandated rematch in case Evander lost, he began to look at the situation differently. In victory and defeat, Evander has always been open to another perspective.

With Katz operating as a peacemaker, Evander eventually apologized for his comments. The biggest misunderstanding came from the fact that Dan Duva was always one of the last ones to leave the party after each of Evander's big wins. This time, after Evander's first loss, Dan spent the evening with Bowe while Evander sat alone. In the emotional heat of the moment, it just didn't seem right.

A Second Look

After a couple months, Evander was rested and rest*less*. He found out that at thirty years of age, rest isn't all it's cut out to be. One of Evander's favorite things about boxing was the work. "I love the work," he said, and watching him, few could doubt it. That attitude made rest all the more difficult. In the few months after his bout with Bowe, Evander had a brief fling at acting school, then bought a motorcycle and some horses. He eventually tired of them, and ended up spending much of his time teaching Evander Jr. how to play football.

Evander saw his son play his heart out to please his dad. The eight-year-old literally became a different player under his father's watchful eye. But Evander knew from his own life what Evander Jr. lacked. Just as Evander had given his all for Morgan, so his son was giving his all for his dad. That would only take him so far.

"It's not good enough for you to want to be good for me," Evander told his son. "You have to want to be good for yourself, to please yourself."

But even as the words slipped out of Evander's mouth, he felt convicted. Wasn't that exactly what he had done against Bowe—focused on pleasing others, fighting the critics' fight, going for the knockout?

It made him think twice about his own retirement.

As Evander's bruises healed and as his rest chased away the weariness—it takes *weeks* to fully recover from such a bout—Evander returned time and again to the tape of his fight with Bowe. Alone in his room, he watched the tape over and over again. He paused the tape just before Bowe's murderous uppercut in the tenth round. The commentator's mouth hung open as Evander stared at the frozen fighters. Then, with a push of the button, he'd let Bowe's fist crash into his head one more time.

Next, Evander stopped the fight one minute into the tenth round, when he so surprisingly came back. He relived the moment, amazed as much as anyone to watch himself come back.

As an objective observer who wasn't sucking for air and feeling the pain and punishment of every single blow, Evander was surprised at how close the fight was. By the way the judges scored it, he assumed he had been torn apart. Sometimes, when you're in the ring, you're too close to your own beating to realize how much punishment your adversary is receiving.

Evander realized he had been in the fight the whole way. In fact, the judges' rather lopsided scoring made him angry. Cortez's failure to call the low blows—obvious, on the tape—also angered him. The fight could have been scored dead even by the eighth round. Evander could certainly have won the ninth round, and though Bowe stunned Evander in the tenth, his comeback rally was sufficient enough to make the round a draw. Bowe gained an edge on Evander in the eleventh round, but Evander easily outscored Bowe in the twelfth. That could put Evander up by one point—and award him the fight.

In Ali's era, a challenger had to knock out the champion or outpoint the champion to such a degree that there was no doubt about who won. In that era, it was understood that all tie-breakers and close battles went to the reigning champion. Ali used to say, "Ya gotta whup the champ to take his title away."

Bowe had fought a hard fight, but this was certainly no "whupping."

Many friends and family members had assured Evander that the fight was close, but at first he felt so exhausted and bruised by the bout that it was hard for him to believe it. Once his wounds healed and his heart rested, however, he was finally able to accept the fact that it *was* a close bout, extremely close.

That's when some people began seeking a "divine" explanation. You hear it all when you win, and you hear it all when you lose. Because this one person knew Evander was a Christian, he insisted that God failed Evander and that it was God's will that Evander lost.

Evander refused to accept this explanation. "I may fail God," he said, "But God never fails me. God would never put me in a position to lose. His will is that I win in the ring and outside."

Evander knew that his loss wasn't attributable to God but to something that had gone wrong on *his* part. He reexamined himself to find out what he did wrong.

His competitive spirit returned, phoenix-like, from the ashes of his disappointment. Now, his reviewing sessions became learning sessions. He stopped the fight just before one of Bowe's major blows, studying Bowe's stance, looking for clues that might announce the release of a particular weapon.

He studied the moments where he made himself vulnerable—occasions in which he overreached, and times when he had the advantage but failed to recognize it and follow it up. He was also able to see where he could have exploded into the advantage if he had had more endurance. *It many ways,* he thought, *Bowe won just because he outhustled me.*

Evander also began evaluating what went wrong *outside* the ring. His first mistake, he realized, was that he had allowed the media to get under his skin. The Bible says, "Pride goeth before a fall," and Evander had let his pride get in the way. The media pounded Evander relentlessly for not knocking out his opponents.

Consequently, during the second round, Evander began fighting the media as much as he began fighting Bowe. Looking at the tape, he realized that he could have outboxed Bowe and won the fight convincingly. Instead, he tried to outslug him, and in that case the judges gave the edge to the bigger, heavier man.

After Evander fought the media's fight, they praised him lavishly. They printed statements like, "Holyfield has the heart of a lion," and one sportscaster referred to him as "Holyfield the warrior." Several writers compared the Holyfield-Bowe fight to the brutal battles of Ali-Frazier. One magazine called it "The Fight of the Decade."

Evander realized that in exchange for the praise and recognition of the critics, he had forfeited his titles. He had let the critics dictate the fight, and that was wrong. It wouldn't happen again.

Again.

The thought almost caught him by surprise. Could there be an again?

Why not? His body was still in good shape. After watching the fight with Bowe, he knew what he needed to do differently to beat him.

Somewhat surprisingly, our mother encouraged Evander to come back. She never liked boxing, and she would have chosen a different career for her son. But Bowe started bragging. He began to embellish his victory over Evander, and then began discounting Evander's abilities. Mother heard all this, and if people wonder where Evander gets his competitive spirit, they should spend half an hour with her. Evander was as surprised as anyone when our mother finally turned off the television, faced Evander, and said, "Son, I want you to whip him for me. That boy just talks too much."

She said five words that jolted Evander, five words that meant more to him than the millions of words penned by critics and pundits: "I didn't raise no quitter."

Many people had come up to Evander shortly after his match with Bowe and urged him not to quit. But Evander knew he couldn't fight for others. Such a motivation would melt in the heat of the ring. He needed to feel the hunger himself, and after watching the tape of his fight with Bowe one more time, that hunger had returned.

"I wanted to prove to myself that I could come back and beat a talented fighter who was better than me on a particular night. I had learned from my mistakes and decided that I was man enough to acknowledge them and come back and clean them up to get back on top."

Evander finally decided he couldn't go out with a loss. He believed that Bowe hadn't won the fight as much as Evander had lost it. He owed it to himself to come back. But first, he had to check it out with the One whose opinion mattered the most.

Evander got on his knees and prayed. Did God want him to move on to other things? In God's still, small voice, Evander sensed that what kept him out of the ring as much as anything wasn't God's will, but fear: The fear his family felt when his head endured so many punches. Fear of returning to the grind. Fear of the grueling schedule of training for a title fight. Fear of working and enduring and persevering, all the while knowing there was no guaranteed payoff at the end. In fact, if Evander listened to the media, victory—regaining the heavyweight titles—was entirely beyond his reach.

But sensing God's approval and direction, Evander decided to face these fears. In fact, he thrived on them.

So it was settled. He'd come back, but he'd do it with a new trainer. George Benton and Lou Duva had moved on, and Evander felt it was time he did too. He interviewed Emanuel Steward, who had trained Ricky Womack years earlier when Evander fought as an amateur. Evander was impressed by Steward's hunger (though successful and well-respected, Steward had never trained a heavyweight champion), and the onetime adversaries began laying plans for a world championship alliance.

"You gotta throw the jab, Evander," Emanuel said. "And you gotta move. You've got the best legs in the business. You don't need to sit there and fight Bowe. Nobody can outbox you, Evander, but you quit boxing and started fighting."

Evander warmed up by fighting and defeating Alex Stewart, setting the stage, to Bowe's chagrin, for a Holyfield-Bowe rematch. Since Lennox Lewis and Riddick Bowe had never been able to agree on a deal, Bowe had been stripped of the WBC belt. Evander would be fighting to regain the WBA and IBF titles.

Not surprisingly, the media didn't waste much time spewing their venom. Suddenly, Evander no longer had the "heart of a lion" but the "mind of a fool." Former team members and advisors— men who had been close to Evander, some of whom had earned a considerable amount of money off him—were quoted as saying, "It's nothing but pure ego. He wouldn't stand a chance in a second fight against Bowe. There's no hope of Evander even going the distance. Even his prayers won't save him this time."

An interviewer finally asked Evander the question point-blank: "Bowe beat you once. He is now stronger and more dangerous than he was the first time you faced him. What makes you think that you can beat him this time?"

Evander responded, "I walk by faith and not by sight. I can do all things through Christ who strengthens me."

The interviewer was puzzled and for perhaps the first time in his life at a loss for words, so Evander explained, "Every setback paves the way for a comeback. Jesus will give me the opportunity to set it right, and go out a winner."

"So what are you saying?" the interviewer asked.

"Through Christ I have already claimed the victory," Evander said. "I am the champ already. Come November 6, I'll just pick up the belt."

Riddick Bowe read the interview and was furious. He called Evander right away. "I thought you were my friend," he half-yelled into the phone. "You said you were going to beat me. You showed me no respect!" Bowe's voice kept rising in its intensity, until finally, he blurted out the threat, "I'm gonna hurt you, man! I'm gonna hurt you!"

In every press conference after that phone conversation, Riddick Bowe would, in Evander's words, "talk noise." He said Evander would be "lucky" to make it to the seventh round. "You can take it to the bank he won't get to the twelfth round," Bowe added. Evander responded by sitting back and smiling.

Evander wasn't trying to dismiss Bowe's skills, but he honestly believed that if he fought his best fight and Bowe fought his best fight, he could win. Since he was confident that God would help him to fight his best fight, Evander fully expected to regain two of his titles.

This comeback became an intensely personal and religious experience. Evander knew he was in God's will, and he believed that God had already given him what he needed to win the fight: the skill, the desire to win, the antipathy to quitting. All of that, he believed, came from his Creator.

So let the other people scoff, Evander didn't care. He had tried to please them before—please them instead of his God—and it had cost him his titles. Now he didn't care. He just wanted to be in God's will, and he was certain that God's will was for him to regain the heavyweight championship of the world. God wouldn't *give* it to him. Evander would have to fight his best and take the titles away from Bowe, but he was prepared to do that.

For his part, Bowe talked as though Evander were nothing more than a nuisance who needed to be "shut up." "Some people do what they want, and some people do what they must," Bowe told a press conference. "At this point, I must fight Evander Holyfield, shut him up, and get him out of the way."

Evander was determined to fight a different fight this time around. He knew he had let Bowe's low blows draw him out of a boxing match and into a slugfest. That wouldn't happen again.

Before the first fight, Evander expected Bowe to tire in the later rounds. In this way, Evander confused his former twenty-year-old sparring partner with the twenty-five-year-old contender. Now, Evander knew exactly what he was facing, and he was ready. He knew he'd have to move more and throw more punches, but he was confident he could do both.

Bowe's manager, Rock Newman, attempted to gain the prefight psychological edge by comparing Bowe to Joe Louis. "Let's match right now Joe Louis in his prime and Riddick Bowe in his prime," Newman said. "I put my money on Riddick Bowe. I'd just about match his punching power with anyone who has ever been the heavyweight champion."

Newman talked past the bout with Evander, as if Evander were just a stepping-stone for Bowe's future defenses. The media shared Newman's perspective. The *Dallas Morning News* said, "There is little reason to doubt the outcome will be any different the second time around." The *Boston Globe* warned that "Bowe is younger, stronger and even bigger than he was when he pounded out a unanimous decision."

Bowe would enter the bout as a 5-to-1 betting favorite. A number of bookies would eventually rue those odds!

CHAPTER 17

THE REMATCH

Holyfield-Bowe II will be remembered as one of the toughest and most bizarre title fights ever. It's a good thing Evander was focusing on spiritual preparation, because only the spiritually strongest could win this fight.

It was a cold evening in Las Vegas as Evander sat quietly in the overcrowded dressing room, getting ready to enter the outside arena.

"Thirty minutes to fight time!" a trainer shouted.

Strangely enough, the announcement made *my* heart leap and elicited a nervous perspiration from my palms and back. I was facing this bout with mixed feelings: elation that my brother might become only the third fighter to regain the title from the man who took it from him; anxiety when I recalled the beating Evander had endured during the first fight. Evander had given Bowe as much as he received, but still, boxing can be a dangerous sport, and I knew this match would be tough.

Evander sat quietly in a corner, the very picture of serenity. It was as if the announcement—thirty minutes to fight time—didn't even register, or if it did, as if it were of no more consequence than a hostess at a restaurant telling a couple of patrons that their table would be ready in another thirty minutes.

Evander's eyes were closed, his head was bowed, and his legs were outstretched. An open Bible rested on his legs. Evander was seeking strength from another world, and all of us knew not to bother him. It's part of his ritual before a fight, an essential element in his preparation.

"A lot of talented fighters are in excellent physical shape," Evander explains, "but in order to win consistently, inside the ring as well as outside it, you have to prepare both physically and spiritually."

Nobody trains as hard as Evander, and I doubt anyone prays as hard either. He always reaffirms, "Boxing is 90 percent spiritual and

10 percent physical. It's the spiritual aspect that gives the edge and an extra burst of energy to draw from when I am in a war. My victories are not achieved by my might, nor by my power, but by the Spirit of Christ who strengthens me."

In the second fight with Bowe, the spiritual and the physical commingled in a powerful alchemy that made history. A Las Vegas pastor, whose church Evander attended when in town, helped prepare Evander right before the fight.

"All right, brother, when you first enter the ring, I want you to say, 'Here I am, Lord. Thy will be done.'"

Evander nodded, his eyes a picture of serene focus. He was preparing his spirit for what would become a physical and ironically brutal act of prayer.

"Every time you hit him," the minister added, "say, 'It is done.'"

Evander nodded, raising his gloves, loosening his arms.

"All right!" a trainer shouted. "Let's go!"

I looked at Evander, whose face now registered confident determination. I was proud of him. Few people outside this room expected him to stand through all twelve rounds, much less to have his arm raised in victory. But Evander was confident the result had already been written. All he had to do was go out and claim it.

He stood, shook his shoulders, and rolled his head. Team Holyfield was ready to roll.

There's nothing to rival the emotion of entering an arena before a title fight. We left the dressing room—security in the front, a few trainers following behind, then Evander, followed by his corner people—and immediately heard the muffled roar of a capacity crowd eager for the show to get started.

The tunnel leading to the arena doors echoed every little sound inside the walkway while muting the sounds outside. Getting ready to walk outside felt like preparing to face a rainstorm. We knew that as soon as we left the cover, we'd be soaked in the crowd's reaction.

Individual voices cried out. "You're the champ!"

"Let's go!"

"Come on!"

Our words bounced off the walls around us, repeating themselves. But once the doors were opened, the muffler was removed, and we couldn't hear ourselves scream. The tiny little sounds that echoed off the tunnel walls just seconds before were lost in the crowd's enthusiastic cacophony. From the sterile walls of the walkway, we were launched into a sea of screaming voices.

The security people looked like Moses parting the Red Sea as they drove a wedge through the crowd, but it was like scooping water at the beach: the spectators closed back in as soon as the entourage was past. The people leaned over as far as they could, pawing and scratching, desperate to touch Evander. If they couldn't touch Evander, they'd touch anybody *near* him, as if we were one giant snake with Evander as the head. People groped and screamed with such intensity that we could literally feel their energy pulsate throughout the arena. If this emotion could be harnessed, it would light an entire city.

As we got closer to the ring, the intensity increased. What sounded like pandemonium just a few seconds before now seemed like merely a warm-up as the entire arena was able to see Team Holyfield climb into the ring. People were on their feet, cheering, shouting, whistling. Evander took it all in, not hesitating a second as he climbed through the ropes.

I'm always particularly moved by this prefight action. Once a fighter passes through the ropes, the only way back out is through the other boxer's fists. Climbing into the ring is the "point of no return."

Remembering his pastor's words, Evander slipped through the ropes and said his prayer. "Here I am, Lord, Thy will be done."

Bowe's camp entered the arena next. The earlier bedlam that surrounded Evander repeated itself, the intensity growing as Bowe made his way toward the ring. Evander turned back toward his corner, praying, moving, loosening up. "Here I am, Lord, Thy will be done," he whispered. "Thy will be done. Here I am."

Evander could tell from the crowd's roar when Bowe entered the ring, so he turned to face him. He caught Bowe's eyes and smiled, patting his gloves, displaying his confidence.

Evander wanted Bowe to see that his prefight talk hadn't scared him. He wanted Bowe to know—before even one blow was struck— that his own talk about walking by faith and not by sight was not a ploy. Evander knew he had trained as hard as he could, physically, to prepare for this fight. But he also knew he was ready spiritually. He wasn't fighting to please the sportswriters. He wasn't fighting to prove he could land a knockout. He didn't care about being a 5-to-1 underdog. If anything, that just made it more exciting. It gave him one more reason to trust, which gave him more confidence.

Bowe had talked confidently before the fight. "I like Holyfield," he said, "we'll still be friends afterward, but I think he has talked himself into a serious whipping."

Yet now, in the ring, Bowe looked away and his trainers worked hard to pump him up. The bell for round one hadn't rung yet, but they knew as well as Evander that the fight had already begun.

I took my seat, preparing myself for the battle that lay ahead.

The announcer's voice pierced the cold, desert air. The arena at Caesar's Palace was open to the dark sky, but intensely bright lights illuminated the ring.

"Weighing in at a solid 212 pounds, with an impressive professional record of twenty-nine wins and one defeat; '84 bronze medalist, the former heavyweight champion of the world, E-*van*-der 'The Real Deal' Hoooolllyfield."

The crowd responded with a mixture of cheers and boos.

"His opponent, fighting out of the Bronx with an impressive record of thirty-four wins and no losses, the un-dis-pu-ted heavyweight champion of the world, Riddick 'Big Daddy' Boooowe!"

Again, the Caesar's Palace crowd erupted. You couldn't tell who the crowd was for. In fact, you can never tell, not for long anyway. Fight crowds are the most fickle of any sport. Except for those who have placed a wager, they want a good bout even more than they want a desired result, and it's not unusual for a crowd to switch its affinity several times throughout a match.

When the opening bell rang, I lost my breath as Bowe unleashed a vicious opening right that caught Evander squarely on the head and shook him. Evander quickly realized that Bowe was attempting to make good on his promise to "hurt him" and take him out early. Suffering such a blow was the type of thing that, earlier in his career, might have immediately drawn Evander into a slugfest. No doubt, Bowe's camp hoped that would be the result. Instead, Evander recovered and began dancing. He was determined to fight *his* fight.

Beginning in the second round, it looked as if Evander was out to give Bowe a boxing lesson. He landed combination after combination. Bowe attempted to trap Evander into a corner and turn the bout into a brawl, but Evander was too fleet-footed and determined to let that happen. Evander would spin around Bowe and then follow up with a punishing combination to his jaw.

In round four, Evander began nailing Bowe with some punishing rights.

"It is done!" he said, as a right connected with Bowe's head.

"It is done!" he yelled, following up with a shot to the body.

"It is done!" he repeated.

Few people knew what the "It is done" was all about, but Evander's most physical form of prayer fed him as he tore into Bowe's body and head, opening up a cut between Bowe's left eye and nose. It was the first time in Bowe's professional career that he had to fight with blood pouring in his face. The match turned personal. The crowd joined in the bedlam, and the noise became so loud that when the bell to end that round sounded, nobody inside the ring—including the referee—heard it. Both fighters kept going. Evander's trainer, Emanuel Steward, finally jumped into the ring. The referee understood what was happening and finally brought the action to an end.

It was intense. What was really going on—especially after the fifth, when Evander almost ended the bout with a mighty blow just before the bell—was that Evander knew he could win, and he was eager to get it done. He had known he could win before the bout started, but now he was more confident than ever. Bowe knew it too, and he just wanted to punch his way out of this growing nightmare. In such a circumstance, it can take superhuman strength to let something as weak as a bell turn off your emotion.

Late in round six, Evander caught Bowe with a wicked combination that rocked him. Bowe wobbled backwards. Evander was on him, but Bowe was spared when the bell rang. Bowe sat down with a pronounced weariness. The effectiveness of Evander's strength training was written all over Bowe's face. His eyes had begun to swell and were in danger of closing. His cut man worked the bruises with fantastic energy, while his trainers tried to talk him back into the fight, offering him some kind of hope against Evander's punishing combinations.

I knew Bowe was troubled when the bell to begin round seven sounded. He took a deep breath before cautiously plodding toward the center of the ring. Evander came out dancing, and he soon began pasting combinations to Bowe's chin and rib cage. Bowe looked tired, and his tiredness seemed to pour more strength and energy into Evander. A blow to the head opened up another cut on Bowe.

The crowd rose to its feet. They sensed a knockout. Evander rocked Bowe again with a right cross and a follow-up hook. Bowe stumbled backwards.

"Oh! Ah!" the crowd yelled and winced along with Bowe.

Evander knew Bowe was hurt, and he began to pursue him with hard, bone-crushing knockout shots instead of combinations. He wanted to finish this fight as soon as possible.

My nephew started nudging me. "There's a guy up there. Look up at the ceiling."

The *last* thing I was about to do was to take my eyes off the ring. I didn't want to miss the knockout. Evander was working on Bowe, and both fighters knew that one forceful strike could end this bout.

As Evander landed another beautiful combination, setting Bowe up for a big blow, Evander's eyes went wide and his concentration was shot. He leapt to the side and entered the most confusing seconds of his life. Bowe saw from the look in Evander's eyes that something weird was happening. For one surreal minute, the two fighters eased up as a parachuter descended into the ring. The parachuter landed behind Bowe, so Evander got a good look at what was going on.

The overhead light started shaking, and Evander was busy trying to figure out which way it was going to fall. A light fixture had recently fallen on Curtis Mayfield, and this seemed like a crazy repeat of history.

Evander also thought about Monica Seles, the tennis player who had recently been stabbed during a tournament. It was so bizzare, seeing a parachuter come down, that Evander assumed the guy must have sinister intent.

The parachutist became tangled in a bank of lights that lit the ring just above Bowe's corner. Spectators yanked him down with vicious force, some of them punching him as they did so. The referee sent the fighters to their corners.

The crowd was like a nest of tarantulas that had been disturbed from their slumber. When the man fell into Bowe's corner, his supporters began cursing and quickly pounced upon the human fly (that's exactly what he looked like, caught in a web), kicking and hitting him with that most modern of twentieth-century weapons—mobile, cellular phones. I saw one or two chairs fly and knew the man was in trouble. He paid dearly for his intrusion, until security finally reached him.

The Rematch

The man looked like he had been beaten unconscious. If even half of the blows that I saw falling had struck him, I thought he'd be in pretty bad shape. The man looked to be unconscious, and security carried him out on a stretcher. (He was later treated for minor injuries and released the same night to a local jail.)

Evander waited impatiently in his corner, frustrated at the turn of events. He had Bowe on the run, and now Bowe would get extra time to heal. Bowe's corner worked furiously to stop a cut. Given enough time, an experienced cut man can stop virtually any wound from becoming a factor. Finally, the Nevada Boxing Commission director stepped in and stopped Bowe's corner from spending any more time on the wound.

The cold night air chilled Evander. The physical exertion required in a boxing match is fueled by adrenaline. Once the excitement builds, you don't realize how badly you hurt or how tired you are; you're just focused on completing the task at hand. But now Evander was forced to stand in the cold as each bruise slowly began to make itself known. Evander's muscles tightened. He felt knots growing on the back of his head. A small cramp started sticking him just above his right hip. Evander asked Hallmark to massage him and relieve the pain. Hallmark's work eventually got the cramp to quiet down, but Evander knew what he really needed was to get back out there. His body had been given a mixed signal. It was trained to accept the punishment, then heal after the fighting stopped. Now, it was being fooled. The fighting had stopped, and his body was trying to heal, but Evander still had half the match to go.

Evander had to work to keep himself from losing focus. He had been in a rhythm and was confident that he could outgun Bowe. As the delay wore on, he had to fight not to become upset and lose focus. It was difficult for him not to believe that the twenty-minute delay wouldn't benefit Bowe the most. The younger fighter's cut was given a chance to stop bleeding. His muscles would recover more quickly. He had been staggered, but now his head would be clear.

Evander knew that when the bout resumed it would be an entirely new fight. In other words, he'd have to beat Bowe twice. Twenty minutes is an eternity in the midst of a boxing match, enough time for a well-trained athlete to recover, regroup, and develop a new strategy.

Evander overcame the mental anguish and challenge by praying. He began pacing in his corner. Out of the corner of his eye, he noticed Bowe watching him. That was a good sign. Evander kept praying. "Thank You, Lord . . . Well, thank You, Lord." Peace assaulted the frustration that had been keeping Evander flustered.

"Thank You, Lord," he kept praying.

Finally Bowe, his eyes trained on Evander, jumped up off the stool and started walking too.

Evander remembered that the Las Vegas pastor had warned him, "Something strange is going to happen in this fight. Satan will try to defeat you with a distraction, but don't let it get your mind off what you're doing."

This was it. God had warned him. He couldn't let the devil have his day. This day belonged to the Lord.

Evander repeated his prayer, "Lord, here I am. Thy will be done."

Steward wanted to do his part to pump Evander up, so he encouraged him with what he knew would be most effective.

"You can win this, Evander," he shouted. "The fight is even right now, but you can get it. There's just one minute left in this round. Go out there and steal it. It's a bargain—you can win an entire round with sixty seconds' worth of work. Take the lead, right here. Just keep winning the rounds and you can go to church in the morning."

That's what Evander wanted to do. That's where he wanted to be. His mother had told him she hadn't raised a quitter. She was praying for him right now. He could picture himself back in Atlanta, sitting in church with his mother by his side.

That's what he wanted to do, and to get there, he had to get past Bowe. He had to win this fight.

The spiritual side of Evander took over. Evander believes that the spirit controls the body. "Your body says, 'I'm tired,'" he explains, "and your mind says, 'Keep going.'"

Now, Evander drew on the strength of his mind as he had never drawn on it before. He had to be ready. He had to make this night count.

Finally, the parachutist was carried out, the referee called both fighters back, and the bout resumed. It took about half a second for Evander to realize he faced a renewed fighter. Bowe came out swinging. The man whose weariness marked the last two rounds suddenly had new energy, and he began sticking Evander with some effective jabs.

My heart sank. I thought Evander had this bout sewn up. Now, he'd have to dig down and find another way to win.

Though Bowe came out strong to finish off the seventh round, Evander eked out a win. "You're up one round," Steward told him when he sat back down. "You're up one. Just keep it going."

Evander won the eighth even more clearly, reopening the cut on Bowe's nose. "You're up two, Champ," Emanuel shouted. "You're up two!"

They traded the ninth and tenth rounds, Evander taking the tenth with a solid right to the head that sent Bowe's mouthpiece flying. At the end of that round, Bowe lifted a weary glance toward Evander, sensing, as Evander did, that he was being beaten.

Evander kept up the pace and dominated the eleventh round. He could feel Bowe getting anxious, and he knew Bowe's corner was telling him he had to go for a knockout or face a loss by points. Bowe's anxiety led him to start telegraphing his punches. Evander could see where Bowe was planning to punch long before the now easily dodged swings came his way.

When the bell sounded, signaling the end of the eleventh round, Evander stood in the center of the ring as if he wanted the round to keep going, while Bowe listlessly walked off toward his corner, looking over his shoulder, wondering whether this was the same Evander Holyfield he had beaten fifty-one weeks ago.

Though it had been a close fight, it seemed clear that Evander had won. Provided there was no knockout in the twelfth, Evander knew the title was his. He came out conservatively while, predictably, Bowe came out looking for the knockout. Evander kept him off, and when the final bell sounded, neither fighter stopped fighting. Steward finally rushed into the ring and inadvertently tackled Evander while the referee pulled Bowe to his corner.

"Ladies and Gentlemen!" the announcer's voice rang out. "By unanimous decision—and for the second time—the New! heavyweight champion of the world, Evander 'the Real Deal' Hoooolllyfield!"

Bowe reached over and hugged Evander. "I was wrong about you," he said. "I am sorry. Let's do it again."

A brilliant smile covered Evander's face as trainers, reporters, officials, and celebrities flooded into the ring. Evander was elated. *Man, God is good,* he said to himself. *That first loss wasn't that bad after all.*

In the minds of the media, this was a story, if ever there was one. A 5-to-1 underdog faces a younger and stronger fighter who had already defeated him, yet he found a way to win. What was his secret?

Evander limited his response to just two sentences. He had told the media before the fight that he would win, and why. Now, he just wanted to remind them.

"First," he said, "I want to give thanks to my Lord and Savior Jesus Christ for giving me the victory. . . . I walk by faith and not by sight."

With those words, Evander left the ring. Everything had already been said and done. He would speak more words later, but for now, Evander enjoyed the sense of personal redemption. Winning back two of the three belts was great, but for Evander, the fight was more about proving himself, refusing to allow the boxing world to remember his career by one night's loss.

With the victory, Evander became only the fourth fighter in history to regain the heavyweight title of the world. He became only the third fighter—joining Muhammad Ali and Floyd Patterson—to regain the title in a rematch.

CHAPTER 18

FIGHTING THROUGH THE PAIN

Ahhh!" As Evander rolled out of bed, every nerve and muscle in his body screamed defiance. Evander could barely move his left shoulder, which felt as if it had been ripped and torn and left hanging. He reached up with his right hand to feel the back of his neck, and the knots he found there were so large and numerous they resembled a topographical map of a mountain region.

Not that he could press very hard. His hands were sore and swollen from the effect of landing several hundred blows on Bowe's hardened body. Scarcely a muscle or joint didn't pulsate with pain. Evander's elbow, his wrists, his legs—all felt weak and abused. There wasn't a spot on him that didn't remind him he had stood in a twenty-foot ring with the second best boxer in the world.

Yesterday morning, Evander could have ripped off hundreds of push-ups and sit-ups, skipped rope, and pounded a bag for hours. One day and twelve rounds later, it hurt to put on a T-shirt and to bend over to slip on a pair of shoes. Even taking a shower was painful.

As a cruiserweight, Evander had taken much less abuse and was usually back in training within a week after a bout. The force of Bowe's beating afforded no such luxury, however. Evander was forced to rest and suffer as his body worked to put itself back together.

As Evander hobbled from room to room, the boxing world swarmed all over the idea of an Evander Holyfield-Lennox Lewis match that would reunify all three titles. (Evander held the International Boxing Federation and the World Boxing Association titles, and Lewis held the World Boxing Council title.) The swelling hadn't even left Evander's hands when reporters began asking him about such a match.

"I'm hurting so bad, I don't even want to think about boxing," Evander replied. When it hurts to hold a glass of milk, it's a bit difficult to imagine pummeling another opponent for an hour and a half.

People like to add up how much money a boxer makes, dividing the minutes in the ring by the millions of dollars he earns. What that equation ignores is the amount of time spent preparing for a fight *and* the amount of time spent *recovering* from a fight.

Evander wanted to fight again, but for the first time in his career, he was seriously concerned about his body. "My body has to heal," he said. "If my body doesn't heal, I can't make a decision." Evander was finally discovering what everyone eventually discovers. A thirty-one-year-old body doesn't put itself back together as quickly as does a twenty-one-year-old body.

Sure he had won, but most people had no idea how much that victory had cost him. Bowe's height advantage had allowed him to pummel the backside of Evander as well as his face, and Evander had the welts on the back of his neck to prove it. "It felt like somebody was trying to pull my head off," he explained.

When a reporter pressed him on whether he would "come back" and when, Evander tried to mollify him by responding, "Fifty-fifty."

"Will it be finances or pride that brings you back?" the writer persisted.

"Neither," Evander said. "The pride's in check." And he had already earned more money at his sport than any athlete in the history of the world.

I couldn't help but compare the wild celebration and demands on Evander's time with the reception he had received after his first loss to Bowe. Everybody wanted a piece of him now. He was the same man, of course, but the interest of the public was radically different. Arsenio Hall wanted him on as soon as possible, and autograph seekers hunted him everywhere. People didn't drop their eyes in the airport after this fight. Instead, they raised their voices and shouted, "Way to go, champ! You did it, man!"

Evander went to a New York party, with plenty of other celebrities around, but suddenly *he was the man*. Everybody wanted to talk to *him*. When he went to a Knicks game, a cameraman put his face on the overhead screen, and the fans roared their approval.

And now David Letterman wanted to put him on his show. Though much of Letterman's comedy seems natural, he is too much of a professional to base everything on chance, so his handlers spent a good part of the day trying to "script" something funny that would occur as soon as Evander appeared on air.

They finally decided to stage a skit that would allude to a good-natured feud between Letterman and morning talk-show host Regis Philbin. As Evander faced Letterman in a mock sparring match, Evander was supposed to scowl and say, "What's Regis's number?"

Evander had never heard of Regis, but Kathy Duva told him it would be funny, so Evander went along with it, and it was funny.

Everywhere Evander went, he sought ways to talk about Jesus. Those around him began to take notice. A writer for *Sports Illustrated* explained it this way: "Holyfield is prodigious in prayer. That's what he does; that's what he's about; that's what defines and confines him. He prays, goes to church, reads the Bible, talks about God."

Evander's faith kept growing with his success. As more and more women threw themselves at him, as more and more businesspeople approached him with the next great money-making idea, as more and more people attempted to build their own careers and bank accounts on the back of Evander's success, Evander realized his one true friend, the One who would never abuse him, leave him, trick him, or let him down, was Jesus Christ. Evander knew that if he had lost his last bout, Letterman would be talking to Riddick Bowe, not Evander Holyfield.

God wasn't nearly so fickle.

So Evander stuck with his faith. When fans asked for an autograph, they got Philippians 4:13 as well.

Evander's one loss had taught him that to the general public, he would only be as popular as his last fight. He enjoyed the acclaim—he had worked hard, after all—but the acclaim wouldn't keep him fighting. He'd have to find something else.

I'm Back

This time, it was for the titles.

As Evander's body healed, his resolve to return to the ring grew. It wasn't for the money. Evander had already earned plenty of that. But because Bowe had lost (by forfeit) the WBC title, Evander had regained just two of his titles, and Evander wanted to "reel that one in too."

"I think it's very important for boxing to have one champion," Evander explained. "There should only be one heavyweight champion of the world."

That's why, even though Evander was offered $20 million to fight Bowe for a third time, Evander didn't bite. "I didn't come back for the money," he said. "I came back for the titles."

Unfortunately, with tens of millions of dollars changing hands, it's becoming increasingly difficult to keep money out of it. Evander wanted the last remaining title back, but his promoters wanted him to fight right away—and to go through Michael Moorer first. That bout would earn millions of dollars before Holyfield and Lewis fought for it all.

Though Moorer was a very skilled fighter, he was no Riddick Bowe. Even so, Evander hesitated to face him right away because his left shoulder, which he had injured in the fight with Bowe, was still bothering him. Evander knew he needed more time to recover before entering another heavy period of training. As soon as he announced he would fight again, however, his promoters began pushing him to make a decision within the next ten days.

Negotiations with the IBF called for Evander to face Moorer, but Moorer had agreed to step aside if he could be guaranteed a shot at the winner of Holyfield-Lewis. Evander's promoters came back to him with the scenario of fighting Moorer in the spring and Lewis in the fall.

Evander balked. He had serious reservations about an April bout. Since his shoulder was still sore—he had fought Bowe less than eight weeks earlier—it would be difficult to begin heavy training, which he would need to start right away for an April bout.

But Evander's promoters insisted that this was the best (meaning most profitable) route to go.

"Look, Evander," the promoters said, "this guy is going to self-destruct. It's not even going to be a tough bout. You can take him out early. This will be a much easier fight."

The boxing world wanted to see it happen, and Evander felt as if he had the entire world pushing him to do something he didn't want to do—face another bout before his shoulder healed. Evander was predisposed to give in. He hates few things more than he hates empty excuses. He had learned long ago that excuses are a top athlete's worst enemy, the first step toward a declining career, so Evander was hypersensitive to anything that even resembled an excuse. He had trained through pain before, he told himself; why couldn't he do it again?

Evander gave in and agreed to fight Moorer in April.

Pleasing others always proved disastrous for Evander. When he tried to please the critics by going for the knockout against Bowe in their first fight, it cost Evander his first titles. Now, wanting to please the boxing world by coming back too soon, Evander was placing his titles in jeopardy for a second time.

Evander was made to fight for God. When he did that, he won. When he fought for others, it became an entirely different story.

Money Mayhem

The Holyfield-Moorer fight was preceded by several controversies surrounding Evander and his management. Whatever the motives, people questioned whether the thirty-one-year-old champ was wise enough to begin making his own decisions. Evander chose to replace his trainer, and former employees of Evander questioned whether the new trainer, Don Turner, would be "strong enough" to direct Evander during a fight. Evander's perspective was clear.

"I've been fighting for twenty-three years. When a person has fought as long as I have, he knows when he wants to hit to the body. I don't need someone telling me. I do listen, but I have to put it together."

People second-guessed Evander, as if he was still a young kid trying to make good. Evander was no longer a young kid, however; he was a multimillionaire and two-time heavyweight champion of the world.

Still, people resent it when an athlete—and let's face it, especially a black athlete—starts to make smart business decisions.

An entire cadre of people had already made their money off Evander's success. He considered many of them to be good friends. Over the years, Evander allowed them to work for a percentage of his earnings. Some of the people were with Evander when he was earning $60,000 a fight, then $600,000 a fight, and now $20 million a fight—and their percentage had stayed the same. The numbers that people were making were getting ridiculous. Evander's cut man— who would work one evening and who might never have to patch a cut—would often make more money for one bout with Evander than he would make with fifty other less-talented fighters throughout the year.

As a good businessman, Evander knew it was time to make a change. He wanted to pay his people fairly, but on the other hand, he didn't want to be taken advantage of, so he approached them and soon discovered who was there for Evander Holyfield and who was there for the money.

"Look guys," Evander said, "I've been fighting ten, twelve, fifteen years. You guys have more than made your money's worth. I could do the whole thing myself, but I don't want to alienate you guys. You're more than my managers and trainers; you're my friends. But I need to cut these numbers down because they're way out of line with the rest of the industry. You're making more money off me than you make working for everyone else the rest of the year. You've already made a ton of money, so let's be fair."

Disgruntled employees who saw their easy cash-in being threatened tried to make Evander look like a miser. The truth is, he was just being a good businessman. Boxing annals are full of talented fighters who took a bruising but ended up with little to show for it, while their trainers and managers lived a life of leisure.

Evander was acutely aware of the fact that he couldn't box forever. His trainers, promoters, and cut man, on the other hand, could work their entire lives. You can train or manage a fighter when you're in your eighties, but you can't fight in the ring when you're in your fifties (and before George Foreman, almost nobody fought in their forties).

Even though the payout for a title fight can sound huge, if a boxer isn't careful, he may end up with less than 40 percent of the purse—and that's *before* he pays taxes. If management is getting 33 percent, and a promoter is getting 20 percent, and the trainer gets 10 percent, and a cut man is getting paid, and training expenses run another 7 to 10 percent, not to mention your own personal expenses, it's not difficult to see how a fighter who earned millions of dollars in his career ends up living off social security.

Evander was the only one who ever got hit, but he wasn't the only one who was becoming wealthy. He was no longer a carefree kid who fought for recreation and respect. He now had an entire business to run, and he was qualified to make the decisions. Also, Evander was two-time heavyweight champion of the world. A trainer could fine-tune him, but the trainer was by no means teaching Evander how to box. Ironically, as less and less became required of his entourage, they expected more and more.

Evander finally offered his trainer, Emanuel Steward, a flat fee—
$250,000 for six weeks' work. Steward said that wasn't enough.
Evander's former cut man asked for $25,000—to be on call for an
hour and a half. Instead, Evander hired Don Turner to serve as both
a trainer and a cut man.

This experience provided a tough lesson. When you're wealthy
and famous, you never really know who your friends are. How do
you know if this person who now always wants to be around you
(and whose livelihood depends upon you) would even go out to eat
with you if you were making $35,000 a year? The truth is, you can't
know, and that's why Evander stays close with family and boyhood
friends, the people who were there before he became heavyweight
champion of the world and the people who will be there long after
his record is just another line in the annals of boxing history.

Stunned

Thirty minutes before the Moorer fight, Evander went through
some of his routine stretches—only this time, while moving his
left shoulder, he suddenly halted and grimaced. Every face in the
locker room became serious. Tim Hallmark stepped forward.

"What's wrong, Holy?"

"My shoulder," Evander responded. The shoulder had continued to bother him during training. When it got really bad, a doctor
was usually able to reduce the discomfort to somewhere between
irritating and bearable, but because of his training, the shoulder had
never been given a chance to fully heal.

Faced with such a serious injury, most fighters would have pulled
out of the bout long before it got this close. Evander had had several
opponents (including Tyson) cancel a bout because of a training-
induced injury. But Evander is incapable of willingly quitting anything. He had always trained through bruises, aches, and pains.
Rather than withdraw, Evander fought through such annoyances, so
he naturally assumed that the sore shoulder wouldn't be any different.

He'd fight through this too.

Evander's sudden halt during routine stretches was not a good
sign. A heavyweight boxer will throw hundreds of blows during a
fight. Those blows either miss, which can stretch the muscles, or

they connect with a conditioned and hardened body, in which case the jarring is enormous. Just try to hit a heavy bag one hundred times, as hard as you can, and you'll see what I mean.

A sore shoulder *before* a fight signals serious trouble, and the Holyfield camp found itself in the position of trying to remain positive just as a tank was driving through its front door. Hallmark immediately began massaging Evander's shoulder, trying to loosen it up. Evander finally shrugged and said he would be fine.

As round one opened, Evander's decision to go forward with the bout looked like the right one. Evander jabbed and scored with combinations that kept Moorer off balance. During the second round, Evander really got moving. His arms resembled pistons as they jabbed back and forth and worked their way over Moorer's head and body.

Moorer was confused. Desperation covered his face as he tried to counter Evander's quickness and darting blows. At first he attempted to dodge Evander's machine-like blows, hoping to follow up with a combination of his own, but Evander rarely missed. The few times he did miss, he recovered so quickly that Moorer was back on the defensive before being able to mount an assault of his own.

Then, during the second round, Evander connected with a strong left hook to Moorer's chin. The challenger dropped like a bowling pin. Just as Evander unleashed his shot, however, he felt an excruciating pain rip through his left shoulder. Suddenly, his upper body felt like it was on fire, and the nerve endings were screaming underneath his skin.

Moorer stayed on one knee while the referee began his count. Evander couldn't believe how badly his shoulder hurt. His adrenaline usually keeps him impervious to most pain, so he has always feared weariness more than he's ever feared another fighter's punch. But this ache was excruciating, the kind that makes you want to scream "Amputate!" just so you can have a moment's reprieve.

Moorer finally rose after the referee counted to seven, and the challenger put his gloves to his chin in the ready position, signaling to the referee that he was able to continue.

Evander knew he had two tasks in front of him: take out the wounded man in front of him and find a way to mask his injury. He didn't want either his face or his swings to signal that anything was wrong with his shoulder, but he had never felt a pain like this before.

As the two fighters reengaged, Evander lifted his left hand and held it out in a pawing motion.

The arm had almost no strength. As far as a heavyweight was concerned, the arm was virtually useless.

I'm gonna have to fight this man with one arm, Evander thought.

The bell rang shortly after Moorer rose, and Evander went back to his corner. Normally, he'd be elated that he had barely missed a knockout, but now he began wondering how he could keep fighting when one arm had stopped working.

"My shoulder's hurt really bad," he told Hallmark.

Hallmark immediately began working the shoulder, but it wouldn't respond. Evander knew it was something much deeper than a cramp or even a slight pull. No amount of massaging was going to bring it back.

When the third round began, the spectators were looking for the final knockout. Evander had dominated Moorer through two rounds, dropping him in the second, and now, with a full round ahead of him, Evander was expected to finish the job.

But nobody knew about the shoulder.

Evander uses his left jab to set up his combinations and hooks. As he gingerly moved his shoulder in the third round, he was unable to get it to respond. Instead of jabbing and following through with a combination, Evander began gently pawing with his left hand, using it only as a distraction, while he waited to unload with his right arm. If he could last one or two more rounds, Evander figured the shoulder might come back.

It never did. Evander was forced to fight Moorer with one arm for the rest of the bout. His courage and resolve were enough to conceal most of the damage, however, and amazingly, Evander stayed in the fight right until the end. In fact, after the eighth round, Moorer returned to his corner, only to find his trainer, Teddy Atlas, sitting on his stool.

"You don't want to do what it takes to become champion," Atlas yelled. "Let me do it. You can go outside and watch."

In the later rounds, Evander's strategy of paw-with-the-left, unload-with-the-right finally met its end. Forced to make his right shoulder do the work of two arms, Evander literally blew it out. He could move it, but there was no strength behind it.

Moorer's trainers finally caught on. They tried their best to inspire the tired challenger just before the eleventh round. Moorer's tiredness and pain made it somewhat difficult for him to believe that the champ was truly hurt, but Atlas was all over him, telling him to take it to Evander.

Without his arms to protect him, Evander's head began to take a terrific beating. At one point, it hurt so much to lift his shoulders, Evander just let Moorer beat his face. He sustained a couple of facial cuts, and his eyes started to swell. What was worse was that Evander felt the pain of each blow he *gave*. His shoulder hurt as much giving a blow as Moorer must have hurt receiving it. This was a bitter injury for a boxer in the midst of a bout.

All of a sudden, the champ offered little defense and only listless offense. Moorer's trainers sensed an upset.

"Mike, go get him!" they told Moorer. "His shoulder is hurting; he's not moving. You can win this fight. He's yours!"

I heard one of them add, "Mike, there comes a time in a fighter's life when he has to seize the moment. This is your moment. Go out and seize it!"

Heartened by Evander's injury, Moorer found new energy and became more aggressive. He ended the twelfth round with a flurry. When the final bell rang, Moorer's people ran out and lifted him in the air as if he had won the fight simply by going the distance with Evander. He had almost been knocked out in the second round, and his trainers were elated that he had been able to recover and hang in here.

For his part, Evander walked back to his corner, looking for a fire extinguisher to put out the flames that now enveloped both shoulders. The pain was excruciating and unrelenting.

I knew Evander was hurting, but I also thought he had done a reasonably good job of keeping it hidden for as long as possible. I felt confident that his strong showing in the early rounds would be enough to pull out the fight. Evander felt that way too. His sore shoulder kept him from defending himself as he would have liked, but he felt confident that he had landed enough blows to retain his title.

In a tough, 3–2 decision, however, the judges went for Moorer. Evander had lost his titles again.

The Moorer camp exploded with delight. Evander was surprised, but in his characteristic fashion, he looked for the positive spin. *Well,* he said to himself, *God just gave me a chance to become three-time heavyweight champion of the world!*

But both Evander and the boxing world were soon to learn that the real fight for Evander Holyfield had just begun.

CHAPTER 19

NOT BY MIGHT

The next few hours were long ones.

Back in the locker room, Evander told his doctor that his shoulders were killing him. The doctor immediately suspected (correctly) a rotator cuff injury. He asked Evander to pass urine, but when Evander tried, he couldn't. He was too dehydrated. The doctor then discovered a kidney bruise, and his medical mind switched to red alert.

Evander was taken to a hospital. As Evander lay on the stretcher, he realized he was entering a different arena. Just minutes before, he was an active participant in the most physical sport in the world. Now he was a passive observer. His body would be poked and probed, tested and stuck, and all he could do was lie there and pray the doctors knew what they were doing.

As soon as Evander arrived, the doctors began pumping him with fluids while giving him morphine for the pain. This combination produced a dangerous effect. The morphine affected the ability of Evander's heart to operate at full capacity as the extra fluids were being plunged into his body.

Evander's lungs began to fill because his heart wasn't strong enough to pump the fluids out. In essence, the overly aggressive treatment was sending him into heart failure.

The physicians ordered that Evander be flown in an air ambulance to the hospital at Emory University, which is nationally recognized for its heart-treatment capabilities. Emory is in Atlanta, so Evander was going home, but it was hardly the homecoming he anticipated or hoped for.

My entire family was shaken when we heard the news. The aftermath of every recent fight had been different—pandemonium after the bout with Douglas, silence and ostracism after the loss to

Bowe, bedlam after the win over Bowe, and now concern over the champ's health after Moorer.

While *we* were concerned about Evander's health, *he* was primarily concerned about the loss of his titles—especially since they were relinquished through such a narrow 3–2 decision. The doctors could tell him he was going into heart failure, but Evander didn't *feel* as though he were.

Instead of worrying about his heart, Evander tried to understand the judges' decision to give the bout to Moorer. As the judges' scorecards became available, Evander found out that there were objective reasons for him to be disappointed with the scoring.

One of the judges had recorded the knockdown in the second round as a "flash" (incidental) knockdown and thus scored the round even. He was the only judge (of five) to do that. (A writer from *Sports Illustrated* wrote, "Holyfield floored Moorer in the second round, something more than a flash knockdown . . .") It's difficult to imagine how a judge could score a blow that kept Moorer on his knees until the count of seven as a "flash knockdown," but that's what he did. Had the judge scored the round 10–9 as the other judges did, Evander would have won.

Evander respected Michael Moorer but also knew he had fought—and defeated—better fighters in the past. While he was still in the hospital recovering from his injuries, Evander called his managers and asked them to arrange a rematch with Moorer as soon as possible.

They were shocked. Here they thought Evander's health was in serious jeopardy, but he was already talking about climbing back into the ring! Evander just assumed that the doctors would be able to "put him back together" and that he could regain the titles. The last thing he wanted to do was end his career after such a fight. In fact, he was eager to follow in the footsteps of Muhammad Ali and capture the title for a third time.

The doctors got Evander through the immediate danger, but they insisted on performing more tests, so Evander was kept in the hospital for several days. It was a sobering moment when the doctors finally came into Evander's room and said they couldn't "fix" Evander at all. They told him he had a nonthreatening, but career-ending, heart problem. In fact, he had not one but two heart problems.

Evander can barely recall receiving the news. The doctors had him pretty drugged up by this point, so his will was weakened.

The boxing world was awed when they heard the news. The *Atlanta Journal* proclaimed, "It was a miracle he finished the fight." Dr. Ron Stephens, Evander's personal physician, agreed. "Mr. Holyfield fought this fight in heart failure, and it's an absolute miracle he could fight this fight for twelve rounds in this condition."

A cardiologist, Dr. Douglas Morris, confirmed Stephens's assessment. "His heart was not functioning at its maximum level."

In layman's terms, what the doctors discovered was that Evander had a "stiff heart." The left ventricle, which is the main pumping chamber, was "noncompliant," that is, it wasn't pumping enough blood. Some experts think this was caused by the overmedication that occurred after the bout. Evander also had an "atrial septal defect," a tiny hole, in his heart. While not life-threatening, the doctors unanimously recommended that Evander retire from the ring.

When his condition was announced, Evander had little choice but to comply with the recommendation. Since his boxing license was immediately revoked, he wouldn't be allowed to fight anyway. He accepted the doctor's comments and was grateful that he could live a normal life. It was still hard for him to believe he had had a sort of heart attack.

If that was a heart attack, he thought, *I done had a lot of heart attacks in my life.*

So while the doctors told him there was nothing they could do for him, Evander silently turned to the doctor who could. *Lord Jesus, please heal me,* he prayed, then repeated the Bible verse, *By the Lord's stripes, I am healed.*

If there is a problem, he said to himself, *it's already taken care of.*

The doctors didn't share Evander's optimism. Every one of them told him in no uncertain terms that his career was over. Evander didn't believe anything was wrong with his heart, but he also knew the doctors were more qualified than he to make that judgment.

"I am a fighter and an expert in the ring," Evander said. "The doctors are the experts in the medical field." Because they were the experts, he thought it best to heed their advice, and called for a press conference to announce his retirement.

People came out from all over the city to attend the press conference. Many of them had tears in their eyes because they thought Evander was going to die if he got overly excited. Though these people were mistaken, I was moved by their concern. Twenty-some years ago, Evander was just another kid off the streets trying to make good. Not too many people cared back then. But God had blessed Evander, and Evander had responded by literally fighting his heart out. The people loved him for it, and they came to show their respect. God had given Evander a stage. What the people attending the press conference didn't realize was that the play was really just about to begin.

Evander and I both believed that God could make something good come even out of this. Some of the fans thought we were crazy, but Evander and I remembered the Bible verse that was often quoted by our grandmother: "All things work together for good, for those that love God and are called according to His purposes."

"Grandmother always told us the emphasis is on 'all things,' especially *bad* things," I explained to one of the fans attending the press conference. "That means loss, sickness, persecution, and even heart problems. When you are a child of God, He will bring something good and positive out of a bad situation if you acknowledge Him and His word."

The guy looked at me like I was crazy. When he saw I was serious, he finally turned his head and looked straight at the platform.

It was then that I realized God had plans even bigger than Evander or I could ever imagine.

During the press conference, Evander thanked God for what he had been able to accomplish. "I thank the Lord that I had twenty-three good years in boxing and that I accomplished all my goals—Boy's Club champion, state champion, making the Olympic team, world heavyweight champion—twice."

He also gave God credit for the miraculous perseverance he displayed in finishing the Moorer fight. "The Lord gives you the strength to finish anything," he said. "You can't quit. I bore the pain."

Evander believed that his accomplishments in the ring could encourage people to succeed outside the ring. If a poor, black, fatherless boy from Atlanta can overcome the obstacles to become heavyweight champion of the world, there was nothing a single mother, an unemployed worker, or a disabled person couldn't accomplish as well. Evander wanted them to know that they could do it. They would have to pay the price, as he had, but with Christ, they could do it.

After the press conference, Evander went home and prayed. It was a familiar, warm, and comfortable feeling to be back on his knees, the posture he assumed when facing all the transitional and difficult moments of his life. His knees were as used to kneeling as his hands were used to being covered by two boxing gloves.

"Lord," he began, "thank You for allowing me to have such a successful career. Thank You for letting me get through the heart problem without any serious injury. I still love You, Lord, and now I ask that You tell me where You want me to go.

"What do You want me to do now, God?" he asked.

The Real Deal Gets a Real Heal

Shortly after Evander offered his prayer for direction, he went to church. His pastor assured him that God had a great calling on his life. "If you think God was using you as a heavyweight champion, just wait until you see what else He has planned."

Evander felt his injured heart leap. He didn't know *what* God was calling him to, but he was elated *that* God was calling him at all.

"Somebody's going to come into your life," the pastor said, "somebody with the spiritual insight you need to achieve God's will."

"Okay!" Evander said. The former champ was elated. He drove home, praising and worshiping God. "Thank You, Lord, for hearing my prayer," he said. "I don't know what You want me to do yet, but I know you've already sent the answer."

Evander parked his car and walked into his house. He began sorting through his mail and felt a spiritual tug when he came across a small white envelope. In it was a letter written by a woman he had never heard of.

"Evander, you don't know me," the letter began, "but I believe God told me to write you."

Evander contacted the woman, and the two began meeting for Bible study. After several sessions, she asked Evander, "Have you ever heard of Benny Hinn?"

"No."

"Well, this man has the touch! I went to one of his crusades, and I was healed."

"What's that got to do with me?" Evander asked.

"Just go ask your pastor about it," the woman said.

Benny Hinn, a Christian evangelist from Florida, often speaks of divine healings during his crusades. Evander believed he had already been healed, but with his pastor's recommendation, Evander was always up for attending a gathering of other Christians. If a large group of people are getting together to worship God, Evander wants to be a part of it.

The problem is, somebody with Evander's notoriety can't just show up and sit in the back. Evander ended up sitting on the stage at Hinn's Philadelphia crusade. His ailment had made national news, and there was an understandable excitement in the crowd as Evander stood in front of Hinn.

Steve Brock, who helped Benny lead the Philadelphia crusade, introduced Evander as the "greatest heavyweight of all time." He informed the crowd that Evander was already thinking about coming back into the ring.

Benny had asked Evander if he came for a healing, but Evander told him, "No. I believe I'm already healed. I came to be close to God."

As Brock stood by Evander's side, Benny told the crowd, "I'm gonna pray that God would heal his heart, if there's anything wrong with it, which I don't think there is. But we're gonna pray anyways, just for blessed assurance."

Evander was given a few moments to address the crowd. He spoke of his faith, then added, "None of my trainers and friends could go into the ring with me—but I always knew that the Lord could."

The crowd leapt to their feet and clapped their hands.

Evander sat down as Benny began the "miraculous" segment of the service. As people sang, prayed, and called out to the Lord, Hinn reached out to a portion of the audience. Benny walked around the crowd, touching and praying for individuals. Near the end of the service, Hinn asked people who wanted to rededicate their lives to God to come forward. Evander's heart quickened. That was exactly his heart's desire.

With Evander standing up front, Hinn walked across the stage. He turned in Evander's direction and shouted out in his "prayer language." Hinn was standing about six feet away from the former champ, and with his right arm made a large, sweeping motion in Evander's direction.

Evander felt himself falling and tried to resist, but his legs didn't respond. His fall was different from anything he had ever felt. Instead of having his knees buckle, as you would expect, Evander dropped directly back, as if somebody had pushed him and he was too unconscious even to move his legs. It was the first time in his life that he had been "slain in the spirit."

Two men standing next to Evander caught him and laid him out on the stage. Evander felt his heart racing, and a warm feeling spread through his chest.

Hinn's voice rose, and he began calling out healings that were taking place. Finally, he turned toward Evander and said, "The Lord is telling me right now He is repairing Holyfield's heart completely."

Evander felt coddled in God's presence. When he heard Hinn say, "His heart is being healed," he rejoiced at the news, receiving it as a confirmation of something that he believed had already happened.

The service went on for hours, but as soon as it was over, a reporter was standing by to talk to Evander. Evander goes out of his way to be good-natured to the press, but this approach on this night was discouraging. He didn't travel to Philadelphia to make a statement or to generate any religious controversy. He just wanted to enjoy an evening of worship. His status as a celebrity, however, never took a break.

The writer seemed eager to capitalize on what he believed could become a sensational headline. "Are you healed?" he asked Evander.

"Yes," Evander responded.

The reporter's words became rushed in their eagerness. "Are you healed because Benny Hinn healed you?"

"No. What Benny did was confirm that I am being healed."

"Are you going to fight again?"

"I don't know," Evander replied.

After the service, Hinn suggested that Evander return to his doctor for an updated prognosis, which Evander already planned to do. His boxing license had been revoked, and Evander didn't expect the boxing commission to accept a miraculous healing from God without verifiable proof.

The next week, he paid a visit to his doctor, confident that God was putting his body back together.

After some tests, the doctor said, "You're getting better."

Evander received this news with confident assurance. He wasn't completely better, but he knew that sometimes healing is a process. God had begun that process, and eventually, he'd be well.

Evander went back to the doctor a second time. More improvement had occurred, but the doctor couldn't yet pronounce him completely healed.

On the third visit, the doctor couldn't believe the X-rays he was looking at and sought a second and third opinion. All the doctors consulted looked shocked and had to be convinced that the "before" and "after" X-rays really were of the same heart. When assured that they were, the doctors agreed that Evander's heart was healed.

Evander was elated, but not surprised. God had already worked major miracles in his life. While it seems extraordianry to some that God would actually heal a person's heart, Evander *expected* it because he had already seen God move in many miraculous ways.

The media couldn't handle it, however. They began lampooning Evander for "seeking out the services" of a "faith healer." Some even suggested that Evander's contribution to Hinn was "payment" for the healing.

There were two misunderstandings here. First, Evander believed God had begun healing him when he and his pastor had prayed shortly after the diagnosis was first made. The fact that the doctor noticed gradual improvement showed that God began the healing, which Hinn later *confirmed*. The healing began before Evander met Hinn, and it wasn't complete until after Hinn left town.

Second, Evander's contribution to Hinn might seem large to most people, but Evander, as a committed Christian, believes in tithing. When you make tens of millions of dollars a year, a contribution of several hundred thousand dollars isn't too large a gift. That's the level at which Evander gives. On several occasions I have found out only by accident about similar gifts Evander has made to schools, churches, and ministries. Evander believes in giving, but his goal is always to give in secret.

Flush with the excitement of his healing, Evander once again sought God in prayer to determine why God had healed him. Was he supposed to fight again? Could he become heavyweight champion of the world for a third time?

However God led, Evander knew that any return to the ring would be a gift. As such, he'd have to return for the Lord, not himself.

"Are you coming back into the ring?" a reporter badgered him.

Evander responded, "If I get back in the ring, it will be to glorify the Lord, not myself. It will be God's will, not mine. If He wills for me to come back, then I will for me to come back too. But I need a sign from Him that it's really His will."

Though Evander believed in God's healing, boxing officials were a bit more skeptical. Randy Gordon, chairman of the New York

State Athletic Commission, said that Evander would have to pass a series of physicals before any state commission would license him to fight again.

Over the next few days, Evander became more and more convinced that God was calling him to return to the ring. This wasn't just a case of wishful thinking. Evander had actually been enjoying retirement. People still called him champ, but he didn't have to get hit to earn the title. People would tell him, "Oh, you could beat so-and-so," and Evander could smile and help himself to another serving of apple pie.

But one afternoon, a little boy saw him eating at a restaurant and said, "Mr. Holyfield, when Jesus healed somebody, didn't they get up and walk?"

"Yes, they did," Evander answered.

"If Jesus healed you, shouldn't you get up and fight?"

Evander smiled, swallowed his sandwich, and said to himself, *Here I go again. I done talked myself into boxing again.*

Evander realized he had an opportunity to make a powerful statement about faith by returning to the ring. It wasn't the money. "What can I do with more money?" he asked. It wasn't the fame. "How can I be more famous?" he asked. Now, it wasn't even the titles—he had held those *twice*. This time, it would be about demonstrating the power of faith and showing people how God could help them overcome their own trials.

The boxing commission insisted that Evander be checked out by the top hospital in the nation: the Mayo Clinic in Rochester, Minnesota. They didn't want a boxer to drop dead in the midst of a fight.

Evander went to the Mayo Clinic and underwent an intense battery of tests. They checked him out from head to toe. They checked out his lungs by having him blow into a tube. He ran on a treadmill while they drew blood. They did stress tests. By the time they were through with him, Evander knew what a laboratory rat must feel like.

Evander was confident throughout the experience, but there was still a great deal of emotion and thankfulness when the doctors gave him the results. "Your heart is not only healthy," Evander heard the Mayo Clinic doctor say, "but you are more healthy than anyone I have ever examined. If any heart can live to be a hundred years old, yours is one of them."

Evander's smile outshone his heart. *God is good,* he said to himself. *God is really good.*

After his tests at the Mayo Clinic, the boxing world was buzzing about a possible Holyfield return to the ring. Evander didn't make them wait for long.

"Now that you've been cleared medically, are you coming back?" a reporter asked.

Evander smiled and said, "Why would God heal me if I wasn't going to fight?" He thought back to the little boy in the restaurant and added, "When God healed the lame man, he didn't continue to lay down, he got up and walked."

Fire and Brimstone

Just days after Evander was cleared to fight again, he began talking about who his next opponent should be. He wanted somebody tough. If he chose a pretender, people might question whether God had really healed his heart. Evander wanted this bout to prove the power of God, and God's power wouldn't be demonstrated by fighting a straw man.

He settled on Ray Mercer. Mercer was a 1984 Olympic gold medalist. He was bigger and stronger than Evander, and nobody could accuse him of being a tomato can. Evander knew that by choosing to fight Mercer he would be sending a clear message to the fans that he was looking for a real fight.

The bout ended up being scheduled for Atlantic City, New Jersey, on May 20, 1995. If anyone doubted why God would want to bring Evander back, the early days of March made that abundantly clear.

God needed an ambassador.

Because Evander was scheduled to return with a fight in New Jersey, he was on many young people's minds in that state. In early March, however, a white police officer fatally shot an unarmed black youth.

Several days of bedlam followed. Protests bordering on riots increased in their intensity. The police couldn't quell the anxiety, because they were a major cause of it. The air was thick with dread, hatred, and tension. Finally, a Baptist pastor asked Evander if he could pay a visit to New Jersey and bring some sanity to the situation.

Evander was pleased to come. His success inside the ring has given him a platform to minister to people outside the ring and Evander feels obligated to God to use that platform wisely. His status as a world-class athlete has given him access to inner-city schools as well as the executives and employees of some of the largest corporations in the world.

"Because I'm a boxer," Evander explains, "there are certain types of people I can get to, people who wouldn't give a pastor the time of day. They see me, and they know I don't want their money, 'cause I have all the money I need. I don't want their vote, 'cause I'm not running for any office.

"So they see me and think, 'Look at this man, he's got money, he's got fame, why is he talking about Jesus? Why would Evander Holyfield, with all that money, why would he try to con somebody? He must really believe what he's talking about.'"

This gives Evander the credibility to address certain situations nobody else wants to touch. The situation in New Jersey in the spring of 1995 was one of those.

The champ was greeted by hundreds of people at the Christ Temple Baptist Church. Evander looked at home in the pulpit. God had prepared him, just as he had prepared the Old Testament Queen Esther "for such a time as this." Evander knew how the residents felt. He had faced racism himself. The sight of his beloved and bloody Lassie would never leave his mind. Evander couldn't forget standing by Lassie's grave with his brothers, unable to understand why a man in uniform would do something that was so clearly wrong.

Most of the people didn't know about Lassie, but they knew Evander cared. And they listened when he told them that hatred never conquers hatred.

"I know the teaching of the Good Book," he began, "and that's always forgiveness. When you love God, you can love yourself, you can love others. When you're violent, you can't win. There are other ways to fight brutality. You can take a badge number and report him instead of fighting and losing a battle. It's a no-win situation when you fight a cop, but you can write a letter about him and get something done."

Evander urged the parents to get involved. Though he was forced to grow up without a dad, Evander remembered how Carter Morgan had helped guide him toward a productive life.

"People ask me, am I a role model? Of course I am, but you are too. You're the parent. Why would you want your kids to look up to me, when you're with them every day?"

Some cynics—displaying a complete misunderstanding of Evander's sport—asked how Evander, a boxer, could possibly speak against violence.

"What I do is not violent," Evander explained. "Violence is when somebody is in a rage of madness. There is no rage when I enter the ring. It's a skilled sport." Evander remembered the hugs after some of his most difficult bouts, and Bowe's comments that he hoped he and Evander could be friends. True fighters were true competitors, but they left their rage in the ring. They never brought it home to the neighborhood.

It's impossible to know how much impact Evander's visit had on Patterson, New Jersey, but already, Evander could see God's blessing on his comeback. Evander had no way of knowing when the bout was scheduled in Atlantic CIty that he would need a high profile in New Jersey to help avert a citywide disaster. But God knew, and Evander felt confident that God was directing his steps.

Evander faced a prepared and well-trained Ray Mercer in May. Though Mercer was an underdog, experts pointed out that Evander was coming to the ring with the baggage of many brutal fights behind him.

"George Foreman, Larry Holmes, Bert Cooper, two fights with Riddick Bowe, Michael Moorer," Larry Holmes said in the prefight analysis, "all tough fights. They had to take something out of him."

What Holmes didn't realize was that he was confirming what Evander had set out to do early in his career—fight the toughest and best boxers of his generation.

Evander dominated Mercer in the early rounds, raising a mouse under Mercer's left eye and using his speed to keep Mercer off balance. The bout became a slugfest in the middle rounds, and Evander became puzzled. He had approached the fight eager to show people how God had healed him, so he entered the ring with great expectations, including a knockout. Now that the fight was half over and Mercer was still standing, Evander didn't understand.

Standing in the middle of round six, Evander prayed, *Lord, You healed me. Why haven't I knocked this boy out?*

No sooner had the prayer escaped his lips than Mercer's head came crashing into Evander's right eye, causing a cut and making Evander bleed.

Evander caught himself. He was doing more thinking than boxing. Here he was, in the midst of the fight—*in the middle of a round*—but he was preoccupied and busy questioning God.

Evander, the champ said to himself, *God healed your heart. That's more incredible than any knockout. You still have to work to win these fights. You've got to quit chatting and start working. God healed you to work, so get busy!*

That's exactly what Evander did, meticulously winning every round that followed. In the seventh round, Evander had Mercer backing up. He dropped Mercer in the eighth round—the first and only time that's happened in Mercer's professional career. Evander opened up a cut below Mercer's right eye in the ninth round, and the two men slugged it out in the tenth and final round.

The *New York Daily News* said Evander's return bout "restored some dignity to a tainted sport." *Sports Illustrated* proclaimed that "Holyfield belted Mercer with fire and brimstone, erasing any doubts about the health of his heart."

Evander had made believers out of doubters. Suddenly, he was once again the top contender, the one every fighter would have to face to prove he earned the title "Champ."

CHAPTER 20

ANOTHER DETOUR: HOLYFIELD-BOWE AGAIN

After Evander lost his two titles to Moorer in April of 1994, the heavyweight division erupted into chaos. Within months, half a dozen men could lay claim to some form of a "world title." Don King began freezing many of the titles in anticipation of Tyson's return to the ring, and there was no longer any one person who was seen as the true champ.

Surprisingly, this resulted in a situation in which both Bowe and Evander were frozen out of a title fight. Neither boxer could find another fighter willing to face him. They weren't ranked in the now disassociated federations, and even though most experts thought of these two men as the best two boxers in the world, they couldn't schedule a fight.

Since neither boxer could find a partner to dance with, they decided to dance with each other, and Holyfield-Bowe III was scheduled for November 4, 1995. Showtime couldn't find a single marquee bout among the now largely meaningless divisions, so they eagerly agreed to carry the "rubber match" (one in which two fighters are fighting for pride, with no title at stake).

Evander was back in the familiar arena of Caesars Palace to fight Riddick Bowe for a third time. Even though no formal title was at stake, the *New York Daily News,* which is seen by many as the official voice of boxing, called the bout the "official heavyweight championship." No less a personality than former heavyweight champion Floyd Patterson agreed with the *Daily News*'s assessment. Even with Don King freezing control of the titles in anticipation of Tyson's return, the boxing world knew a title fight when they saw it.

Bowe was heavily favored. Again, experts pointed to his relative youth (five years younger than Evander), his two-and-a-half-inch height advantage, and his weight. For the first time in his career, however, Evander predicted a knockout.

Ironically, this prediction was born by an uncharacteristic lack of confidence. Shortly before the fight, Evander had been suffering from the flu, and his weakened body made him question whether he could go the distance.

Well, if I can't go the distance, he thought, *I guess I gotta knock him out!* A knockout represented his best—and perhaps his only— chance to win. Without the stamina, Evander knew he'd have to bring the bout to an early end.

That's what he was *thinking* anyway, but once the media got hold of the words, his "prediction" sounded much different.

Oh man, not again, Evander thought. Bowe would be out for blood.

Evander was strong in the early rounds, but he began feeling the boxer's biggest demon—weariness—get its claws into him as early as the end of round one. Though he lacked the energy that character- ized his earlier fights, Evander was still able to to take control of the bout. Whether or not he got the knockout, Evander was clearly outpointing his bigger and heavier opponent.

Bowe unleashed a characteristically low blow in the fifth. He was penalized a point, and Evander was given all the rest he needed, up to five minutes, to recover. He took ninety seconds.

Evander responded, early in the sixth, by unleashing a horren- dous left hook that caught Bowe in the head. Bowe's knees buckled, and his body crashed upon the canvas. Evander had swung so hard that he almost fell on top of Bowe. It was the first time Bowe had ever been knocked down.

If anybody doubted Evander's comeback, all doubts ceased at this point. A younger Holyfield had beaten, but never dropped, Bowe. Now, in one year, he had knocked down two heavyweights—Mercer and Bowe—whose knees had never tasted the canvas before. Evander hit Bowe so hard that one sportswriter described Bowe as "a standing dead man in the neutral corner."

Bowe climbed up on the count of seven. Evander saw his oppor- tunity—maybe his prediction of a knockout wasn't so bad after all— but his punch-weary arms and flu-depleted body failed him. It was a frustrating moment. Evander knew what he had to do. He could see how badly Bowe was hurt. But his body wouldn't respond. He was just "bone-tired." Bowe had riddled him with body shots throughout the bout, and now, when Evander reached down to come up with the blow that would end it all, he just couldn't find the strength. His arms lacked the power. Bowe used left jabs to keep Evander away and survive into the seventh round.

As the bout entered the eighth round, Evander was leading on all the judges' scorecards. He still felt, however, that things weren't going as well as he would have liked, so he decided to adjust his strategy. In order to avoid Bowe's jabs, he began keeping himself close to Bowe's chest.

It proved to be a disastrous adjustment. By staying so close to Bowe, Evander gave the heavier man a decided advantage.

In heavyweight boxing, the only thing separating you from the canvas is one unexpected blow. In baseball, football, or tennis, a losing opponent can only gradually work his or her way back toward victory. In boxing, a fighter can be behind on all scorecards and still pull out a sudden and stunning win by coming up with a knockout punch.

That's why Evander has always feared weariness in the ring more than he fears pain. After you've been fighting for several rounds and tiredness kicks in, you have to fight to keep your mind clear. You may have your opponent reeling and wobbling, but you must learn to pursue him with caution. If you let your guard down, you can lose it all. Even a wounded heavyweight carries the potential to do serious damage if he gets a clear shot.

Even so, Evander knew he was fighting with limited time. Because of his weakened condition, the later rounds would prove to be dangerous. The decision to come up on Bowe like he did was a bold gamble—knock out or be knocked out.

Early in the ninth, Evander suffered a sharp left hook that kept him moving forward. He then walked directly into Bowe's vicious right cross. The blow was devastating, and Evander fell face forward. He hadn't seen the first hit coming and did nothing to blunt its force. The second hit fogged his mind, and he dropped to the ground.

Fighting to regain his senses, Evander instinctively stumbled to his feet. His knees felt weak. He could hear the referee, Joe Cortez, count his way toward ten. The crowd was screaming. Through sweat-filled eyes, Evander saw Cortez looking at him, and Evander did his best to show Cortez he could go on. Cortez motioned for the two fighters to begin again.

Evander's head hadn't cleared. With Bowe outweighing him by twenty-five pounds and with Evander's quickness temporarily removed by a punch-induced fog, Bowe had him back against the ropes in a matter of seconds. Cortez stepped in and stopped the fight.

Evander thought he could go on, but he doesn't hold ill feelings toward Cortez. "Look, I knew how I was feeling. I knew I wasn't seriously hurt, but a referree can't know that. It's his decision to stop it. I take everything as a blessing. I didn't get punched up too bad, so I still have an opportunity to come back.

"If you have an opportuntity to come back, why complain?"

It was the first time in his career that Evander was knocked out.

Still, the writers praised the legendary duel. *Sports Illustrated* proclaimed that "Bowe and Holyfield have been delivered straight into Ali-Frazier country, their careers forever defined by their repeated and concussive collisions."

Evander had always wanted to fight the best of his day, and in doing so he had become the best of his day, earning the respect and admiration of pundits and fans around the world.

Fighting for the Cherry

After the loss to Bowe, the boxing world assumed that Evander would again retire. He had started on the comeback trail, but, after a win against Mercer, he tasted another defeat. Boxing is unique in that one loss—especially one suffered by a fighter entering his mid-thirties—inevitably leads to talk of retirement. Two or three losses, and retirement is considered almost mandatory.

What the writers didn't know, however, was that Evander was fighting for other reasons, ones they knew little about. This comeback was between him and God.

When Evander lost his title to Moorer and was then "medically forced" into retirement, he descended into one of the deepest valleys of his life. Everything was going wrong. Boxing had been his life, but now that was over. To make matters worse, Evander's business interests were becoming more of a liability than an asset. Evander was building a 57,000 square-foot mansion and was involved in several other business investments, all of which required a constant out-flow of cash. In addition, the boxing commission revoked his boxing license after their medical examination, which took away Evander's most reliable source of income.

What am I gonna do? he thought.

He went for a long walk on his estate. As he mulled over future scenarios, he realized that, although he had major endorsements and wise business investments in place, his primary and most lucrative source of income was boxing.

Evander kept this journey through the valley to himself. Dozens of people depended on him for their livelihood—the groundskeepers, the personnel at Holyfield management, business partners, and the like—and he didn't want them to have to shoulder his burden. This was *his* valley. He'd have to find his own way out of it.

During this troubled time—"one of the lowest points of my life," Evander says—his greatest solace was going to church on Wednesday nights. Sunday brings out everybody, but Wednesday night is church for the most serious Christians. Sitting in the pew, being around Christians who were trusting and worshiping God, Evander felt a light break into the depth of his valley. He'd be refreshed and able to face another week.

One particular Wednesday, Evander arrived at church only to find out that, instead of the usual service, there was going to be a "financial seminar."

I don't need no financial seminar, Evander thought. He turned to go back out the door, but a voice inside him said, *Stay.*

Evander tried to resist, but the feeling was strong.

All right, God, he prayed. *You want me to stay, I'll stay.*

The pastor began talking about tithing. He opened his big black Bible to Malachi 3:8: "Will a man rob God?'" the pastor read with emotion. "You ask, 'How do we rob God?'"

"In tithes and offerings," the pastor continued. Evander felt his heart fall. He sat back in his seat as if somebody had just clubbed him over the head. God had been so good to Him. Could it be true that he had then turned around and robbed Him?

"You are under a curse, the whole nation of you, because you are robbing Me. Bring the whoooollle tithe into the storehouse." The pastor was expressive now, bending over, stretching the words, sending the music of its truth out to his enrapt congregation.

"'Test me in this,' the Lord says. 'Test me in this, and see if I will not open the floodgates of heaven and pour out so much blessing that you will not have room enough for it.'"

The pastor spoke for some time, but Evander's mind was racing with the first few words. "Will a man rob God?" He began thinking about the tens of millions of dollars he had earned. Although he had given away well over a million dollars to different churches and charitable organizations, he wondered if he had been tithing properly. He wondered if a person could inadvertently rob God by giving improperly.

Because Evander's earnings are so large, he often partitions his giving: so much to the church and so much to charitable organizations. Oftentimes, what is given to the church is more than a tenth of his earnings. But the problem resided in the few times that he had given in this manner and the church received less than "a whole tithe into the storehouse."

Finally, the pastor's voice broke once again into Evander's thoughts. "Have you robbed God?" he asked. "God will forgive. God's a forgiving God. Jesus said we should pray, 'Forgive us our debts, as we forgive our debtors.' God will forgive us, because he expects us to forgive others. Do you want this forgiveness?"

"Yes!" Evander wanted to shout, but didn't.

"Amen!" a woman cried out.

"Yes, brother," another person said.

"Then stand up," the preacher said.

Evander stood. He had walked into this church carrying more weight on his 6-foot 2-inch frame than he could ever remember. It was time to put it down.

Here I am, Lord, he was praying. *I want your forgiveness.*

The pastor led those who stood through a prayer asking for God's forgiveness. Evander felt a huge release, as if a concrete spiritual dam inside him had just burst apart, allowing the river of God's joy to flow unimpeded.

"Now," the pastor concluded, "don't play games with God. He's forgiven you, but don't keep robbing Him. Bring your whooollle tithe into the storehouse."

When Evander got home from church, he fixed himself something to eat and sat down with his mail. He opened an envelope from his management team. Inside was a check for $1.2 million dollars, a late windfall from the second Bowe fight.

Evander held the check in the same hand that had once held

the pay stub of a coworker from Epps airport. God had been so good. Evander could take two steps out the door and see the frame of a dream house begin to take shape. His landholding was so large that he could barely see to the end of his property. Along the way his eyes would survey horses, a baseball field, tennis courts, a gymnasium, a large garage with half a dozen cars, many of them costing more than some people earn in an entire year . . .

Who would have believed it? He thought back to the days following the death of Carter Morgan. How easy it would have been to quit, keep working at Epps, and "just get by" for the rest of his life.

Evander looked at the check. *One million, two hundred thousand dollars,* it said. *This is a test,* Evander thought.

First thing the next morning, he went to his secretary and told her that he had received another check from the Bowe fight and wanted her to write out a check for $120,000 and give it all to the church.

"But Evander," his secretary protested. "You know we've been really tight, don't you?"

"I know that," Evander said. "And the reason why is, I haven't been tithing. Now, I'm gonna do more than tithe. I'm gonna bring my offering too."

The conviction of his tone was enough to convince the assistant that arguing wouldn't do any good. She cut a check for $120,000.

Within weeks, Evander had his boxing license back. His general health improved. His outside-the-ring business interests took off. He was soon in the best physical, financial, and spiritual shape of his life.

Wow! he thought. *I wish I woulda heard that sermon sooner!*

Evander experienced complete restoration. He had his career back, his business back, and his health back. Only one thing was still lacking.

His titles.

"That'll be the cherry on top of the sundae," Evander said. "I believe God wants to restore it all, and that means I have to fight to get my title back. Then everything will be restored."

That's why Evander's loss to Bowe ended up being a detour, not a dead end. To Evander, it was just another obstacle. He wasn't about to eat God's sundae without that red cherry to chew on.

Little did he know, however, that the loss to Bowe was absolutely insignificant compared to the loss that lay just ahead.

CHAPTER 21

THE REAL DEAL

E vander was playing in a celebrity basketball tournament in North Carolina when our sister, Eloise, pulled out of the New Saint John Baptist Church in Atlanta. Eloise was driving our mother home, something that occurred four to five nights a week. If something's happening at the church, Annie Holyfield wants to be there.

The celebrity basketball tournament, sponsored by Coca-Cola, was a prelude to Evander's going into training for an upcoming bout in Madison Square Gardens. Evander was scheduled to fight Bobby Czyz as part of "The Triple Header of Heavyweights" in May 1996.

Eloise entered an intersection and a car pulled out right in front of her. To avoid hitting the car, Eloise pulled the car sharply to the right. The passenger side front tire hit the curb and burst. When the tire burst, Eloise lost control of the car, and the black Jaguar she was driving spun back out into the intersection. At the same time, a pickup truck was entering the intersection and plowed into the passenger side of the car.

Eloise was knocked fifteen feet out of the car. Mother was trapped inside.

There was a rush of activity as Eloise, semi-conscious, lay on the ground. Finally, ambulance personnel arrived and asked her where she wanted to be taken. They had already decided to take our mother, who was also semi-conscious, to the nearest hospital. Eloise opted to go to the same place.

Emergency personnel tell us our mother talked during the trip to the hospital. She asked about things, such as "Where is my lipstick?" But when the doctors began to ask her questions: "How many fingers am I holding up?" she slipped into a coma.

It was a shock, but all the family members remained positive. Mother had survived a couple heart attacks, a triple bypass, and the raising of eight children (without a husband to support her). We just assumed she'd get through this too.

Since the members of our immediate family were with Mother, one of our friends called Evander with the news. He was immediately alarmed when told about the accident, but he wasn't sure about the severity of it, so he asked, "Do I need to come home?"

"No," he was told. "It's not that bad. She'll be all right."

Evander still opted to fly back into Atlanta the next day. When he found out just how badly Mother was hurt, his face changed in front of me. It was covered with hurt. Evander felt like he had been deceived. If his mom was in danger, he wanted to be there. If a coma wasn't danger, then what was? Why hadn't he been told?

Evander rushed into Mom's room, and the hurt he had felt over being deceived felt like nothing compared to the hurt he felt looking at the body of our mother. She was badly bruised and very swollen. For a second, Evander even wondered if she was still inside the bodily shell that had carried her through her earthly life.

The first day after was a quiet blur, but gradually it melted into the longer ordeal of a vigil. Mother was never left alone at the hospital. She had been there for all of us, and we weren't about to abandon her in her time of need. When she woke up—and we felt confident she would—we wanted one of us to greet her.

Evander took his turns, often playing music and singing to her. Though his bout with Czyz was getting ever closer, Evander opted to stay in Atlanta. He didn't want to leave our mother. One afternoon, while sitting by Mother's bed, Evander's prayer was jolted by an outside thought: *What exactly are you praying for?*

"I'm praying for her to come back," he said. Over the next few days, Evander would begin to understand why his prayer was being questioned.

Hours later—it was now about two weeks after the accident— the doctors warned us that there was evidence of internal bleeding. They wanted to drill holes behind Mother's ears to allow the blood to drain. It was a risky operation, but the doctors said if we didn't do it, she would die.

We had no choice. We wanted Mom to have every opportunity so we said, "Yes, of course."

Though the operation was successful, it didn't solve any of the underlying problems. While it allowed the blood to drain, it didn't stop the bleeding itself, so the doctors recommended a second operation that would attempt to remove the damaged tissue.

"Now, once we do this," the doctor told us, "I can't guarantee that your mother will be the same woman that you knew. There's no way to tell. But if we don't do it, she's going to die."

Evander went back to his knees. "Lord, I know my mother is Your child. If You allow her to come back, then please, heal her. If not, then allow her to be taken to Your better place."

Evander knew that heaven wouldn't be a loss. Mother was a Christian, and heaven would be a better world. He just wanted Mother to be healed—whether that healing took place on earth or in heaven really didn't matter.

Suddenly, a great peace washed over Evander. He rose from prayer, his concern for Mother supernaturally lifted, confident that God had heard his request. *She's gonna be healed either way,* Evander thought. *It's just up to God.*

As Evander's grief was lifted, the practical concerns surrounding her injury found a window into his soul. *If Mother's going to get the best care,* he thought, *then I'm gonna have to pay for it.*

He couldn't afford to take his upcoming fight for granted. Evander felt spiritually released to go into training.

Before Evander left, he talked to the doctors. "I want Mama to stay on the machines as long as possible. I don't care what it costs. You just give her the best chance she has, and I'll pay for it."

Evander traveled to Houston and began his heavy training for the Czyz fight. Unfortunately, training in the midst of grief was becoming all too familiar for Evander. Just before he had fought in the Olympics, Evander had to face the death of our grandmother. Then, just before he fought for the heavyweight championship of the world against Buster Douglas, he was served with divorce papers. Just a few fights later, shortly before his toughest title defense against Riddick Bowe, Evander had to endure the death of Willie. And now, on a mission, fighting for God to regain the title for the third time, Evander learned that the mother he loved—the only real parent he ever had—might be gone forever. This one cut even more deeply than the others. This was our mother.

Much to our relief, mother seemed to respond very well to the second operation. She opened her eyes, and her face lightened up when I read her the Twenty-third Psalm, but there was still a glassy, faraway look in her expression.

I had to know if she was there. "Mama," I said, "squeeze my hand if you can hear me."

I felt her gentle, precious squeeze. She couldn't talk, but at least I knew she was still with us, and at least I knew the Scriptures could still bring out the brightness of her faithful soul.

"Mama, I know this must be frightening for you," I said, "because it's frightening for me. But we're here for you, Mama, we love you." I read her the psalm once again.

Evander was relieved when I told him what had happened. He said he couldn't wait to get back on the weekend.

The doctors told us that we had now entered a waiting game— the only thing we could do was wait for Mother to wake up. It might be a day, it might be a week, it might be a month. All we could do was wait for the woman who gave birth to each one of us to come back to life.

Several days passed, and Mother's health took a bad turn. Her vital organs began to deteriorate as her brain stopped telling them what to do. With the kidneys and liver not functioning properly, our mother's life was severely threatened.

The doctor's face was grim as he faced our family. "Even if she makes it through this," he warned, "she'll likely be in a vegetative state for the rest of her life. The only thing that's sustaining her is the appartus that she's on."

The doctor paused and looked at us before continuing. "I recommend we remove her from the life support and see what happens."

We didn't even have to discuss it. "Absolutely not," we said. "Keep her on life support as long as possible. We want to give her every chance to make it." Evander's resources gave us the opportunity to afford what other families could not, and Evander had already said he was willing to spend whatever it took to give Mama her very best chance.

It was a sobering time, but we still believed that somehow, Mother would pull through. She always had.

When Evander heard the news, he called Benny Hinn. Benny invited Evander to attend another crusade where they would pray for Mother. Evander went, eager to see what God would do. He sat through another session of worship and preaching, and then, after everyone had left, finally got to do what he had come for. Just after midnight, Benny, Evander, and some other Christians joined in earnest prayer for Mother's healing.

When Evander got back to his hotel, he called me. I was thankful, because I had been trying to call him.

I had been woken up just a bit earlier, right around 2 A.M. Nothing good has ever come from a call past midnight, and I braced myself for the worst as I reached for the phone. Eloise was on the other end and I knew what she was going to say. She had virtually become Mother's personal assistant, and as Mother took a turn for the worst, Eloise didn't want to leave her side.

Her voice was broken, but her message was clear.

"Mom has passed."

I told Evander the news and was surprised by the almost casual way he said, "Oh, okay."

Then, after a short pause, Evander asked me, "What time did she pass?"

"About 1:30," I said.

Evander had looked at his watch when he and Benny had started praying. If mother was healed, he wanted to know the exact time the prayers were lifted. The crusade was held in Memphis, Tennessee, which is one hour behind Atlanta's time, which meant they began praying at about 1:30 A.M., Atlanta time.

God heard our prayers, Evander said to himself. *Mother is healed, now. She's all better.*

I've seen few people handle their grief as well as Evander did. "Don't you see how good God was to us?" he said. "God allowed us to have Mama for a little while after the accident, so that each one of us could spend some last time with her, to tell her how much we loved her, and to say good-bye. Then, He took her to be with Him, where she don't hurt no more.

"If Mother would have passed directly at the car accident, it would have hurt me a lot," he said. "But because I got a chance to sing to her, hold her hand, and tell her I loved her, it made it a lot easier."

The chance to spend some last few precious moments with Mother meant a lot to Evander. Early in his career, Mama had complained to him that he didn't see her as much as he used to.

"You don't love me, anymore," she had said.

"I love you, Mama, I just gotta work out."

"No, you don't love me," she said.

Evander decided to settle that real quick. He bought a new house for her—right across the street from his own.

"Now you can see me whenever you want," he said. And instead of having to drive across town, Evander could just cross the street for a drop-in visit.

Knowing he had done everything he could, Evander felt released at her passing. God had heard his prayers, and decided to heal Mother by taking her to heaven. Ironically, his fight was scheduled on the Friday before Mother's Day.

Triple Header

E vander fought on the third card of a triple-header. Lennox Lewis scored a controversial and widely booed decision over Ray Mercer, and Tim Witherspoon knocked out Jorge Luis Gonzalez in the fifth round.

Evander entered the ring against Bobby Czyz, a former middleweight champion. It was the first time in a long time that Evander fought somebody who weighed the same as he did. Usually his opponents outweighed him by 30–40 pounds. As the bout got under way, Evander was amazed at how easy it was to hit his opponent, and Czyz paid the price for standing in.

Just as I expected, the emotion Evander carried into the ring proved decisive, and he completely dominated Czyz throughout five rounds. Czyz was literally being pounded, and was forced to take a standing eight-count in the third round. Evander pinned him against the ropes in the fifth round and hurt him with a right hand to the head just before the bell rang. Czyz wasn't able to begin the sixth round.

It was an emotional night for Evander. He had won a boxing match, convincing the boxing world he was still in good enough shape to lay claim to the title for the third time. His showing was sufficient to convince Don King that it was time to finally let Evander and Mike Tyson rumble in the ring. Yet Evander had won the bout knowing that this was the first fight our mother hadn't spent on her knees, praying for his safety. Even so, Evander was confident she had been praying (but still not watching!) in heaven.

Mother's Day—without Mom

Back in Atlanta, we all gathered at Mother's church on Sunday. We went to her church every Mother's Day, and saw no reason to do any differently this year. The church had gained a good bit of unasked for publicity when HBO ran a special spot on Mother just before Evander's bout with Czyz (HBO actually sent a gift to the church in honor of Evander's mother). The pastor asked Evander to share a few words.

"A lot of people love to bring bad news," Evander began, "but this morning, I have good news. At my mother's funeral, we had a lot of people who had been to a lot of funerals. But I was told by many that this was the first funeral service they had ever been to where they came in with their head held down and left it with their head held high."

The congregation came alive. "Amen!"

"That's right!"

"Glory to God!"

Evander went on. "My mama had a hard life, but she always said, she made her bed hard, and she had to sleep in it. I thank God that my mother never gave up. She had eight kids and I was the youngest and she instilled Christ in me. All that I have is what my mother instilled in me.

"It's Mother's Day, and we can be proud of our mothers. Without our mothers we wouldn't be here. Our mothers tell us that we get out of life only what we put into it. Well, my mother put a lot into me. What you're hearing, and what you're seeing, is what my mother put in. My mother's life was tough coming up, but she imparted all those godly attributes in me, and it came back to bless her. When my mama left here, she had everything she wanted: she had the home she always wanted; she could spend as much time in church as she liked, and she never had any more pressure about whether the bills would be paid."

"That's right," the congregation shouted back. Heads nodded vigorously.

"We're all like a bank," Evander continued. "We can walk by a bank as many times as we want to, but we can only take out what we have first deposited. Kids are banks. You deposit as much as you want to, but remember to deposit good, because whatever you deposit is going to come back to you."

Evander paused. Every heart in the church was beating with his. "Life is wonderful!"

"Amen!"

"That's right, brother!"

"You tell 'em, Champ!"

"I just pray that God would give me the strength to do the same thing for my kids that Mama did for hers. She never complained that she had too many. Instead, she did what she had to do."

She did what she had to do.

If you could sum up Evander's career in one sentence, I don't know if you could find a better one.

He did what he had to do.

Born in Atmore, Alabama, raised without a father, *he did what he had to do.*

Moved to Atlanta, living in a crowded and tiny house, *he did what he had to do.*

Joined the Boy's Club, and when at first Carter Morgan wouldn't let him on the boxing team, Evander wouldn't give in. He asked to be let on, every day, for weeks . . .

He did what he had to do.

Fighting in a city that gave amateurs little exposure, working with trainers who weren't nationally reknown, clawing and climbing his way into a top ranking . . .

He did what he had to do.

Lacking a sponsor, facing debt, raising a family, yet fighting to keep his Olympic dream alive . . .

He did what he had to do.

Winning the Olympics, turning pro, facing a bruising initial fight, then fighting his way through the ranks until he became the junior heavyweight champion of the world . . .

He did what he had to do.

Unifying the cruiserweight titles, then making the decision to go pro, working long hours in the gym to build his body into that of a bonafide heavyweight . . .

He did what he had to do.

Beating bigger fighters, stronger fighters, and heavier fighters, until finally he became heavyweight champion of the world . . .

He did what he had to do.

Overcoming the death of his grandmother, the death of his older brother, returning to the ring after he lost his title to regain it once again . . .

He did what he had to do.

Coming back for a third title shot, proving he could still win, signing for a major fight with Tyson . . .

He did what he had to do.

And if you asked him what his secret was, how he overcame, how he kept coming back, how he managed to do what he had to do, well, surely you know by now what he'd say. If you were in his gym, he'd point to the sign on the wall, the sign under which he trains, the sign that contains the motto of his life.

> "I Can Do All Things Through Christ
> Who Gives Me Strength"
> Phil. 4:13

THE 1996 OLYMPICS

As Atlanta prepared to welcome the world to the 1996 Olympic Games, it was perhaps inevitable that Evander Holyfield's name would come up as a prime candidate to carry the Olympic torch during the opening ceremonies. Evander had done much to put Atlanta on the sports map to begin with, and he has long been considered a favorite son.

The Olympics have always owned prime real estate in Evander's heart. His experience in 1984 was spiritually and emotionally intoxicating. The 1976 Olympics rekindled his boxing dream; the 1980 Olympics gave him a boost; the 1984 Olympics gave him his fame.

What did it mean to Evander to carry the torch in 1996? From a spiritual perspective, Evander couldn't wait to have the eyes of the world watching a *Christian* carry the Olympic flame into the stadium. "Everything I am, and everything I do, eventually somebody's going to point out that it reflects on me being a Christian.

"I can imagine fathers and mothers turning to their children and saying, 'See, your friends talk about how Christians are wimps, and here Evander Holyfield is, a *fighter,* and a Christian, and he's carrying the Olympic flame. He's not a wimp.'"

Evander is passionate about removing the stereotype of Christians as poor, depressed, uptight, and unhappy people.

"They drive by my house, and they know somebody's been good to me. If they listen, they know that that somebody is God."

To Evander, the Olympics will show the world the glory of following Christ. "I don't care how good an actor you are, if you're struggling at home, if you can't pay your bills, if you're depressed, people are going to know it, and they're going to assume that it's because of your faith."

Now that God has made him more successful, more famous, and more wealthy than he ever could have dreamed, Evander is eager to point the finger right back to God. "He's the cause, He's the reason, *He's the man!*

"Too many think only bad people get something nice. They're wrong. All they got to do is drive by my house!"

Evander's concern for young people shows through. "You know, young people, they think they gotta do bad acts to get nice things. If all they see when they see Christians are people who look poor and unhappy and who act like everything's bothering them, why would they want to get to know Jesus?

"As Christians, we've got to learn how to *live* life, and to live it abundantly."

So for Evander, the 1996 Olympics in Atlanta, Georgia, represented a spiritual as well as a literal homecoming—the story of how God took hold of a poor child born in Atmore, Alabama, and raised in Atlanta, Georgia, and lifted him up to become two-time heavyweight champion of the world.